W9-DFA-978

The Managed Hand

The Managed Hand

RACE, GENDER, AND THE BODY
IN BEAUTY SERVICE WORK

MILIANN KANG

UNIVERSITY OF CALIFORNIA PRESS
Berkeley   Los Angeles   London

University of California Press, one of the most distinguished university presses in the United States, enriches lives around the world by advancing scholarship in the humanities, social sciences, and natural sciences. Its activities are supported by the UC Press Foundation and by philanthropic contributions from individuals and institutions. For more information, visit www.ucpress.edu.

University of California Press
Berkeley and Los Angeles, California

University of California Press, Ltd.
London, England

Portions of this book have been adapted and reprinted from Miliann Kang, "The Managed Hand: The Commercialization of Bodies and Emotions in Korean Immigrant-owned Nail Salons," *Gender and Society* 17 (2003): 820–39, and Miliann Kang, "Manicuring Race, Gender, and Class: Service Interactions in New York City Korean Nail Salons," *Race, Gender, and Class* 4 (1997): 143–64. Reprinted by permission.

Excerpt from "Anatomy of a Fish Store" by Ishle Park, from *The Temperature of This Water* (New York: Kaya Press, 2004), reprinted by permission.

Library of Congress Cataloging-in-Publication Data

Kang, Miliann.
    The managed hand : race, gender, and the body in beauty service work / Miliann Kang.
        p.   cm.
    Includes bibliographical references and index.
    ISBN 978-0-520-26258-4 (cloth : alk. paper)
    ISBN 978-0-520-26260-7 (pbk. : alk. paper)
    1. Beauty culture—Social aspects—United States.   2. Korean American women—Employment—United States.   3. Women immigrants—Employment—United States.   4. Asian Americans—Social conditions. 5. United States—Race relations.   I. Title.

TT958.K36   2010
391.6—dc22   2009035369

Manufactured in the United States of America

19 18 17 16 15 14 13 12 11 10
10 9 8 7 6 5 4 3 2 1

This book is printed on Cascades Enviro 100, a 100% post consumer waste, recycled, de-inked fiber. FSC recycled certified and processed chlorine free. It is acid free, Ecologo certified, and manufactured by BioGas energy.

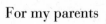

For my parents

Contents

List of Illustrations		ix
Acknowledgments		xi
	Introduction: Manicuring Work	1
1.	"There's No Business Like the Nail Business"	32
2.	"What Other Work Is There?": Manicurists	57
3.	Hooked on Nails: Customers	96
4.	"I Just Put Koreans and Nails Together": Nail Spas and the Model Minority	133
5.	Black People "Have Not Been the Ones Who Get Pampered": Nail Art Salons and Black-Korean Relations	165
6.	"You Could Get a Fungus": Asian Discount Nail Salons as the New Yellow Peril	201
	Conclusion: What Is a Manicure Worth?	239
	Notes	255
	References	275
	Index	301

Illustrations

Photographs by Jeeyun Lee

1. Manicurists in nail salon — 14
2. Buffing foot for pedicure — 19
3. Nail polish display — 34
4. Display of airbrushed and hand-painted nail designs on acrylic nails — 39
5. A nail salon owner sits at her reception desk — 60
6. Back room of a nail salon — 69
7. Male customer argues with manicurist — 89
8. Pedicure as pampering body labor — 97
9. Customers at nail art salons — 117
10. Manicurist hand-paints designs on acrylic nails — 131
11. Storefront of nail spa — 136
12. Spa chairs and sanitizing machines — 149
13. Storefront of nail art salon — 168
14. Packed waiting room in nail art salon — 188
15. Worker mixing chemicals — 221

Acknowledgments

I owe a personal and intellectual debt to many people who supported and tolerated me throughout the many years of working on this book. While I take full responsibility for any mistakes or misrepresentations, I hope this book does justice to their contributions.

Most of all, I am deeply grateful to all the nail salon workers, owners, customers, and advocates who welcomed me into their worlds and shared their lives and knowledge with me. Their generosity in answering questions, allowing me to look over their shoulders, and trusting me with their stories has overwhelmed me. I am also grateful to the community leaders and organizations that contributed their perspectives. Some are named, others asked to remain anonymous. While they did not directly participate in this research, the work of the Korean Immigrant Workers Alliance in Los Angeles and the Committee against

Anti-Asian Violence in New York City has shaped my understanding of Asian immigrant communities and the meaning of relevant and engaged research.

The University of Massachusetts Amherst, New York University, Grinnell College, and the Social Science Research Council's International Migration Program have provided much-needed research support. At my home institution of the University of Massachusetts Amherst, I am grateful to the Asian and Asian American Studies Certificate program, Office of the Dean of the College of Humanities and Fine Arts, Labor Relations and Research Center, Office of the Vice Provost for Research, and especially the Women's, Gender, Sexuality Studies Program for multiple forms of assistance. Sociologists for Women in Society, the Eastern Sociological Society, and the American Sociological Association's Section on Race, Gender and Class recognized this research with awards and connected me to audiences for this book.

Naomi Schneider, my editor at the University of California Press, has been a strong and patient advocate. The anonymous reviewers offered informed, constructive critiques that moved my project forward without asking me to make it into something else. Emily Park shepherded it through production, and Polly Kummel provided expert copyediting. I am especially pleased that UC Press allowed me to include photographs and am indebted to Jeeyun Lee for capturing such beautiful and evocative images, and to the subjects who gave permission to publish them. Those depicted are not the people whom I interviewed nor were they located at the research sites, but they capture the spirit of these salons.

This book began as my doctoral dissertation for New York University's Sociology Department, under the steady guidance of my adviser, Craig Calhoun (who "got" what I was trying to do and helped me develop tools to do it better), committee members Jeff Goodwin and Ruth Horowitz, and readers Troy Duster and Kathleen Gerson. NYU graduate students who provided feedback and friendship along the way include Vanessa Barker, Chris Bonastia, Tina Fetner, Drew Halfman, Gloria Ho, Carrie James, Miranda Martinez, Steve Pfaff, Louise Roth, Michael Young, and members of the "Woodenfish" working group. Herbert Gans at Columbia University, Philip Kasinitz at the City University of New York's Graduate Center, and John Kuo Wei Tchen, director of NYU's Asian/Pacific/American Studies Program and Institute, also shaped this project in important ways during its early incarnations. Sections of this book were adapted from journal articles and book chapters and were improved by feedback from Chris Bose, former editor of *Gender and Society;* Jean Ait Belkhir, editor of *Race, Gender and Class;* and Martin Manalansan, editor of *Cultural Compass: Ethnographic Explorations of Asian America* (Temple University Press). Although I published an article on a different subject with Jeff Goodwin and James Jasper, former editors of *Contexts,* they gave invaluable advice on how to write both rigorously and accessibly.

Conferences and individual presentations have provided opportunities to hone my thinking on this research, and I am grateful to the organizers for inviting me. These include the Intimate Labors conference at the University of California, Santa Barbara (organized by Eileen Boris, Rhacel Parreñas, and Elizabeth Shermer); the Body Work Seminar sponsored by the Economic and Social Research Council at the University of Warwick, Coventry, England (organized by Carol Wolkowitz, Julia Twigg, and Rachel Cohen); the Ford Foundation's Project on Low-wage Work, Migration and Gender (organized by Nilda Flores, Anna Guevarra, Hector Cordero Guzman, and Pallavi Banerjee); the Feminist Foundations seminars of the Women's, Gender, Sexuality Studies Program at the University of Massachusetts Amherst (organized by Banu Subramanium); the meetings of the Asian Americans in New England Research Initiative (organized by Michael Liu, Shauna Lo, and Paul Watanabe); the Five College Asian Pacific American Studies seminars; the Feminist Seminar and Race Seminar at the University of Wisconsin–Madison (organized by Myra Marx Ferree and Mitch Duneier); the Social and Demographic Research Institute at the University of Massachusetts Amherst (organized by Michelle Budig and Doug Anderton); the Crossing Borders, Bridging Gaps Series at Michigan State University (organized by Andrea Louie and Marilyn McCullough); the Gender and Inequality Workshop at New York University (organized by Jo Dixon); and the annual meetings of the American Sociological Association, the Association for Asian American Studies, and Sociologists for Women in Society.

My home in Women's, Gender, Sexuality Studies at the University of Massachusetts Amherst has challenged me to bring an interdisciplinary, intersectional feminist lens to my research. I am indebted to my chair, Arlene Avakian, and colleagues Alex Deschamps, Ann Ferguson, Dayo Gore, and Banu Subramaniam. I have also benefited from the incisive critiques of my colleagues in sociology. The network of feminist and Asian American scholars in the Five Colleges has pushed me to engage seriously with transnational, postcolonial, and ethnic studies frameworks. I owe special thanks to Floyd Cheung, Joya Misra, and Robert Zussman, who gave detailed feedback on all or nearly all of the manuscript, from its larger ideas to the nuts and bolts. Others whose contributions have improved it considerably include Karen Cardozo, John Chin, Nora Choi-Lee, Richard Chu, Michael Chwe, Dan Clawson, Debra Gimlin, Jung-hwa Hwang, Nancy Folbre, Naomi Gerstel, Alice Julier, Juliana Kim, Eunja Lee, Eunju Lee, Jennifer Lee, Namhee Lee, Sara Lee, Sueyeon Juliette Lee, Pamila Ginyoung Lew, Vijay Prashad, Victoria Robertson, Cora Roelofs, and Susan Walzer. This research was supported by research assistants who helped with contacting respondents, translating, transcribing, coding, and running to the library. Thanks to Jessica Brooks, Daniel Cheng, Yeowool Huh, Michelle Kozlowski, Yoon Hee Lee, Jiwon Lee, Ji-hyun Seo, Sandy Yu, and the ablest and most enthusiastic assistants of all, my parents.

I am a social writer and rely on the good company of writing partners. Millie Thayer has shared comments, great food, and even snowshoes on retreats in New Hampshire. Lisa Papademetriou meets me for weekly coffee and dueling computer dates. I have holed up in cafes and libraries with Lisa Armstrong, Mari Castaneda, Barbara Cruikshank, Tameka Gillum, Debra Immergut, Lili Kim, Laura Lovett, Lorena Munoz, Nitasha Sharma, and Diana Yoon. The writing support programs offered by Mary Deane Sorcinelli and the staff at the Center for Teaching at the University of Massachusetts Amherst have been invaluable. Writing groups led by Carol Edelstein and Nerissa Nields have brought the fun back to the writing process—I recommend them highly. The practice and practitioners of Vipassana meditation have helped me remember to breathe throughout this process.

C. N. Le, my partner in crime, has been there throughout all the ups and downs of writing this book. He has an amazing set of skills, which include educating about Asian American communities (check out his Web site, www.asian-nation.org), formatting endnotes, raising one eyebrow when he is skeptical, and getting us all out the door in the morning. Our daughter, Sangha, has grown up with this book and has helped us to do the same. She adorns my desk with beautiful pictures and notes scribbled with such words of wisdom as, "Finish your book because I want to hang out with you." She insisted that I acknowledge Zendo, our shi tzu mix, for serving as my faithful foot warmer. My hope is that this book will help my daughter and her generation understand and feel a sense of pride in the struggles and accomplishments of their parents, grandparents, and communities. We are blessed to be part of a generous circle of family and friends—I can't list them all but hope they know how much their support has meant along the way.

Introduction

> For all the migrations in this gender-revolutionary century, care
> still remains largely in women's hands.
>
> Arlie Hochschild, *The Commercialization of Intimate Life*

> Our bodies are invested with social meaning. . . . Whether a body
> is handled with reverence or contempt, whether it is nourished or
> starved, whether its owner has control over it or must succumb to
> others' control—these are all determined by the intertwining of
> communities, families and individuals.
>
> Judith Lorber and Lisa Jean Moore, *Gendered Bodies*

> Forging a political agenda that addresses the universal needs of
> women is highly problematic not just because women's priorities
> differ but because gains for some groups might result in a corre-
> sponding loss of advantage and privilege for others. . . . This does
> not mean that we give up on the goal of concerted struggle. It means
> that we give up trying falsely to harmonize women's interests.
>
> Evelyn Nakano Glenn, "From Servitude to Service Work"

Two women, virtual strangers, sit hand in hand across a narrow table,
both intent on the same thing—the achievement of a perfect manicure.
From the touches to the smells, a manicure is a visceral experience. When
the experience includes creamy hand massages, acupressure, and aromatherapy, the embodied dimensions of the manicure greatly enhance
its appeal. The exchange shifts dramatically, however, when the touches

result in misfiled nails, bleeding cuticles, and fungal infections, and the smells involve toxic chemicals, sweaty feet, and the exhalations of recently digested lunches across an eighteen-inch-wide table. The carnality of the manicure sets it up as an unpredictable exchange that can lurch suddenly from relaxing to uncomfortable, if not alarming. These embodied interactions are yet more complex because they occur between women who usually would not find themselves in the same social circles, let alone touching each other.

The clipping, filing, sculpting, and polishing of nails entails not only the manicuring of the physical body but also the manicuring of the women who perform this work and receive these services. This work requires both technical expertise and adroit emotional skills to finesse strong reactions of customers to the servicing of their bodies. Like much work in the service economy, this work is mostly invisible. It largely goes unnoticed and unappreciated and shows up only when it is performed unsatisfactorily. Nail salon interactions demonstrate how women inhabit bodies differently as well as how women's bodies are differentially valued and employed. In particular, while some women's bodies are manicured into objects of beauty, other women's bodies serve as tools for enacting these beauty regimens.

The Latin roots of the word *manicure* mean simply care of the hands. However, contemporary manicures and the establishments in which they occur involve much more than this bare definition suggests. While I use the term *manicure* to refer to a specific set of beauty service practices, I also use manicuring as a powerful metaphor for the individual and social processes that shape women's bodies, emotions, relationships, and lives. At the same time the metaphor of being *nailed* is also apt, as women are not completely free agents who construct their bodies and their bodily care according to their own will and whims. Instead, they are nailed to social positions and structures that shape not only their own bodies and the bodies of others but also the terms of commercialized embodied services.

Recent sociological and feminist scholarship has experienced a marked turn toward "bringing bodies back in" to theory and research.[1] As Mary Margaret Fonow and Judith Cook argue, "Contemporary feminist theory has added new ways to think about the body, and feminists now speak of writing the body, reading the body, sexing the body, racing the body, enabling the body, policing the body, disciplining the body, erasing the body, and politicizing the body."[2] I add to this list manicuring and nailing the body as new ways to think about the multiple forces shaping gendered bodies.

Because the intimacy of manicuring work engenders complex feelings, this work requires both physical labor and the extensive management of emotions, or what the sociologist Arlie Hochschild refers to as "emotional labor," in which "the emotional style of offering service is part of the service itself." The title of Hochschild's 1983 groundbreaking study, *The Managed Heart*, provides a rich metaphor for the control and commercialization of human feeling in service interactions. I play on Hochschild's title to coin the term *the managed hand*, which addresses the commercialization of both human feelings and *bodies* in manicuring work.[3]

Building on Hochschild's concept, I introduce the concept of body labor to designate the provision of body-related services and the management of both feelings and bodies that accompanies it. While service work increasingly involves managing the emotional work of the heart, it also involves managing the physical work of hands and the bodies they touch. Despite the many dimensions of emotional labor that scholars of gender and work have addressed, the body-related contours of low-wage service work dominated by immigrant women of color, particularly in the beauty industry, demand further research. Thus Asian-owned nail salons serve as a rich empirical site to develop the concept of body labor as a new theoretical lens through which to study gender, migration, race relations, and the emotional and embodied dimensions of service work.

While domination by Koreans of the nail salon niche in New York City is unusual in some ways, in other ways it reveals similar experiences among Asian immigrant women throughout the United States. My project emphasizes the specificities of Korean-owned nail salons in New York City while also exploring commonalities and differences among Korean, Vietnamese, and other Asian women based on their work in this industry.[4] Thus it both recognizes and problematizes the strong tendency to lump all Asians together, despite multiple differences.

This book is not meant as a comprehensive overview of the nail salon industry in the United States. Instead, it focuses on the work of Asian women in this niche, specifically, Korean women in New York City, in order to illuminate the nature of the services provided and the social relations that shape them. Specifically, it theorizes new forms of body labor that unfold in the delivery of nail salon services to a broad range of customers, and it contextualizes these within shifting racial and gendered constructions of Asian immigrant women.

MANICURING IMAGES VERSUS INTERACTIONS

Popular culture would have us believe that beauty service establishments are homes to a universal and uncomplicated sisterhood. Dolly Parton's beauty salon in the film *Steel Magnolias* serves as a refuge in which privileged southern white women bare their souls. *Beauty Shop*, starring Queen Latifah, offers a multicultural version of a similar story.[5] Manicurists also appear as women's best friends and therapists, most famously, when Reese Witherspoon as Elle Woods in *Legally Blonde* retreats to her manicurist after battling it out in the trenches of Harvard Law School. These media representations ignore the reality that beauty salons, and nail salons specifically, are not simply women's community centers, although they may in limited circumstances foster that impression. Instead, they are, first and foremost, places of employment, and the relationships forged within them are not simply between friends but are labor relations dictated by the protocols of the service industry.

Contrary to the popular representations of women as naturally and universally invested in the pursuit of beauty, many complex factors shape nail salons as feminized, globalized, postindustrial work sites and Asian immigrant women as the labor force most represented in this niche. Describing a process which she calls the "racialized feminization of labor," Lisa Lowe writes, "Asian immigrant and Asian American women are not simply the most recent formation within the genealogy of Asian American racialization; they, along with women working in the 'third world,' are the 'new' workforce within the global reorganization of capitalism."[6] Like Lowe and other scholars, I argue that gender is central to racial constructions of Asian Americans and shapes their incorporation into U.S. labor markets.[7] Racial ideologies feminize Asian American women and men into particular jobs and reinforce notions of Asia itself as feminine. For Asian men this means that they gain acceptability by forfeiting their claims to conventional ideals of masculinity. In contrast, the terms of Asian women's racial acceptance require their enactment of forms of femininity grounded in subservient work. These complex social processes propel thousands of Asian immigrant women into nail salon work, and thousands more customers literally into their hands, but stereotypes that "Asian women are just good at nails" normalize their clustering in this niche. Thus everyday manicuring interactions both conceal and reproduce racial inequalities, labor migration flows, and the expansion of the global service economy under the veneer of women's supposedly common investment in beauty and beauty practices.

Racialized representations are simultaneously linked to gender and embedded in the racial imaginary through what Patricia Hill Collins refers to as "controlling images."[8] As such they become taken-for-granted frameworks that serve to justify social arrangements. In the case of nail salon relations, controlling images pose certain women as the "natural" providers of manicures and other women as the entitled recipients of these services. These controlling images, however, are played out in face-to-face interactions in unpredictable ways, as women uncritically reproduce them in some situations and actively resist them in others.

In her 2003 "Revolution" tour, stand-up comedian Margaret Cho satirized the controlling image of the subservient Asian (Korean American) manicurist through her depiction of the Hollywood roles that she has been offered but refuses to play.[9] Rather than begin with the well-known stereotypes of Asian women as dragon lady seductress, submissive China doll, or model minority television newscaster (although some of these appeared later in her show), her first act portrayed a manicurist. She would cock her head obsequiously to one side, pretend to hold a hand gingerly in front of her, and croon, "You have pretty nail." In the brazen comedic style that catapulted her to international fame, Cho captures the fawning behavior associated with Asian women in service jobs while critiquing this depiction as a caricature.

Seated in the audience of her standing-room-only show, I was not sure whether to cheer or wince at Cho's performance. I applauded how she deftly played on the image of the Asian manicurist as a widely recognizable cultural stereotype while smashing it. At the same time her representations of the women who work in and patronize Asian-owned nail salons are oversimplified. During years of researching these sites I have lost the ability to accept such facile depictions of manicurists and their customers, even for the sake of a good laugh. The complexity of these women's lives and their relations with each other have challenged me to rethink my feminist, sociological, and Asian American consciousness. Can Margaret Cho's stand-up act even begin to hint at the contradictory relationships of manicurist and client, friend and confidante, caregiver and cultural translator negotiated across the manicuring table?

I hope it is obvious that I am setting this iconic comedian up as a straw, holding her to standards that no stand-up performer, however brilliant, could be expected to meet. While Cho's performance powerfully exposes demeaning stereotypes of Asian manicurists, it also shortchanges the women who participate in these exchanges. Thus I invoke her performance as a jumping-off point to delve into women's manicuring practices and the ways that they manicure themselves and each other. As I watched Cho's performance, I wondered—what would the women in my study have to say about her representation of manicuring work? I think of Nancy Lee, the pseudonym I have given a manicurist at a Manhattan salon I call Uptown Nails; she provides intensive caregiving for her many elderly, middle-, and upper-class white customers.[10] This includes massaging their arthritic hands and feet, helping them to the bathroom, and propping them up against the wall when they fall asleep while their nails are drying. On several occasions I heard Nancy make blunt comments to her coworkers about her clients, all veiled by a placid expression and uttered in her native Korean—"This one gives three dollars and thinks she's a BIG tipper." My guess is that Nancy would respond to Margaret Cho's depiction of manicurists with the same candor with which Nancy responded to my incessant questions about her experiences in nail salon work: "I probably wouldn't have come to the U.S. if I knew this is what I would be doing. But after a few weeks, you get used to it. . . . I want to send my children to college."

Next I thought of Goldie Chun, the feisty owner of Artistic Nails, a bustling nail salon in a predominantly black neighborhood in Queens. She sports ornate nails and low-rise jeans while directing customers to stations for acrylic tips, airbrushing, and hand-painted nail art. In the course of a day I have seen her chase rats with a broom, grab a cell phone from a customer arranging a drug drop-off, joke with customers about their boyfriends, and give candy to children. "When I first got here," she told me, "I was so surprised. I thought 'Oh—my—God, how I am going to work here? How can I get the business here?' . . . Because [of] all the blacks. I could not even open the door of my car. . . . I had such a hard time, all the time fighting. I had to call the police. . . . Now, I know how to handle that. When they say something, I say, 'Oh, these people want these things.' Then I talk to them, this and that. I know how to do that now." Goldie's work in the nail salons wrought major changes in her identity, from a college student in Seoul to a struggling immigrant mother to the owner of a profitable business in a neighborhood where she once was afraid to get out of her car. She summarized the impact of nail salon work on her life: "I got more hot tempered, and not listen to people, and I was like that even in my home. When my sister and mother visited me, they were surprised about my change. If the members of my church could see me at work, they would say, 'What happened to you!' They wouldn't believe how tough I can be."

What about the customers, who are invisible in Cho's comic performance? The first who came to mind was Alia, an African American grocery store cashier who prides herself on her long nails adorned with rhinestones and hand-painted flames. She explained, "My hands are real big and rough. With my nails done, they don't look so chopped up. You know women, you know the way we are—we want to look ladylike. I used to be embarrassed about my hands but now I hold them up." Alia sees her nails as the ticket to claiming membership in a club from which she has been excluded for most of her life—the club of women who take pride in their appearance. Her nails also connect her to women with whom she otherwise would have little contact. "Everyone who gets on my line has to look at my nails, and some of them will spend two, three, four minutes asking me, 'Oh, where you get them done?' . . . I would have on sweat pants, but if my nails are done, it makes me feel like I have on a whole new outfit. I can't dress up everyday, but I can have my nails done all the time." And the proliferation of Asian-owned nail salons is one of the main reasons that she can—in styles she prefers and at prices she can afford.

Similarly, Patti, who identifies herself as a Jewish American native of Brooklyn and a chronic nail biter, applauds the growth of Asian-owned nail salons for enabling her to have her nails done weekly in order to repair the damage of her constant gnawing. "The best is when I come here with my fingers hurting from my biting them. I cannot stand it. I cannot stand looking at them, and I cannot stand biting them because it even keeps me up at night—biting, biting, and biting. So . . . leaving after I get done with all my nails on—that is the best." Patti works as a hospital social worker and credits her weekly nail salon visits with helping her to survive the daily physical and emotional stressors of her job. In return she has provided regular and tangible support to the salon owner, Charlie Choi, by mediating with upset customers and helping to translate English-language conversations and documents. Charlie values Patti's patronage, but she also acknowledges that Patti's emotional neediness and physically demanding nails can be stressful. "I'm very happy to see her because she is kind and I know she really needs my help, but when we are very busy and I don't have time to spend with her, I feel bad," Charlie told me.

Controlling images of Asian manicurists, as well as the disruption of these images in performances such as Margaret Cho's, illuminate one-dimensional representations of Asian immigrant women. This book complicates these images by asking questions about the social relations from which they emerge and that they in turn influence. In exploring the variation in manicuring services, this book examines three different forms of body labor at Asian-owned nail salons: "pampering body labor" in nail spas serving mostly white upper- and middle-class women; "expressive body labor" in nail art salons serving mostly black working- and lower-middle-class women; and "routinized body labor" at discount nail salons serving racially and socioeconomically mixed customers. Like the emotional labor that Hochschild documents, pampering body labor involves catering to the needs of customers, but it is complicated by differences of language, culture, class, and race. This form of body labor enforces the treatment of white women's bodies as both special and normative, thereby upholding these women's racial and class privilege. Simultaneously, it disciplines Asian women's bodies to display deference and attentiveness in line with the controlling image of the Asian "model minority." In contrast, expressive body labor in nail art salons serving a mostly black working-class clientele disrupts dominant racialized discourses regarding "Korean-black conflict," which emphasize tensions and hostility between these groups. Instead, Korean and black women can create respectful, reciprocal, and even affectionate relations through service interactions, although these ties remain fragile and tenuous in the face of pervasive racial and class divisions. Finally, discount nail salons reframe manicures from a luxury product to a one-size-fits-all consumer good. However, the scaled-down aspects of routinized manicures kindle fears of disease and contamination that resuscitate negative views of Asians as the "yellow peril." Interactions in these different sites are shaped but not determined by racial relations and economic positions. Instead, they are negotiated through particular practices of gendered work, specifically, the exchanges of body labor between diverse women in various types of nail salons. Furthermore, these different kinds of salons do not exist in isolation from each other but are part of a constellation of social relations in which Asian immigrant women are incorporated into existing divisions within U.S. society and culture in complex and contradictory ways. The different kinds of services and service relations in the range of salons that Asian immigrant women operate illustrate how they simultaneously play the roles of idealized minority citizen, racialized outsiders, and economic and cultural threat.

ACROSS THE MANICURING TABLE: STRUCTURE AND AGENCY

No individual woman suddenly wakes up with the idea that manicured nails are central to her identity. Years of socialization, along with the messages of her immediate social worlds, coalesce in her determination that her nails say something important about who she is and that it is worth paying someone to make the statement that she desires. At the same time women are not simply puppets acting out social dictates through their beauty practices and their relations with their beauty service providers. Women make choices, not only about how, how often, and from whom to purchase beauty services but also about the ways that they define themselves and others in relation to these practices. While most customers insist on seeing their manicures as purely private rituals, their manicuring practices emerge at the nexus of historical and contemporary forces that have fostered a booming global niche in nail products and services.

Similarly, no individual woman simply wakes up to find herself seated in the manicurist's chair.[11] Forces beyond her control, such as global patterns of feminized labor migration flows, the growth of service-related industries, racialized job structures, and the resources of her family and ethnic community shape the conditions of her employment. Yet within these large-scale structural conditions, women make choices about the work they do and the terms under which they do it, although these terms reflect numerous constraints. Manicurists construct new identities in the salon (the women often christen themselves with a new "American name"—Eunju becomes Eunice, Haeran becomes Helen) that ultimately demand conformity to their status as service workers, even as the women themselves are incorporating competing identities as mother, wife, student, professional, immigrant, Korean, Asian, and American.

Social interactions in particular sites, such as nail salons, are simultaneously patterned by external forces and negotiated by individual actors. As a feminist sociologist I seek to understand dominant patterns of social relations, particularly those that relate to women and the persistence of gender inequality, but I am equally interested in departures from and resistance to these patterns. I am also concerned with identifying the mechanisms through which these various patterns are reproduced and disrupted, often in surprising and unpredictable ways.

What kind of relations do women forge in this exchange of manicuring services? How have Korean women in New York, and Asian women throughout the United States, become the de rigueur providers of nail services, and why have customers from across the racial and class spectrum flocked to their doors? What factors shape the lives of Asian immigrant manicurists and their customers and the complex interactions that unfold between them? In what contexts do entrenched hierarchies of power and privilege prevail, and in what contexts are individuals able to contest and rework them? What happens during the manicure, and what explains the variation in manicuring practices and relations? How does this fleeting encounter shape these women after they leave the manicuring table? And what is the significance of these encounters for relations between the different groups to which these women belong, specifically, Asians, blacks, and whites, immigrants and natives, consumers and service providers? In exploring these questions my study is grounded in an ethnographic tradition that seeks to see the global through the local, to capture the larger workings of society by understanding how they play out in the mundane happenings at a specific site.[12] I believe that the answers to these questions lie not so much in individual women's psyches, nor in the media onslaught of beauty advertising or the rising cultural standards for women's appearance. These factors play an important part, but the larger story of why so many women seek manicures and why their manicuring practices vary so widely must address broader social shifts, especially the expansion of the global service economy, increase in women's paid participation in the labor force, flows of feminized migrant labor, and persistent racial and class inequalities. Centrally implicated in all these processes are women's bodies, both as the tools and the targets of new forms of work, which I characterize as body labor.

In what ways is nail salon work gendered? In what ways are these gendered work processes remolded by race and class? Nail salon work is gendered in that it involves mostly women as both service providers and customers; it focuses on the construction of feminine beauty; it is situated in feminized semiprivate spaces; and it involves gendered work practices, specifically, the performance of emotional and body labor between women.[13] But it is not solely gendered work. Patterns of body labor conform to the racial and class positions of the customers and the associated feeling rules that define their service expectations. Building upon Paul

Gilroy's assertion that "gender is the modality in which race is lived," I argue that race, as well as class, are lived in nail salons, and other body-service sites, through differences in the gendered performances of body labor.[14] These performances reveal that the simplistic framework of "sisterhood is global" does not hold in women's relations across the manicuring table and in beauty service work more generally. Instead, these relations demonstrate intractable divisions between women.

FEMINISM, BEAUTY, AND INEQUALITIES BETWEEN WOMEN

While surfing the Internet for nail-related articles, I stumbled upon a piece and was immediately disturbed by its jarring depiction of Asian manicurists as simultaneously exoticized sexual objects and maternal caregivers. One moment the author is sexually aroused by her manicurist, the next she regresses to an infantilized state of passivity. Even more unsettling is her insistence that this exchange somehow qualifies as an empowering experience simply because it occurs between women. I was about to dismiss this as the unfortunate ranting of some adolescent blogger, when I noticed the name of the author. Jennifer Baumgardner, who penned this reflection on her nail salon experiences, is widely recognized as a feminist author and leader in the Third Wave feminist movement.[15] I found myself depressed and infuriated by her piece—and in a quandary as to how to respond. These feelings were compounded by my overall respect and admiration of her work. I asked myself, if a leading feminist writer and activist could engage in a manicure with such uncritical self-aggrandizement, what chance is there that the average customer will recognize the problematic aspects of this exchange, let alone strive to change them? Baumgardner writes:

> But finances and love aside, long, well-tended nails are sexy. And, the process that gets them that way has a nice sensual intimacy that is rare in a $6 service. . . . The manicurist kneads your palm and slides her fingers up and down on the fleshy nook in between your pointer finger and thumb. As she pulls on your hand and wrist, your fingers splayed open,

arm vertical, palm toward her, you rock slightly in your chair from the force of her rubbing. . . . When it's over, if it's cold out, your manicurist has to help you into your coat. Standing in front of you, she zips or buttons you in, and wraps your scarf around your neck like she's your mom and you're suddenly six again. . . . A big reason that the manicure transaction works the way it does—as safe, inexpensive carnality—is because it is a relationship among women. . . . I'd be lying if I didn't note that there is a class and race overtone to the New York manicure experience: the manicurists are small ladies who speak loudly in Korean to one another; the clients are yuppyish, mainly white, and talk too loudly into cell phones to other yuppyish, mainly white people.[16]

Unfortunately, Baumgardner's stature as a prominent feminist thinker stands in stark contrast to her objectification of the Korean immigrant woman who performs her manicure. While Baumgardner concedes that this service is shaped by race and class inequalities, this concession does not lead her to consider the manicurist's perspective and what this exchange means for her. Instead, Baumgardner goes on to commend herself for turning the supposedly unfeminist obsession with her nails into what she sees as a pleasurable and empowering act.

By criticizing Baumgardner—and other educated white middle-class U.S. feminists who may share her limitations in understanding women's lives very different from her own—I find myself, like many women of color, transnational and postcolonial feminists, caught in a difficult position. I do not want to deepen divisions within the feminist movement and provide further ammunition to those who are already too eager to invalidate its intellectual and activist goals. At the same time I find her self-congratulatory comments not only offensive but also indicative of attitudes that stand in the way of any kind of meaningful gender solidarity. Thus I hope that critics do not dismiss this book as a long rant that diverts attention from the work of feminist social change; rather, my hope is that this book exposes a persistent blind spot in many women's lives. That is, certain women benefit from the intimate body and emotional labor of other women at great cost to both those who serve them and the goal of more egalitarian relations—not just between women and men but between women across multiple boundaries of race, class, immigration, and citizenship.

Figure 1.   Asian women's work in nail salons reveals complex relations between women as well as their own agency in creating and performing these services.

With these concerns in mind, I hope this book serves as an invitation to explore difficult and uncomfortable issues of power and privilege between women—issues that are central to forging an inclusive feminist scholarship and movement. As Evelyn Nakano Glenn writes in this chapter's epigraph, confronting privilege and inequality between women is a painful but necessary process to end oppressive working conditions in jobs such as housecleaning and other services. Likewise, a better understanding of the dynamics of nail salon work can illuminate the lives of women who provide manicures and their customers, as all women stand to gain from greater equality in the social relations that shape these sites.

BEAUTY MYTH VERSUS BEAUTY WORK: WHO DOES THE THIRD SHIFT?

Instead of addressing the inequalities between the providers and purchasers of beauty services, a major focus in the popular and scholarly literature on beauty has been on the ways that the "beauty myth" under-cuts privileged women's professional and political advancement by shackling them with unattainable expectations regarding their physi-cal appearance. The author Naomi Wolf is perhaps the best-known articulator of this argument. She asserts that beauty ideology and the beauty industry are important tools in orchestrating the backlash against women's rising social, political, and economic power: Wolf regards the heightened standards for women's physical appearance as the "replace-ment shackle" to domestic work. Invoking the sociologist Arlie Hoch-schild's concept of the "second shift," which refers to women's double duty as wage earners and homemakers, Wolf asserts that beauty work has become women's "third shift" and functions as an additional tool to subvert women's increasing power. "The backlash was provoked," Wolf writes, "because even when they were weighted with the 'second shift' of domestic work, women still battered inroads into the power struc-ture. . . . *Someone had to come up with a third shift fast.*"[17] Thus she argues that contemporary beauty culture imposes unattainable standards and regimens that divert time, energy, and money from career advancement while lowering women's confidence in pursuing various goals. Wolf's book has served as a call to arms for individual women and the feminist movement to take seriously the cultural dictates of beauty as a major force in the ongoing subordination of women.

Unfortunately, Wolf and her supporters have ignored the many women who do not do their own beauty work. Instead, they pass off sizable portions of this third shift onto the shoulders of less-privileged women. Whereas Hochschild followed up her analysis of the second shift with *Global Woman: Nannies, Maids, and Sex Workers in the New Econ-omy* (with Barbara Ehrenreich, 2004), which explores the transnational inequalities that allow professional women in industrialized nations to rely upon women from poorer countries for their domestic duties, few scholars have focused on these global inequalities in beauty work. This book addresses this gap, arguing that, like the domestic work of the second shift, the beauty work of the third shift is not laid solely on the shoulders of educated powerful women. Just as immigrant women, predominantly from Latin America, the Caribbean, and the Philippines, pick up the second shift of raising children, cooking food, and cleaning homes, the third shift of beauty work also increasingly relies upon the labor of immigrant women of color.[18] Parallel social and historical conditions that push certain immigrant women into the work of housework and child care channel other women into the work of beauty services. Like domestic service, beauty services are regarded and remunerated as unskilled labor, when in fact beauty work entails highly skilled procedures as well as the exercise of extensive emotional labor. Furthermore, just as domestic workers trade care work for a paycheck at the expense of nurturing their own families, the women who perform beauty work often sacrifice caring for their own families and their own physical and emotional health in the service of other women's beauty.

While contributing incisive critiques of the contradictions involved in women's search for beauty, the literature on beauty has focused mainly on the experiences of middle-class white women consumers and their physical and psychological exploitation by the male-dominated beauty industry.[19] More attention needs to be given to the substandard working conditions, unequal power relations, and complex emotional lives of the women who provide these services.

WOMEN, BEAUTY, AND THE LIMITATIONS OF GENDER

When do commonalities based upon gender take precedence, and when are they subordinated to, or fragmented by, other categories of difference? Intersectional, transnational, and postcolonial feminist scholars have identified the problematic assumptions of gender essentialism in academic and popular discourse that treat gender monolithically and fail to account for its fluidity and variation in local and global contexts.[20] Instead, the presumed commonalities between women, particularly around their investment in feminine beauty practices, unmistakably break down when examined in specific sites in which women interact.

Whereas feminist scholars have often focused on gender to the neglect of race, class, and immigration, scholars of race, class, and immigration have often neglected gender. This study bridges these literatures by showing how gender, as enacted through body labor in the feminized niche of nail salons, can both disrupt ideologies of race and immigration as well as reinforce discrimination and exclusion. In particular, gender is an understudied factor in explaining the presence or absence of racial conflict in immigrant-owned small business establishments.

Race, class, and immigrant status also do not operate monolithically in their intersections with gender, as women of the same racial and immigrant groups do not necessarily cluster predictably into simplistic groupings or experiences. For example, middle-class white women are not all equally privileged nor are they identically demanding of pampering treatment. Likewise, working-class black women do not all uniformly desire long acrylic nails nor do they all experience tensions with their Asian nail care providers. Asian immigrant women en masse do not find the same motivations and meaning for pursuing this work, nor do they uniformly relate to their customers based solely on racial markers. Instead, distinct patterns emerge and are renegotiated by individual actors within the constraints of their social contexts.

While scholars of intersectionality have convincingly argued that gender operates in conjunction with multiple categories of difference, this theoretical understanding often flies in the face of the commonsense ways that people live these categories as separate and unbridgeable—you are either a woman or you are black; it's either about gender or about race.[21] This "one-or-the-other" framing is ubiquitous in mundane interactions as well as in contemporary politics.[22] Therefore, while I firmly assert an intersectional framing of gender and race as simultaneous and interconnected categories, I also explore why most people stubbornly adhere to seeing these as either/or constructs. In order to disrupt these commonsense dichotomies of gender and race, I seek to theorize ways that race, gender, and other forms of difference intersect and to examine specific ways that these intersections are forged and contested in concrete social settings.

Which intersections are most salient in any given context? While I recognize the importance of multiple forms of difference, including age, sexuality, and disability, I focus mainly on the intersections of gender, class, race, and immigration for several reasons. First, this framework captures the understandings that respondents in this study most often articulated. Second, both public discourse and academic explanations of relations between Asian immigrants and other groups have prioritized heavily racialized understandings of relations between immigrants and native-born Americans. While class and economic relations are clearly central to all the questions that I address here, they are often rendered invisible and rewritten in terms of race, foreign status, or general notions of "otherness." Thus I attempt to show not only how race, class, immigration, and gender intersect but also why and how these particular intersections are visible or hidden in performances of body labor.

FROM THE MANAGED HEART
TO THE MANAGED HAND

The concept of body labor that I develop in this book is indebted to Hochschild's foundational work on emotional labor, which mapped the terrain of commercialized feelings but still left much ground to be explored. One of the many reasons that the concept of emotional labor hit such a resounding chord is that it provides language for a phenomenon that many people, particularly women, recognize as an integral but invisible part of their everyday work life. *Emotional labor* serves as a shorthand for the ineffable but constant attention put into smiling, complimenting, exchanging pleasantries, and smoothing over conflicts that comprise an inordinate chunk of the workday for those in subordinate positions—particularly, women serving men. Building upon Hochschild's work, studies of emotional labor have illuminated the increasing prevalence of emotional management in specific occupations and industries, the gendered composition of the emotional labor force, wage discrimination, job burnout, and other occupational health issues.While scholars of emotional labor have examined certain embodied aspects of emotional labor concerned with gendered bodily *display*, ranging from control of weight to smiles, the study of bodily *contact* in service interactions deserves greater attention. In addition to neglecting embodied aspects, the concept of emotional labor has been less plastic in capturing the experiences of those subordinated on the basis of race, class, and immigrant status, in addition to gender.[23]

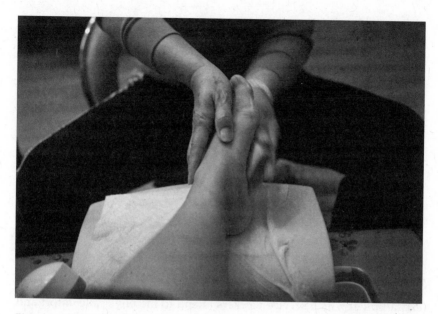

Figure 2.   Body labor brings diverse women into intimate embodied and emotional exchanges.

Similarly, the scholarship on gender and the body, while offering many important critical interventions, has largely focused on deconstructing the body itself, rather than examining work sites where actual bodies and their gendered meanings are constructed. Although feminist scholars have long been engaged in the project of "putting the body on the intellectual map," Kathy Davis argues that they have neglected the day-to-day interactions involving actual bodies.[24] By bringing an embodied perspective into the study of gendered work, this book highlights the intricate everyday practices of enhancing the appearance of women's bodies in body-related service-sector work. Exploration of the multiple dimensions of body labor in nail salons can illuminate other body-related service jobs, including nurse, nanny, plastic surgeon, massage therapist, sex worker, and cosmetics seller.[25]

In addition to illuminating studies of gender and work, the lens of body labor can also bring new perspectives to the study of race and immigration. In *Silent Travelers: Germs, Genes and the "Immigrant Menace,"*

Alan Kraut writes, "While scholars have paid considerable attention to negotiations between newcomers and native-born in matters of politics, religion, music, food, and social behaviors of various kinds, insufficient attention has been paid to the ongoing conversation between aliens and Americans over matters of the body."[26] Kraut has coined the term *medicalized nativism* to describe the justification of anti-immigrant sentiments based on fears of bodily contagion. While this embodied pathologizing of immigrants has been explored from a public health perspective, few have analyzed the embodied dimensions of everyday contact between immigrants and natives by looking at gendered work in the global service economy. Thus, by "bringing the body back in" to the study of race, immigration, gender, and work, the concept of body labor as applied to manicuring work reveals new dimensions of everyday social relations.

How, then, do I define *body labor*, and how does this concept relate to emotional labor? The term *body labor* designates commercialized exchanges in which service workers attend to the physical comfort and appearance of the customers, through direct contact with the body (such as touching, massaging, and manicuring) and by attending to the feelings involved with these practices. Furthermore, body labor requires that service workers manage their own feelings regarding the corporeality of their work while instilling their work with a sense of caring for their customers. Thus I use the term *body labor* to incorporate both emotional and embodied dimensions of body-service work, whereas the term *emotional labor* specifically references Hochschild's concept and related scholarship. While Hochschild distinguishes between emotion work and emotional labor, I adapt her concepts to draw distinctions among body work, body labor, and physical labor but also acknowledge overlap in these concepts.[27] I use *body work* as a general term for referring to commercial and noncommercial efforts directed at maintaining or improving the health and/or appearance of the body. This can include caring for one's own or another's body, whether paid or unpaid. *Physical labor* refers to work enacted *by* the body as the tool or form of labor. In contrast, the term *body labor* focuses specifically on the exchange value of services performed *on* the body for a wage or other form of compensation. Body labor entails extensive physical labor in which the body serves as the vehicle for performing service work, but it also incorporates the body as the *site* or *object* upon which services are performed. It also involves the management of commercialized *feelings*, which is the defining character-istic of emotional labor, but *body labor* emphasizes the management of commercialized *embodied* exchanges and thus examines feelings as they are related to the servicing of bodies.

These two arenas—feelings and bodies—are often referenced as pri-mary components of women's shared experiences and are framed in opposition to men's presumed commonalities in the domains of intellect and action. These outmoded binaries stubbornly persist, further mistak-enly enforcing beliefs that women's feelings and bodies are not only dis-tinct from men's but similar to each other's. An intersectional analysis is again important here, as it highlights differences between women, as well as parallels and distinctions in emotions, bodies, and the work they entail.

Hochschild's definition of emotional labor focuses on a particular form that "requires one to induce or suppress feeling in order to sus-tain the outward countenance that produces the proper state of mind in others—in this case, the sense of being cared for in a convivial and safe place."[28] However, rather than being regarded as one form of emotional labor, this kind of caring attentive service has often been applied as a general definition. Asian-owned nail salons thus serve as a rich site to explore the range of emotional labor in work sites that are differently gendered, raced, and classed and are not necessarily governed by the feeling rules of white middle-class America. Furthermore, these salons can illuminate other sites in which emotional labor incorporates bodies as well as feelings and involves women serving women (as opposed to mainly women serving men).

DESCRIPTION OF THE RESEARCH

I began this project as my dissertation research in 1997–98, with four-teen months of intensive fieldwork in New York City nail salons. While drawing from this early research, the data in the book include much more recent research during the summers of 2003, 2006, 2007, and 2009.

Data collection for this project has thus spanned more than a decade, thereby documenting patterns of both change and continuity in these sites. I have served as a receptionist, shared meals, and socialized with the owners, workers, and patrons, including visits to employees' homes and churches and several impromptu visits to *noreh-bang* (Korean-style karaoke clubs). I sought employment as a manicurist, and although I found one owner who was generous (or naive) enough to let me work in her salon, I abandoned this strategy, in part because I lacked proper licensing but mostly because of my thorough technical ineptitude. (Even for the sake of better research, it is hard to justify having someone pay you to do their nails when you cannot even make your own look presentable.) I thus pursued another strategy to gain access to the salons—cooperation with a community-based Asian American organization, the Committee Against Anti-Asian Violence, to offer English-language workplace literacy classes to manicurists.[29] Initially, these classes gained me access and offered some reciprocity for respondents' support and cooperation, but I increasingly incorporated many of the insights and interactions from these classes into the data collection. While my presence as a researcher invariably altered the naturalistic setting, our shared ethnicity (I am a second-generation Korean American woman) allowed me to blend into the site, despite our class, immigration, and generational differences; that I was able to blend in is evidenced by some customers' mistaking me for the daughter of the owner of one salon.

The research design for the study included ethnography at six sites: "Uptown Nails" and "Exclusive Nails," located in predominantly white middle-class and upper-class neighborhoods; "Downtown Nails" and "Artistic Nails" in predominantly black (African American and Caribbean) working- and lower-middle-class neighborhoods; and "Crosstown Nails" and "Convenient Nails" in racially and socioeconomically mixed neighborhoods. In addition, the research included in-depth, semistructured interviews ($N = 77$) with thirteen Korean nail salon owners, fifteen Korean nail salon workers, twenty-three black customers, and twenty-six white customers. I also conducted more than two dozen key respondent interviews with representatives of Korean business associations, reporters for the Korean ethnic press, New York State licensing officials, administrators at the New York City mayor's office, instructors at Korean-operated nail schools, employees of Korean nail supply stores and distributors, and staff at several local community organizations and national advocacy groups. To provide comparisons based on gender and ethnicity, I interviewed two Korean men who are nail salon owners, two Korean male manicurists, three white male customers, two black male customers, two Vietnamese nail salon owners (one man, one woman), and one Chinese, one Russian, and two Ecuadoran women manicurists. To provide comparisons to other Korean-owned small businesses, I engaged in limited participant observation in a Korean-owned grocery store and interviewed the owner and manager. As part of extended participant observation, I engaged women in dozens of informal unstructured interviews about nails on subways, at parties, waiting in lines, and in the myriad locations in which New Yorkers find an excuse to strike up a conversation. Research followed the institutional review board protocols of the sponsoring institutions.

In-depth interviews averaged ninety minutes to two hours for owners and workers and thirty to forty-five minutes for customers. I interviewed owners and workers in Korean or English, depending on their preference and level of fluency. Several bilingual research assistants helped with locating respondents, translation, transcription, and follow-up interviews. Rather than editing participants' and translators' grammatical errors, I have preserved their use of English as it shows the natural speech patterns of Korean immigrants. I interviewed customers in English at the salon while they were having their manicures, and in some cases I arranged a follow-up meeting or telephone interview. I tape-recorded interviews when interviewees consented to the procedure (approximately two-thirds of the interviewees). In cases where respondents refused or where tape-recording was difficult, I made extensive handwritten notes and typed them immediately afterward. I use pseudonyms for customers and service providers that approximate the names they use in the salons. As many Korean women have adopted American-style names in the workplace, I follow this convention. I have also changed the names of nail salons. I refer to key respondents according to a description of their positions and, if they gave permission, by their names and organizational affiliations.

RESEARCHING ONE'S OWN: REFLEXIVITY
AND FEMINIST METHODOLOGY

Where does the urge come from to barge into strangers' lives and pick apart the meanings of their words, gestures, random thoughts, and most hidden feelings? It has become standard practice in ethnographic and feminist research for the author to provide a biographical account of the experiences that drive her interest in the project. These practices are sometimes misunderstood or dismissed as self-indulgent and superfluous to the study, perhaps satisfying readers' curiosity but a distraction from the real data and analysis. In the eyes of its harshest critics, reflexivity is regarded as an excuse for relativism or sloppiness. I do not agree. On the contrary, recent theorizing in various disciplinary and interdisciplinary fields, especially feminist methodology, emphasizes the importance of situating the researcher vis-à-vis the research sites and participants in order to acknowledge biases and account for them in data collection and interpretation.[30] Practices of reflexivity have evolved to include not only reflections on the researcher's social location and its impact on the research but also evaluation of the multiple perspectives of participants and audiences and how the context of academic institutions and political discourse impact this process. While I do not address all these dimensions of reflexivity, I have written myself into the text at various points in order to make my perspectives and role in shaping the research transparent and to allow readers to assess the validity of the findings and consider alternative interpretations.[31]

Several biographical experiences shaped the ethnographic impulses behind this project, not the least of which is shared ethnicity with many of the research subjects. I am the daughter of Korean immigrants. Like many of the women in this study, my mother entered into immigrant entrepreneurship, pouring the family savings into a small business, an Asian gift shop rather than a nail salon. Working in the shop as a child, I witnessed her struggles to negotiate not only everyday relations with customers but also her own multiple roles as self-employed businesswoman, wife and then ex-wife of a minister, mother of four young children, supporter of extended family in Korea, and new U.S. citizen.

I tell this story to acknowledge that my immediate sympathies tend to lie with the Korean women who work in and own the salons. Their struggles to earn a living, negotiate a new culture, and find meaning in their lives as immigrants resonate with my parents' story of displacement and uneven assimilation into U.S. society. At the same time I have often inwardly criticized these women for their discriminatory behavior, ethnocentric views, traditional gender norms, and unrealistic expectations for their children's achievement. While I feel strong ties to my Korean heritage, my upbringing has been largely outside the Korean community, and I identify most strongly as Asian American. My experiences illustrate that the terms *Korean* and *Asian American* do not refer to homogeneous groups but are undercut by multiple divisions, including citizenship, religion, class, political ideologies, and gender and sexual politics. I have also worked as an activist with several community and labor rights organizations, experiences that shape my concerns about the working conditions in the salons. Chinese and Latina workers of various ethnicities are increasingly employed to perform the dirtiest, most undesirable, work for the lowest pay and in the most undesirable working conditions. Lacking Spanish- and Chinese-language ability and research support, I regret the limitations of this study in addressing their experiences. I was able to conduct only a few interviews and engage in limited participant observation with these workers.

My indebtedness to the Korean owners for allowing me to conduct research in their salons necessitated that I maintain cordial relations with them and respect their viewpoints. This was most challenging when they expressed openly racist or antifeminist views. I was often torn between not saying anything and appearing to validate their perspectives or confronting them, at the risk of altering the naturalistic setting and losing access to the research sites. Early in my research I mostly kept my mouth shut, but as the level of trust with participants increased, I became more open about expressing my views. Several interesting and revealing interactions resulted, and I have included these as part of the data presentation throughout the book. One story in particular is worth highlighting here for its theoretical and methodological significance for this study.

To get to know the manicurists and reciprocate for their participation in my research, I offered to give English lessons during breaks at one salon, Uptown Nails. Although initially this was a gesture of appreciation to the women for agreeing to participate in my study, I found that the classes I held transformed my research questions and the dynamics of knowledge and power in the research process. For the first class I presented a lesson on how to ask for directions, copied from a beginner text for teaching English as a second language. The women participated dutifully, reading handouts, repeating phrases, and even good-humoredly acting out role-plays. However, the following week, when I arrived with another lesson, the women balked. Nancy tactfully told me that they appreciated my willingness to teach them, but they preferred that I just do my research. As I tried to hide my hurt feelings for their rebuke of my attempt at feminist reciprocity, I inquired, "Are you too busy, or do you not think it is important to learn English?" Stacey, the manager, instantly blurted, "Oh, no, we think it's very important to learn English, just not the English that you are teaching us." My curiosity sparked, I ventured, "So, what English do you think is important?" Stacey looked me in the eye and said, "I want to know how you say, 'You look like you lost weight.'" Nancy then chimed in, "How do you say, 'This color looks good with your dress'?" Another manicurist interjected, "*This* is the most important thing to know how to say—'Your boyfriend will think you look pretty!'" We all burst out laughing, and for the next half hour they bombarded me with questions about ways to compliment customers, including comparing them with various movie stars. I felt as if scales had fallen from my eyes. Rather than obsequiously catering to their customers, the manicurists are strategic in their delivery of emotional pampering and revealed that they understand the skills that they need to fulfill this aspect of their work.

At the time this interaction took me by surprise, but looking back several insights are now obvious to me. First, manicurists at this upscale salon clearly understood the expectation that they attend to their customers' feelings, and they did so consciously and at times humorously, rather than as victims or blind followers of the dictates of beauty service. Second, their conformity to their customers' expectations does not signal a blind desire to assimilate but instead derives from the conditions of gendered service work, specifically, pampering body labor at nail spas. In other words, their emotional and embodied performances, rather than cultural traits, are adaptations to the kind of labor they engage in as immigrant women workers. At the same time their accommodations to body labor end up reinforcing the controlling image of hardworking, eager-to-please Asian immigrants. Finally, these strategic negotiations are often invisible to customers who benefit from them and even to somewhat detached observers like me. They became apparent only when the women took it upon themselves to confront me, in this case with the total inefficacy of the formal English that I was attempting to teach them, and instead asserted their need to learn colloquial forms of flattery and banter. Thus, instead of the researcher's bestowing her superior knowledge upon the researched, these women demonstrated their more nuanced understanding of the work that they perform on a daily basis.

Likewise, I have also had to challenge my hidden biases toward nail salon customers as dupes of oppressive ideologies of beauty and femininity and instead recognize their active participation in shaping the meaning of their manicuring practices. I must admit that in the beginning I saw the customers as mostly vain and frivolous. I had never had my nails professionally manicured and could not fathom the investment these women had in maintaining their fingertips. Also, my first paid nonfamily employment as a teenager had been in a suburban beauty salon that catered mostly to well-heeled elderly white women. While I have some fond recollections of customers, my strongest memories are of unremitting requests to adjust hair dryer settings, bring cups of coffee, and assist with handbags and coats, accompanied by frequent comments about my diligent work ethic and unaccented English. Thus my initial orientation toward customers could best be characterized as distant and somewhat dismissive.

Over months of conducting research, however, I came to know the nail salon customers and to understand the multilayered significance to them of manicured nails. Early in my research I engaged in forays around the city, receiving manicures and pedicures. While the purpose of these visits was to scope out sites and develop relationships with potential participants, I confess that, like many customers, I quickly took to these services. In one salon the women insisted on giving me free manicures, and I recall the warmth I felt toward them as they massaged the tensions of graduate school and city living out of my hands. When people complimented my newly polished nails, I felt surprisingly flattered. Once I splurged on acrylic extensions and designs and basked in the feeling of power I felt drumming my long airbrushed nails on tabletops and subway railings. While my own manicuring phase was short lived, it was enough to engender an appreciation for the allure of nice-looking nails and the services that accompany them, especially for women whose bimonthly manicures may be the only thing they consistently do for themselves.

Are such beauty practices parasitic to women's self-esteem and a diversion from other more worthy pursuits or do they offer women a potential source of pleasure and power? In the women's studies, sociology, and Asian American studies courses that I have taught, I often find students intensely divided in these debates regarding beauty culture. While I agree that contemporary standards of feminine beauty have reached ridiculous extremes and fuel the exploitation of women, I also recognize that beauty and its regimens can provide meaning and opportunities for certain women. While I am critical of the distorted images of women's bodies used by corporate advertising to boost profit, I doubt that the multibillion-dollar beauty industry will disappear anytime soon. In addition, employment and self-employment in nail salons will remain one of the more attractive job prospects for Asian immigrant women as long as they are deterred from other jobs. I also think that it is important to understand the various needs that manicured nails fulfill for customers while not giving up on possibilities for women to fulfill these needs other than cosmetically. Thus, rather than condemning or dismissing the enterprise of manicuring nails, I regard these exchanges as a rare window through which to view women and the complex forces that shape their bodies, feelings, and relations with each other.

OVERVIEW OF THE BOOK

This book uses nail salons as a site to examine the patterns of commercialized emotional and embodied exchange and the contexts of these interactions, both inside and outside salons. The lens of body labor illuminates how and why the actions, beliefs, and feelings that seem so natural and justified for one party in this exchange can strike the other as rude, demeaning, or simply incomprehensible. As a sociologist, I focus not so much on individuals' internal processing of these exchanges, which is more the work of psychologists, but on the social structures that shape them and give them meaning. My purpose in describing and analyzing nail services is not to valorize or condemn women on either side of the manicuring table. Nonetheless, I believe that inequalities in power and status allow some women greater choice, and hence responsibility, in shaping these exchanges.

The chapters in this book address multiple dimensions of manicuring exchanges. Chapter 1 examines the growth of the nail salon industry, focusing on New York City and the clustering of Asian women, particularly Koreans, in this employment sector. How have nail salons and the services they offer become so prevalent? Who are the women who engage in these service interactions, and what factors have led them to either side of the manicuring table? In short, what can a manicure tell us about the larger society in which it is performed? This chapter situates the burgeoning nail salon industry within the expansion and globalization of service work. The conditions that have fueled Asian women's domination of the nail niche in New York City include gendered employment patterns, labor migration flows, ethnic community resources, racialized representations, and political and economic relations between South Korea and the United States.

Chapter 2 documents the stories of particular Korean women working in the salons. Who are these women, and how did they find this work? Why do they stay? How does this work affect their lives? This chapter examines in-depth narratives of Korean owners and workers, situating them within debates in the study of gender and immigration, particularly regarding the mixed gains and losses that migration, paid work, and reconfigured family relations bring to women.

Chapter 3 focuses on the customers. Who are the women who patronize these salons, and what are the factors that influence them to get their nails done? Why do they choose particular nail styles, and how do they understand their own manicuring practices? Customers' narratives illustrate that beauty is not monolithic but that women in different racial and class locations construct and reconstruct the meaning of the manicure according to contrasting norms of femininity and beauty.

The next three chapters shift attention to relations across the manicuring table among customers, workers, and owners in different kinds of nail salons in diverse racial and socioeconomic settings. How do virtual strangers negotiate relations that involve semi-intimate physical and emotional contact that traverses lines of race, class, immigration, and gender? Varying forms of body labor emerge in distinct settings, and the contours of this work shape racial constructions of Asians and their relations with other groups.

Chapter 4 examines "nail spas" serving predominantly white middle-class and upper-class customers through "pampering body labor." Interactions at these sites demonstrate the gap between one-dimensional representations and the actual complexities of relations between Asians and whites. Gendered service practices intersect with dominant representations of the Asian "model minority" in ways that uphold the racial and class privilege of white middle-class and upper-class customers while reinforcing notions of Asians as a laudable but still marginalized group.

Chapter 5 explores "nail art salons" serving mostly black working-class customers through "expressive body labor." This type of service offers original creative nail designs while expressing respect and reciprocity toward individual customers and the communities in which these salons are situated. Expressive body labor contradicts representations of "Korean-black conflict" that naturalize racial tensions between these two groups. Instead, interactions in these salons demonstrate how Asian immigrant service providers and black customers negotiate shifting gender, race, and class alliances in these salons. The gendered performance of expressive body labor can subvert racial hierarchies, in ways that mitigate but do not transcend dominant racial discourses.

Finally, the focus of chapter 6 is "discount nail salons" serving racially and socioeconomically mixed clientele through "routinized body labor." The conditions of gendered work reflected in these sites fuel negative racial stereotypes of Asians as the "yellow peril," who spread disease and bring down wage and living standards. The forms of body labor that Asian women enact in discount salons aim to disrupt this discourse of contamination by delivering services that are neither special nor objectionable. However, the provision of even these scaled-down manicures is hampered by toxic products, labor rights violations, and customers' demands for fast inexpensive service.

The conclusion addresses the question "What is a manicure worth?" and situates nail salon interactions within current debates about the desirability of new immigrants and their impact on U.S. society and culture. While the chapter underscores the persistent divisions between women even in interactions involving intimacy and interdependence, it also explores prospects for understanding and improving women's lives on both sides of the manicuring table through efforts to upgrade nail salon work as well as to address the various needs that manicured nails fulfill in customers' lives.

Writing a book such as this is both immensely rewarding and frustrating, as it requires excluding many worthy and important avenues of inquiry in striving for a theoretically and empirically coherent analysis. I take responsibility for the limitations of this study and look forward to engaging with scholars whom I hope will delve into other dimensions of this intriguing niche.[32] By fleshing out the implications of embodied service work for social relations among diverse women, I hope to provide those who regularly purchase and perform manicures with new insights into this complex social exchange. In addition, I would be pleased if those who have never set foot (or hand) in one of these establishments decide to venture into the fascinating worlds that unfold in their corner nail salon.

One ## "There's No Business Like the Nail Business"

In this most manicured of metropolises—there is a nail technician for every 1,000 New Yorkers—inexpensive nail service, for some women, borders on becoming an inalienable right.

Christine Haughney, 2003

The old American dream with a special Korean polish . . . an American classic with a rich New York overlay. For it's about immigrants, with few English language skills, no great capital, but lots of hard work and widespread success. It's also the old-fashioned dream, for there are no SBA loans, no setasides, no subsidies.

Alair A. Townsend, 1989

A manicure is no longer a purely private ritual that a woman gives herself, her daughter, or a girlfriend in the quiet of her own bathroom. Instead, it is something she increasingly purchases in a nail salon and from an Asian manicurist. In the buying and selling of manicuring services, women both implicate their own bodies in intimate commercialized exchanges and expand the boundaries of the service economy to encompass regimens of hygiene and physical adornment that were once private. In so doing, they also encounter at close range women whom they would normally regard only from a safe social distance.

Why have nail salons cropped up on city blocks and in suburban strip malls across the United States? Why do so many women get manicures? Why have these services proliferated in specific cities, such as New York?

Why do so many Asian women, and Korean women in particular, own and work in these salons? These questions recognize the simultaneous ways that supply, demand, and location shape the growth of the global service economy and the development of a specific ethnic-dominated niche like nail salons within it. While these are distinct questions, they are also closely interrelated. The question of why so many Asian women work in nail salons can be answered only in relation to the question of why so many women in the United States desire and purchase these services. Furthermore, in order to understand the proliferation of nail salons in a specific site such as New York City, it is important to examine not only the individual consumers who purchase these services and the providers who offer them but also the economic, political, and cultural contexts in which these exchanges occur.

In this chapter I respond to these questions—why nails, why New York, and why Asian women?—by examining the appeal of nail services to diverse customers, the growth of the nail salon industry in New York City, and the clustering of Asian women, particularly Koreans, in this employment sector. The politics of race, class, and immigration in the United States and the shifting dynamics of the global service economy provide the context that shapes the relations that women forge around the manicuring table. The growth in manicuring services reflects a general expansion of capitalist markets, the specifically gendered processes relating to the commercialization of women's bodies, and the positions of women in the labor market. The influx of women into the paid labor force has increased the demand for such services, because more women can now afford them. However, another important factor is heightened desires for beauty as a commodity. The purchase of body-related services is fueled by ramped-up social standards for women's appearance, as well as by women's own longing for the accoutrements of beauty, including the pampering services associated with it.

At the same time women's desires for beauty services would simply be longings rather than daily enactments if it were not for the presence of a ready fleet of immigrant women workers to provide these services. The lifestyle that many urbanites take for granted in cities such as New York is possible only because of the influx of new immigrants and their

Figure 3. Asian immigrant women have expanded the nail salon industry by offering a range of services and products, such as the array of polishes in this display.

willingness to work long arduous hours for minimal pay in jobs that many native-born Americans view as beneath them. While immigrant women from specific ethnic groups are not the sole creators of these jobs or the terms under which they perform them, they contribute to creation of these specialized niches by capitalizing on the limited choices available to them.

The formation of New York City's nail salon industry and its domination by Asian women simultaneously draws on and contests two competing racial discourses. On the one hand, representations of Asian success in this industry exemplify praise for the innovation and diligence of Asian Americans and their independence from government "special treatment," as referenced in the Townsend epigraph. On the other hand, their success fuels the anti-Asian and anti-immigrant sentiments held by those who blame these groups for downgrading U.S. working conditions. Neither of these discourses, which are discussed in-depth in later chapters, adequately accounts for the composite factors that drive nail salon growth in New York and other cities. While Asian immigrant women are indeed hardworking and resourceful, these characteristics alone cannot account for their domination of the nail salon industry.

Rather, it is the context of the "global city" that shapes the consistent demand for inexpensive and convenient beauty services and the terms of who does this work.[1] In other words, while customers' desire for manicured nails and manicurists' need to earn a living are certainly important factors in the increase in nail salons, these factors are driven by larger processes pertaining to the postindustrial transformation of cities and city life. Through a fortuitous convergence of global and local factors, rather than through their unique cultural traits, Korean women have successfully mobilized individual and community resources to sustain entrepreneurship and employment in this service niche.

WHY NAILS? MANICURES AND THE COMMERCIALIZATION OF THE BODY

Why do more and more women now pay for manicures instead of doing their nails themselves? The answer to this question, far from a simple story of women's innate longing for physical beauty, instead pulls back the curtain on the surreptitious but revolutionary reorganization of social life in the late twentieth century. Arlie Hochschild describes this sea change as "the commercialization of intimate life," in which more and more human activity that was formerly engaged in by family, friends, and community members has been subsumed into the global capitalist economy.[2] In short, capitalism has expanded geographically to hinterlands previously untouched by commodity markets as well as into areas of human life once viewed as private and even sacred. Other scholars have similarly explored how formerly unpaid activities, such as raising children, caring for the elderly, preparing food, doing laundry, and mowing the lawn, are now routinely farmed out to paid service workers.[3] In addition, market capitalism has spawned new occupations, ranging from on-line matchmaker to personal assistant, home organizer, party escort, and life coach. These services are designed to meet the emotional and social needs formerly met by friends, churches, bowling leagues, neighborhood associations and community groups and reflect an overall decline in civic ties.[4] Most important for this study, a new range of service providers—personal trainers, massage therapists, plastic surgeons, and manicurists, to name a few—have staked out the body, its appearance, comfort, and health, as a profit-making venue.

Whereas Hochschild's study focuses on the commercialization of human feelings, the interactions in nail salons illuminate the complexities of buying and selling services that cater to both human emotions and bodies. These interactions are not unique to nail salons but reveal how the routine upkeep of the body and its appearance have spawned an array of purchasable services. Indeed, the growth in nail salons has been impressive—and the overall growth in beauty services has been staggering. Like the manicure, a child's first haircut is no longer a ritual performed on a stool in a family kitchen but is farmed out to hair-cutting chains around the country.[5] Rather than giving each other backrubs at the end of a long day, two tired spouses can opt for a fifteen-minute chair massage on the way home. A child's diaper or an elderly parent's bedpan are increasingly changed by paid caregivers rather than family members. The process of assigning market value to bodies—their appearance, functions, and the forms of contact between them—generates new forms of work, which I refer to as *body labor*. By examining how body labor exchanges occur, and what the participants gain and lose through them, the study of manicures can illuminate similar patterns in other embodied services.

While the levels and kinds of consumption of these complex embodied and emotional services increase, the means to purchase them has been eroded for most segments of the population. However, rather than decreasing the demand for body services, these economic pressures can fuel the market for them. Just like going to the movies, indulging in body services can be the ideal escape in a recession. With unemployment and downsizing looming as constant threats, workday concerns take over more and more of individual and collective life. Rather than turning away from market solutions, people increasingly turn to the power of consumption, not only to obtain material goods but also to purchase services that provide care and connection, especially for tired and stressed bodies.

This process of seeking commercialized solutions for intimate needs, however, is far from fluid and care free. As Viviana Zelizer writes in *The Purchase of Intimacy*, while the arenas of intimacy and economics have long intermingled in various forms, the negotiation of the terms of this intermingling is often confusing and fraught, and increasingly so in new venues where social conventions are not fully worked out.[6] Thus social actors must negotiate new forms of intimate relations within existing frameworks, even when these frameworks are not fully up to the task of making sense of how commerce and intimacy mix in both uncharted and ubiquitous ways.

Into this brave new world of commercialized intimacy enters the nail salon. In a day devoid of touch and beauty, the nail salon provides a taste of both. For $15 or less customers can brush their cares away while their manicurists dote on them, massaging the day's tensions out of their hands and putting polish on their cracked or lackluster nails. This belief in the manicure as cure-all is expressed simply in an evocative greeting card that depicts a young woman soaking her fingers. The caption: "Life is tough. I recommend getting a manicure and a really cute helmet."[7] A manicure thus can serve as a quick fix to a host of problems, ranging from demanding children, nagging spouses, critical bosses, and needy friends to larger anxieties about seemingly unsolvable personal and social problems.

While the avenues for relief or distraction from the cares and demands of domestic, work, and social life are many and varied, the combination of emotional and physical attention offered in a haven of women who cater to the needs of other women carries a particular appeal. The changing dynamics of women's place in the home and workplace, as well as their substantial increase in earnings, are thus important pieces in understanding the growth of the nail salon industry and, more broadly, the commercialization of the body and body-related services. Since the late 1960s women have entered into the paid labor force in historically unprecedented numbers.[8] While their paychecks are usually central to maintaining basic economic survival for themselves and their dependents, women's paid labor also gives them greater control over discretionary spending. Work provides them with income to purchase nail services but also fuels their consumption of these services, as many women feel that professionally manicured nails are an expected part of their work attire (see chapter 3). Even in workplaces where such appearance standards are not explicit, well-manicured nails can augment professional appearance and give some women a confidence boost.

Manicures can also be a way of reassuring women and those around them that they do indeed conform to norms of traditional femininity, even as they challenge and redefine these standards in various areas of their lives. On the other hand, some women use original nail designs to express an identity that is distinct from or in opposition to mainstream feminine norms. Given the wide-ranging needs that a weekly manicure can fulfill, is it any wonder that nail salons have become a major growth industry?

NAIL SALONS AS A GROWTH INDUSTRY

"There's No Business Like the Nail Business" trumpeted the headline in a Vietnamese community newspaper, *Nguoi Viet*, reporting that revenues from nail salons in the United States topped $6 billion in 2004 and the number of nail salons in the United States grew from 32,674 in 1993 to 53,615 in 2003, an increase of more than 60 percent in a decade.[9] In 2006–2007 *Nails* magazine estimated the United States had 58,330 nail salons and 347,898 nail technicians in a $6.16 billion industry.[10] Even the much more conservative figures from the U.S. Bureau of Labor Statistics projected 28 percent growth between 2006 and 2016.[11] Despite this tremendous growth, the job of manicurist and the workplace of nail salon easily slip below the radar of both official statistics and everyday perceptions.[12]

Nail salon growth has also been fueled by two technological innovations—the electric file and acrylic nail products—often to mixed reviews. By adding speed and versatility to the manicuring process, while also fostering dependence on regular salon visits, these innovations have substantially increased the volume and kinds of services the salons offer, enabling them to reach out to a much wider consumer base. Of the nail

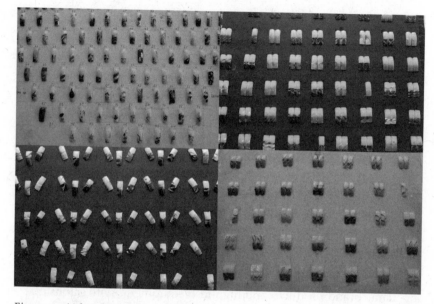

Figure 4. Airbrushed and hand-painted nail designs on acrylic nails have fueled the growth of nail salons.

technicians who responded to a *Nails* survey, 63.2 percent use an electric file, and such use is no longer disparaged as a "symbol of a lazy nail technician or an assembly-line salon. What used to be called a drill is now used by even old-time filing purists."[13] These technological break-throughs have revolutionized the techniques and products available for nail care and design. Unlike old-fashioned press-on nail tips, acrylic compounds form a durable, thin, and natural-looking surface that holds various colors and applications.[14] Acrylics can be used to repair broken nails, smooth out uneven or damaged nail surfaces, discourage nail bit-ing, and to create long and thick nail extensions. However, they require particular skills to apply and maintain, necessitating frequent return vis-its to the nail salon.

While greatly expanding the overall industry, advances in technology and products have not necessarily translated into greater profits for indi-vidual nail salons or technicians. Mass marketing means more customers who pay less. By speeding up and slashing the price of a manicure, the electric file allows a faster turnover in the salon chair, thereby expanding the market for potential nail care customers. At the same time the number of dissatisfied customers increases with this assembly-line style of service provision (see chapter 6).

Furthermore, the increase in customers also draws more competitors into the industry. Whereas many major cities once had one nail salon for every three or four blocks, now it is not uncommon to see several salons on a single block. Long-time nail salon owner Jean Hwang lamented, "There are too many nail salons today. When I first started there weren't as many. However, the number of people getting their nails done have increased tremendously. Everyone, from little children to grandmothers, are getting their nails done. But the prices have gone down and my income remained pretty much the same. The only way it could go is down." In aspiring to keep up with competitors, many salon owners have upgraded their services to include massages, eyebrow and leg waxing, name brand products, and high-tech equipment. With salons opening up across the street from each other, a 2001 *New York Times* headline proclaimed, "Success, at a Price, at Nail Salons; Anxiety Tempers Good Times for Koreans in Business."[15]

In this climate of intense competition, salons must adopt different strategies to stay competitive. They can cut their prices, along with wages and other costs, to the bare minimum; they can justify higher prices by offering higher quality products and services; or they can create new products and services. In other words, nail salons must not only tap into existing demand but must generate new demand by reaching out to customers who otherwise would not purchase these services on a regular basis. In attempting to expand their consumer base, nail salons have targeted different kinds of customers with different kinds of services. The three main types of salons on which this study focuses are: nail spas catering largely to middle- and upper-class white women; nail art salons serving mostly African American working-class customers; and discount salons targeting a mixed racial and socioeconomic clientele. These different kinds of salons, which are the focus of later chapters, reflect the innovation and resourcefulness of individual salon owners and the fluidity of the industry as a whole as well as the shifting dynamics of consumption in the global service economy. In understanding the importance of gender, race, and immigration in shaping the divergent patterns of consumption and provision of beauty services, it is illuminating to compare contrasting patterns in nail salons versus hair salons.

HAIR VERSUS NAIL SALONS: "ONLY BLACK WOMEN CAN DO BRAIDS"

What is different about doing nails and hair? Or, to put it another way, how do ethnic-owned nail salons differ from ethnic-owned hair salons? One glaring difference is that nail salons attract customers from diverse racial and ethnic groups, whereas many beauty salons, especially those that are ethnically owned, cater overwhelmingly to coethnic customers. For example, Julie Willett describes how beauty salons in African American communities have fulfilled the needs of clientele who historically have been excluded from mainstream beauty salons or whose hair requires care that mainstream salons cannot provide. As one African American customer whom I interviewed commented, "Only black women can do braids." Furthermore, black beauty salons have also served as centers for social networking and, in some cases, political organizing. Similar dynamics emerge among Latinas, as Ginetta Candelario shows that Dominican-owned salons in Washington Heights, a neighborhood on the Upper West Side of Manhattan, import specific styles and procedures from the home country while also providing newcomers with social contacts and information that is crucial to negotiating jobs, housing, and schools.[16] While these establishments serve important community functions, they are also largely dependent on patronage by members of their own ethnic group. This limits their customer base and their location to ethnic enclaves and, hence, their overall profit-making ability.

But why do hair salons cater mostly to members of the same racial and ethnic group, while nail salons have been able to attract diverse clients? The answer lies partly in the differences between hair and nails and their racial meanings and partly in the differences between the representations and resources of the groups that operate these enterprises. Interestingly, in stark contrast to Asian-owned nail salons, which proliferate in a wide range of urban, suburban, and even small-town settings, Asian-owned beauty salons are a very circumscribed phenomenon, visible mainly in Asian ethnic enclaves in large cities. The contrast in the patterns of clients who support Asian-owned beauty salons (same race or ethnic group) versus nail salons (diverse customers) suggests that hair, even more so than nails, emerges as a primary signifier of racial identity, both in appearance and care. Hairstyles, textures, and treatments are markers of racial and ethnic identity, and the experience and skills to attend to particular kinds of hair emerge as forms of racial differentiation. Thus hair stands out in both practical and symbolic terms as a racial marker.[17]

Nails also carry racial meanings, as I discuss in chapter 3, with pastel French manicures carrying associations with white womanhood and airbrushed acrylic nails signaling black and Latina femininities. However, the knowledge necessary to create certain kinds of nails is not seen as limited to members of the same racial and ethnic group as that of the customer. Instead, as the following chapters explore, diverse customers intentionally value and seek out Asian women *because* of distinct racialized characteristics that they regard as desirable in their manicurists.

These racializations of Asian women as preferred nail service providers emerge in the specific context of large urban centers, such as New York City, that receive many immigrants. Furthermore, customers' willingness to invest regularly in a range of nail services is notably higher in large cities, where appearances carry a particular kind of cachet.

WHY NEW YORK?

New York, New York—in a city that specializes in specialties, a thriving business niche based on the single product of manicured nails is an extension of the same cultural and economic mix that has produced such eclectic services as dog walking, bicycle delivery, and street corner massage. What factors have shaped the growth of the nail salon industry in New York City, and how are they similar to and different from the same industry in other cities? In retrospect, it seems obvious that manicuring mania would first have flourished in New York. New Yorkers are conditioned to want and expect instant access to a vast array of essential and nonessential products and services, and the mushrooming of nail salons is an outgrowth of this pervasive service culture. Janice, a thirty-year-old accessories importer who gets her nails done "religiously every ten days," explained, "New Yorkers are more fashion conscious. It's all a matter of appearances here. Part of it is keeping yourself well groomed, part is being able to have them done for you. It's relaxing at the end of the day to get your nails done. I would say half of the women in New York get them done." Gail, an African American customer, singled out New York for its highly developed nail art forms: "If I go somewhere else, in another state, then I would say . . . I won't see as much design or as much creativity as here, no. I definitely think, at least in the big cities, you'll see it, but New York is up there, probably near the peak."

In addition to the extent and kind of services, convenience and price are also distinctive to the New York nail scene. The reputation of New York's Korean-owned salons as a "great deal" is so widespread that Jill, a customer who works as a flight attendant, told me about coworkers from cities around the world who arrange stopovers in New York City exclusively to take advantage of "the $15 manicure/pedicure specials at the Korean stores." This testimony reflects the globalization of the service economy and the position of New York City as a hub.

Nail salon growth in New York began in the 1980s and took off exponentially in the 1990s. In 1991 nail industry sources counted 1,132 nail salons in New York State, and ten years later the number had nearly tripled to 3,236. While growth has slowed, the number has steadily increased, to 3,798 in 2004.[18] According to U.S. Census Bureau statistics on nail salons, in 1997 New York had the largest collective payroll for nail salon salaries—$1.93 million—and claimed 14.06 percent of total nationwide receipts for nail businesses, a close second to California at 14.22 percent.[19] These figures reflect a New York–specific context, as well as more general social and economic factors throughout the United States in the late twentieth century.

Despite competition from other cities, particularly Los Angeles, New York still maintains its position, symbolically if not actually, as both the fashion mecca and the immigrant-receiving capital of the world. New

York's status as what the leading immigration scholar Saskia Sassen calls a "global city" is unquestioned.[20] These global cities serve as command centers of national and transnational economies, drawing both the highly skilled, highly paid workforce at the top of the capitalist financial chain as well as the low-skilled and low-wage immigrant workers who provide the everyday support services to maintain this economy. This "servicing of the service sector" takes on distinct characteristics in New York City in light of the size and diversity of the advanced service sector—which includes finance, hotels and restaurants, fashion, advertising, and consulting.[21] Thus New York, while an iconoclastic city, also represents general trends in the shift from a manufacturing to a highly professionalized service economy and the incorporation of new immigrants to meet the low-wage service needs of this sector.[22]

The factors that have contributed to the growth of the nail salon industry in New York City play themselves out in similar but distinct ways in other cities. In particular, Vietnamese have dominated the industry in California and Texas. Chinese women have also made significant inroads into the niche in different cities. New York and most other states do not collect information about the ethnic breakdown of license holders, so statistics are difficult to find. Nonetheless, industry sources estimate that Vietnamese comprise up to 80 percent of the nail technicians in California and 25 percent nationwide.[23] Thus the New York City nail salon niche is, on the one hand, a unique phenomenon in terms of scale, timing, and its domination by Koreans and, on the other, fits a pattern of new Asian immigrants' establishing nail salons throughout the United States and other countries.

In sum, nail salons have emerged not as an anomaly but as part and parcel of the service-on-demand culture of New York and other urban centers. Without the workforce to meet these demands, however, most services that New Yorkers and other urban residents take for granted would simply be fantasies rather than actual thriving industries. A large and consistent influx of new immigrants willing and able to do the work is a necessary but not sufficient precondition. Favorable political and regulatory conditions allowing them to move into this work must also be present.

When Korean women first began to establish and work in specialized nail salons, they were able to acquire the necessary skills on the job and bypass the training and licensing requirements of full-service beauticians. Mary Lee, fifty-three, the owner of Mary Nails on Manhattan's Upper East Side, emigrated in 1978, found work in the nail salons immediately, and opened her own salon in 1982. College-educated, with a degree in physical education, she described the ease with which she gained her manicuring skills and was able to translate them into entrepreneurial success: "In the beginning, anyone could open a nail salon. We just needed a few tables and basic equipment. We just learned as we did it." The ability to gain skills on the job without having to receive formal training attracted many women, and strong social networks further channeled coethnic women into this niche. Given their limited time and resources for education and training, this open regulatory atmosphere was crucial to attracting Korean immigrant women.

In its early years nail salon work, lacking regulation, constituted informal sector employment that offered a ripe opportunity for new immigrants, and women in particular. Saskia Sassen argues that, contrary to popular belief, the growth of the informal economy in advanced societies is not the result of emigration from underdeveloped countries, but instead that informality is endemic to postindustrial economic restructuring.[24] While the informal economy can create opportunities for new immigrants, these opportunities open and close quickly depending on the local business climate, state policies, and the general levels of social tolerance. Most states have implemented credentialing requirements for manicurists.[25] However, New York State did not require licenses for nail technicians until 1994 (subsequent regulation and its impact are discussed later in this chapter and in chapter 6). Even in consideration of these later trends, the initial informality of nail salon work created opportunities for small business entrepreneurship and service employment, into which Asian immigrant women stepped.

WHY ASIAN IMMIGRANT WOMEN?

Who dominates a service niche and why? The domination of one immigrant group in any given employment niche is the outcome of long, complicated, and shifting rhythms of the global economy and the ability of individuals and ethnic communities to dance to its changing and irregular heartbeat. Various innovations such as electric files and acrylic nails, and conditions such as the increasing commercialization of body services and an unregulated business niche, may have opened up a market opportunity for expansion of the nail salon industry, but a small group of Korean immigrant women in New York turned this opportunity into an actual thriving business niche. The trade industry magazine *Nails* reported in 1992, "Nail salons have long been a stronghold for immigrant employment in larger cities, but the Koreans' entry into the industry has had the greatest impact."[26] More recently, Vietnamese emerged as a dominant force in the industry. Larry Gaynor, CEO of Nailco Salon Marketplace, told a reporter in 1997, "The nail industry was virtually flat for three years, and now it's starting to grow again because of the Asian salons."[27]

How and why have nail salons drawn in such a large supply of immigrant service workers, mostly women, from Asia? These questions demand a synthetic response that considers how immigrant employment niches are simultaneously gendered and dominated by particular racial and ethnic groups. This intersectional approach to gendered work addresses why women (and not men) work in particular niches, as well as why immigrant, not native-born women, take these jobs; why women from certain countries take up this employment; and why they choose a particular niche and not another? In unraveling the puzzle about why Asian women cluster so heavily in the nail salon industry, it is important to ask why women from other racial and ethnic groups have not been as successful in this niche. Certainly, Asian women, and Koreans in particular, have not been the only ones to recognize and pursue manicuring work as a potential profit-making venture. Various factors, ranging from individual motivations and skill to ethnic community resources to state regulation to racial and gender stereotypes, situate some women in more favorable positions than others to succeed in this line of employment. While certain factors push immigrant women in general into this line of work, other factors are specific to Asians and to Koreans in particular.

Instead of parsing the complex forces that have led Asians to dominate the nail salon niche, media and popular representations reference simplistic framings of Asians as the industrious and hardworking "model minority." These representations combine with gendered stereotypes of Asian women as docile, subservient, and well suited to detailed handiwork as an easy but erroneous explanation of their clustering in service work generally and nail salons in particular. These essentialist portrayals of Asian immigrants as naturally industrious and service oriented neglect the specific conditions that push them into beauty service work.

To understand why so many Asian women have entered into nail salon work, it is also important to ask why they have not entered into other kinds of work. When I asked one Korean woman why she worked in a nail salon, she gave the succinct response, "What other work is there?" Other respondents voiced similar sentiments (see chapter 2). The openings in nail salon work are the flip side of barriers in other traditionally gendered professional and semiprofessional occupations, such as nursing, teaching, and secretarial work. Unable to enter into these white-collar niches because of language and credentialing requirements, many Asian immigrant women turn to employment and self-employment in small business. Working in and potentially owning a nail salon becomes an attractive alternative, given the other low-wage jobs available—such as jobs in garment factories, domestic service, restaurants, bars and nightclubs, and working as unpaid family labor.

WHY KOREANS? GENDERED PATTERNS OF MIGRATION AND WORK

Young Ku Chang, a Korean American attorney, jokes that the job a new Korean immigrant finds upon coming to the United States "depends on the occupation of the person who picks up the immigrant at the airport."[28] Like all jokes, this one is funny because it strikes a chord of reality. Referring to the process of ethnic niche formation, it speaks to the centrality of social networks in determining the field of employment into which a new immigrant enters. These social networks establish and connect new immigrants to particular kinds of jobs and normalize work that might otherwise be stigmatized. Chang's comment takes on particular meaning when combined with another oft-heard sentiment in the Korean American community that emphasizes the gendered dimensions of Korean immigration to the United States: "If Korea is a country for men, America is for women." As Kyeyoung Park notes in *The Korean American Dream: Immigrants and Small Business in New York*, this saying refers to the pattern of "women-initiated migration" that has driven Korean immigration to the United States.[29] Thus Korean women's concentration in a particular employment niche such as nail salon work illuminates gendered patterns of global economic restructuring as well as specific historical relations between the Republic of Korea and the United States.

Gendered migration flows from South Korea to the United States have emerged through the political, economic, and military relations between these two countries, as wars, rapid industrialization, and state policies have had particular impacts on women. World War II, the Korean War, and the ongoing north-south division generated fears of war and political repression and served as major "push" factors for South Koreans in general to emigrate, but specific labor and family immigration policies favored Korean women, particularly nurses and wives of U.S. servicemen.[30]

Processes of uneven economic development in South Korea also served as an impetus for women to migrate. Since the 1970s the Republic of Korea (South Korea) has rapidly transformed itself from an impoverished country to one of the newly industrialized "Asian tigers," by relying upon foreign capital and export-oriented trade.[31] While spawning the rise of a large urban middle class, higher levels of consumption, and a modern infrastructure, this development model also fuels authoritarian state powers, class polarization, antiunionization, and a strong foreign military presence, all factors that have affected women in particular ways.[32]

Seungsook Moon calls the South Korean development model one of "militarized modernity" and "gendered citizenship" that defines male citizens by mandatory military service and women through their roles as reproducers and household managers.[33] Gendered citizenship limited women's paid work mainly to poor women who were forced into low-wage factory jobs. With the decline of the military dictatorship in 1987, women forged other models of citizenship through participation in the women's and labor rights movements, often in the face of violence and repression. While Moon does not explicitly analyze this pattern of gendered citizenship as a factor influencing gendered migration flows from South Korea to the United States, her research provides important background for understanding the context in which Korean women have come to the United States. Faced with pressure to conform to constraining domestic roles, limited job opportunities, and the dangers of engaging in social movements, women desiring greater economic, political, and social freedom have found the option of migrating to the United States attractive.

These incentives for middle-class South Korean women to migrate in the 1960s and 1970s resulted in relatively high levels of educated professionals in the Korean immigrant community in the United States. Although the class dynamics of Korean migration shifted in the 1980s to include more laborers, earlier immigrant waves came with substantial financial and human capital.[34] Their inability to enter into professions because of language or credentialing requirements caused many to channel their resources into small business ownership.

Yet even with these significant "push" factors on the South Korean side, Korean women's migration required corresponding "pull" factors on the U.S. side, and the most important were changes in U.S. immigration policy. The Immigration and Nationality Act of 1965, which removed the national origins quota system that had been in place since 1924, finally overrode nearly a century of anti-Asian exclusion laws and opened the doors for large numbers of Asian immigrants to resettle permanently in the United States.[35] The resulting increase in South Korean emigration was substantial: from 1976 into the early 1990s it averaged more than thirty thousand per year, peaking at 35,776 in 1986. Since then it has varied, depending on several factors, including economic conditions in Asia, but emigration from Korea averaged about 19,500 annually through 2007.[36]

Several factors led to a slowdown in Korean emigration beginning in the 1990s. As the South Korean economy flourished and the standard of living rose dramatically, fewer people found it necessary to emigrate to obtain well-paying jobs and an urban middle-class lifestyle, as they could secure these in the rapidly expanding metropolitan areas of Seoul and other cities. The 1988 Olympics, the democratic election of a civilian government, and signs of rapprochement with North Korea also have contributed to a greater sense of South Korean national pride and international status. In addition, the American dream has become tarnished, as stories of the economic hardship, racism, and social and cultural marginalization that Korean immigrants encounter in the United States are disseminated through the growth of international telecommunications and transnational return migration. Most striking, the 1992 acquittal of four Los Angeles police officers in the beating of Rodney King and the resulting civil unrest in Los Angeles, which led to the looting and burning of more than two thousand Korean-owned stores (see chapter 5), not only shifted the consciousness of the Korean American community throughout the United States but also sent negative reverberations about Korean immigrant life back to the homeland.

Then, in 1997–98, South Korea, along with other Asian countries, suffered a major financial crisis that resulted in capital flight, failures of major conglomerates, currency devaluation, and joblessness, leading to a controversial multibillion dollar bailout from the International Monetary Fund. According to a United Nations report, the Asian economic crisis had a disproportionate impact on women as a result of their concentration in low-wage, unstable jobs, thus precipitating the "rapid feminization of growing unemployment."[37] While the direct impact of the crisis on Korean women's emigration to the United States is difficult to measure, the overall increase in the number of immigrants suggests that the unstable economic situation stimulated women to leave Korea for the United States into the early 2000s.

Throughout these ups and downs of developments in the home country and the resulting ebbs and flows in emigration to the United States, New York City has continued to serve as a major destination of South Korean emigrants. Upon arrival, Korean women's pathways into nail salon work are determined partially by their own skills and resources, as well as by blocked mobility, labor market discrimination, occupational sex segregation, and their racialized position vis-à-vis the U.S. mainstream.

KOREANS AND NAIL SALONS IN NEW YORK CITY

"Can you imagine? Ten thousand Korean women earn about $500 per week in nail salons in New York City. This is $5 million added not just to the Korean community but to New York's economy. This money supports other Korean businesses—restaurants, dry cleaners, grocery, etc., because if Koreans make more money, they buy more things from each other," said Kye Song Lee, editor of the *Korean American Nail and Beauty Journal*. His comments capture the substantial economic contributions of the nail industry to New York's Korean community, although his esti- mates of the number of Korean women and their earnings are higher than those in other official sources.[38]

Koreans in New York have clustered in the Borough of Queens, most heavily in Flushing but also in the adjacent areas of Elmhurst, Bayside, Whitestone, and College Point. Pyong Gap Min reports that in 1990, roughly 150,000 Korean Americans lived in the New York–New Jersey metropolitan area. New York State was home to 12 percent of the Korean population in the United States, and New Jersey claimed 5 percent.[39] According to the U.S. Census Bureau, in 2000 the Korean-ancestry popu- lation (both foreign and U.S. born) in New York City was 86,473, with 46 percent men and 54 percent women. As of 2006, the Census Bureau reported New York City's Korean population at 91,561.[40] Second only to the Korean community in Los Angeles, the high concentration of Koreans in New York City has enabled them to consolidate their dominance in nail salons and fend off threats from regulation and interethnic competition.

Unlike in Los Angeles, where Vietnamese and Chinese have posed stiff competition, nail salons in New York City remain predominantly Korean owned. As one Vietnamese nail salon owner attested, "Kore- ans are the best. Everyone got trained by the Koreans. Vietnamese are very fast and have good designs, but Koreans are still the best." Koreans have been able to maintain their dominance through their reputation of providing superior services, even at higher cost. A Korean ethnic press reporter interviewed for this study described the continued dominance of Koreans, even in the face of ethnic competition: "About 80 percent of nail salons are run by Koreans—about 2,500 salons. The other 20 percent are Vietnamese, Chinese, Spanish and Americans. Russians tried to start but most didn't make it because they don't have the skills of Koreans."

While the early inroads into this entrepreneurial niche were through the efforts of Korean women, Korean men and male-dominated institutions have nonetheless contributed important resources to maintain this domination. A significant number of men are legally the sole or co-owners, although most do not do manicures and instead provide maintenance, accounting, and background support. Furthermore, men are also the direct and indirect beneficiaries of nail salon prosperity, as the industry generates demand for suppliers and manufacturers of nail products. Far from being marginal or superfluous enterprises, the nail salons rival the grocery stores as bulwarks of the Korean immigrant community's economic security. As such, nail salon entrepreneurship has garnered the support of typically male-controlled resources in this community, including ethnic media, business associations, and training schools. The income generated from nail salons enables other Korean-owned businesses to thrive. The channeling of both Korean immigrant women and men into this form of feminized labor is a result of their exclusion from mainstream occupations; as Yen Espiritu notes, they are "barred from decent paying jobs in the general labor market."[41] Thus Korean-owned nail salons thrive not only because of their owners' hard work but also as a result of gendered work processes that limit employment options and foster ethnic group efforts to sustain Korean domination of this niche.

The importance of the resources of the entire Korean community in maintaining ethnic control of this niche is apparent in its successful negotiation of proposals by New York City and State licensing authorities to increase regulation. In 1991 the New York State legislature began to regulate nail salons. According to the original bill, the law would have required six hundred hours of education and a qualification examination in order to receive the nail specialty license.[42] This bill held the potential to devastate Korean immigrants' hold on the nail salon industry. Most Korean women not have been able to afford the time and expense of completing the education requirements, and many would not have been able to pass the examination in English. In the face of this threat the Korean Nail Salon Association of New York mobilized to propose an alternative bill, as An Sik Nam, former president, explained to me: "The key is that we quickly organized this association so they [Korean nail salon owners] had something to lean on to help with all the regulations. The nail salon association provides a center where Koreans can organize in united efforts to solve problems."[43] The association successfully lobbied for a grandfather clause that allowed those who could prove one or more years of experience working in the nail salons to obtain licenses without additional training classes or examinations.

When the early conditions of an unregulated industry disappeared and the state instituted strict requirements, the Korean community responded with Korean-run nail schools that provide training and licensing. The Christian Nail School on 34th Street near the Korean business enclave in midtown Manhattan and the Flushing Nail School in the Korean community in Queens provide instruction in various techniques as well as information about state regulations regarding health and safety standards, tax reporting, and workers compensation. Furthermore, by increasing the attention given to customer service and English-language instruction, these schools provide immigrant women with socialization into the values and practices of the mainstream society, as well as technical training to become manicurists. The establishment and operation of these schools has developed into a new entrepreneurial niche for Korean women who provide language instruction, translation, exam preparation, and business consulting in addition to technical nail training.

Another important Korean community institution is the informal rotating credit association (kye) in which groups of friends, family, or people from the same hometown pay into a common fund and take turns drawing from it. These associations have provided many small business owners with start-up capital, and one community leader, who requested anonymity, told me, "Most of the women [nail salon owners] . . . raise money from another family business like a grocery store or through kye."

Korean churches have also played a significant role in building networks that help women to find work and establish nail salons. Immigrant churches also fulfill the practical role of employment brokers for ethnic-dominated industries. Mary Lee, a pioneer in the nail salon industry who worked in one of the first Korean-owned nail salons beginning in 1978, described how her church facilitated her first job in a nail salon: "I had to work somewhere so I asked the church minister's wife to find a job for me. . . . I didn't know anything. I didn't even know that it was a nail salon. I just followed the minister's wife and found out." Similarly, many new Korean immigrants, whether they are Christians or not, flock to the well-established network of Korean churches to seek support from coethnics to secure jobs and housing and meet other basic needs in the process of settlement.

The network of Korean churches legitimates women's participation in this work, making it palatable for women who otherwise might shun it. One manicurist commented, "Even Jesus washed people's feet—why should I feel bad about it?" Several respondents invoked this metaphor of Jesus washing the disciples' feet, appealing to their Christian faith as a source of sustenance in this job. One worker explained that while at first she did not like the idea of using an "American name" in the salon, choosing a salon name from the Bible eased this transition. "I use Ruth in the salon. I worked with a pastor's wife when I first began and she picked this name for me from the Bible. I don't use this name outside of the salon [with Koreans], but I use it when I deal with Americans outside of the salon. I like this name now." Thus churches and Christian beliefs ameliorate the often difficult negotiations of identity that nail salon work entails.

Korean women also are channeled into nail salon work by job ads in the vibrant ethnic press as well as news of openings passed along by word of mouth. Asked how owners find workers for their salons, An Sik Nam explained, "When someone has a job opening in their salon or needs a job, they ask their neighbors or friends or family or they look in the Korean newspaper. . . . In Korea the nail salon business is also growing, I think because of the influence from the U.S. People heard about what is going on in the U.S. and how successful it is."[44] Transnational telecommunications and travel have sent word of nail salon work back to the homeland, and many new immigrants arrive already aware of the high rates of employment of Korean women in nail salons and quickly fill openings.

These various ethnic community resources—business associations, rotating credit associations, churches, and ethnic newspapers—have sustained the dominance of Koreans in nail salons. In addition, they have influenced favorable state policies and provided training and other forms of business support. The relatively high education levels of Korean immigrants give them access to various class and community resources. These two factors, the availability of ethnic resources and mainstream occupational barriers, channel the labor of both immigrant women and men into this feminized entrepreneurial niche. Thus Korean domination of the nail salon niche in New York has relied upon the effective mobilization of ethnic group resources in the face of limited opportunities, rather than merely reflecting their innate industriousness or propensity for service work.

CONCLUSION

The city that inspired the idea of the melting pot still can brew up an enterprise as unlikely yet as commonplace as the stand-alone nail salon. The factors that make up this mix include the downsizing of manufacturing work and the expansion of service-related jobs, increased participation of women in the paid labor force, influx of new immigrants into low-wage ethnic labor markets, and growth of service sectors in global cities. However, without an available workforce to meet these demands, accessible and affordable manicures would have remained just another unmet desire instead of a thriving niche for new immigrants.

Macrostructural forces shape opportunities for immigrant entrepreneurship and employment. Among those forces are patterns of global migration, ethnic community resources, and the racialized structures of U.S. society. Immigration flows, along with ethnic concentration in specific niches, are responses to mechanisms in national and global economies that draw certain workers into certain jobs in certain geographic areas while excluding them from other employment and migration trajectories. Just as important, Koreans have been able to attract diverse customers outside their own community instead of catering to coethnics, as is the case with most other ethnic-owned beauty establishments, such as those operated by Latinas and African Americans.

Nonetheless, while the context of the receiving society is the main factor in determining gender, racial, and ethnic clustering in this line of work, employment outcomes also reflect the agency of particular women and groups and the choices they make to channel their resources and skills into specific enterprises. In the next chapter I delve into these stories of individual women who create, find, and perform this work and the gains and losses that they incur in the process.

Two "What Other Work Is There?"

MANICURISTS

[Relations with my husband] are better than before, and because I'm at the salon for most of the day, my family tries to be nicer. My daughter and husband prepare dinner, and so when I get home, I just eat. . . . People who work in the nail salons learn English and adjust to life here in America faster. Koreans who work in dry cleaners and groceries don't have the opportunity we have to sit face to face and talk with Americans. . . . I like America. In Korea, you have to be self-conscious of people, but here you don't. I'm left alone to live my life, my own way.

Jackie Hong, owner, Brooklyn

The owner asked how I felt after washing feet for the first time. She asked if I was okay. As soon as she asked, I felt so sad . . . and I started to cry. In the beginning, I thought that there was nothing I couldn't do, "As long as I have a determined heart, I can do it!" But it was another story when I started doing the work; I started to doubt myself. I had a good job in Korea, and I couldn't believe that I was doing this. I felt like I was moving backward here.

Joanne Shin, manicurist, Manhattan

To understand why most immigrant women have only nibbled at the margins of patriarchy, we must abandon the notion that gender hierarchy is the most determinative structure in their lives.

Patricia Pessar, "Engendering Migration Studies"

Who are the women who work in nail salons, how do they get there, and how does this work affect their lives? Contrary to media pronouncements about Asian women in the nail salon industry as the ultimate immigrant success story, these women tell ambivalent stories of long hours, hard and at times degrading work, conflicts with spouses and children, and uneasy assimilation into their new country. Some, like Jackie Hong, feel that despite the hard work and long hours, nail salon work has helped them to assimilate into their new country and has made family relations more egalitarian. Others, like Joanne Shin, see themselves as "moving backward" by performing low-wage work that extracts a high emotional and physical toll. By exploring the range of ways that nail salon work shapes Korean women's lives, in this chapter I delve into central questions in the study of gender and immigration. What do women gain and lose by emigrating to the United States? How does employment in a particular ethnic niche, such as the nail salons, transform or reproduce gendered patterns of inequality within households, communities, and labor markets?

In chapter 1, I explored the economic and political factors at the local, national, and global levels that have fueled the growth of the nail industry and have channeled Asian immigrant women into it. In this chapter I move from this bird's-eye view to experiences on the ground, highlighting the everyday lived experiences of women as they find, learn, and perform this work. The narratives in this chapter contest pervasive beliefs that non-Western women gain freedom and riches by fleeing their poor backward countries and achieving the American dream of upward mobility. This ideology of liberation through emigration to the United States emphasizes the "model minority" stereotype of Asian immigrants who succeed through hard work, self-sufficiency, and strong family values.[1] In this chapter I critique the ideology of Asian-run nail salons as the ultimate success story by demonstrating the contradictory and uneven gains of Asian women through entrepreneurship and employment in this niche. I demonstrate how a stronger gender analysis illuminates important and often neglected dimensions of immigration, specifically, those related to bodies and emotions in work and identities.

Pierrette Hondagneu-Sotelo, the gender and immigration scholar, explores these mixed gains and losses of women through migration, particularly with regard to transforming traditional gender roles and relations. She explains that in seeking to rectify the invisibility of women in migration research, some scholars have privileged gender while marginalizing race and other structures of oppression. Rather than focusing solely on differences between men and women in terms of who migrates, when, where, and under what conditions, she emphasizes new gendered dimensions of immigration that emerge in daily practices and institutional structures. Recent gender and migration scholarship addresses topics such as sexual identities and practices, constructions of childhood, transnational connections through the sending of remittances and participation in hometown associations and politics, responses to immigration laws, access to U.S. institutions, such as schools, health care and social services, and negotiations of the meaning and terms of citizenship.[2]

I hope to add another dimension to this burgeoning research on gender and migration by illuminating understudied embodied and emotional dimensions of immigrant women's lives. The lens of body labor focuses attention on gendered aspects of immigration and work that have been neglected, particularly the centrality of women's bodies and feelings in their work, families, identities, and patterns of assimilation. While no single woman's experiences can be deemed typical, I develop two in-depth profiles in this chapter that dramatize consistent and central themes articulated by other women in the study regarding how immigration and nail salon work have shaped their lives.

The case studies of Charlie Choi and Jinny Kim reveal the intimate lived experiences of nail salon owners and workers but also raise important theoretical questions about how women's bodies and feelings are shaped by the crosscutting influences of race, gender, class, and immigration. Charlie Choi, owner of a profitable upscale salon in a posh, mostly white, section of Brooklyn, recounted a mixed story of pride in operating her business, combined with difficulties in her family relations and in life as an immigrant. Her story dramatizes the complexities of "success" for Korean women entrepreneurs as they stretch to accommodate the new responsibilities and expectations of working in the nail industry while also meeting the traditional demands of family life. The

Figure 5. A nail salon owner sits at her salon's reception area, which displays handwritten thank-you notes from customers, signs about acceptable salon behavior, and baskets of free candies, all attesting to the high levels of emotional labor involved in running a nail salon.

second case profiles Jinny Kim, who emigrated as a college student with ambitious plans to pursue a career in corporate America but was working without a license or legal status at a nail art salon in a low-income, predominantly black, neighborhood. Her story reveals a not uncommon experience of blocked mobility leading to long-term employment as a manicurist. With little time or energy to develop relationships or pursue additional education, Jinny occupied an in-between position, regarding herself as an outsider from both the U.S. mainstream and the Korean American community and her former life in South Korea. Charlie and Jinny challenge the one-dimensional framing of Asian manicurists as immigrant success stories. Instead, they dramatize the simultaneous gains and losses of immigration and employment in the gendered ethnic niche of nail salon work and the daily performance of intensive body labor.

CHARLIE CHOI—THE MANICURIST IN THE WINDOW

A professionally dressed white woman stood in front of Exclusive Nails, appearing to talk to her reflection in the window. "Don't my nails look great with this bag!" she said with exaggerated gestures. As I approached, I realized that she was not talking to herself but was having a pantomime conversation with Charlie, who was sitting behind the window. While doing research at this salon, I observed this as a common occurrence, as customers regularly passed by and waved or mouthed greetings to this popular manicurist and salon owner. Charlie smilingly participated in this intermittent game of window charades and appeared to relish the role. Even her name suits the part. Charlie, whose given name is Hae-jin, earned her "American name" when a customer misunderstood the pronunciation of her surname. "Choi is my last name, and one customer misunderstood Choi as Charlie, but I liked Charlie a lot. Charlie is the name of a perfume designer." Indeed, she lives up to her fashionable name; as Reverend Kim, the Korean minister who introduced us, commented, Charlie is "the most beautiful, friendly, and devout Korean woman working in a nail salon."

The first time I met Charlie, I was accompanied by Reverend Kim and a newly arrived Korean immigrant woman who had contacted him in search of work. Although Charlie was busy with a customer, she welcomed us into her salon as if it were her living room. She greeted her countrywoman, putting her at ease by saying, "I know how you feel, this work looks very strange, doesn't it? . . . I don't have any job openings now, but if you want to sit and watch and ask questions, that is fine." Similarly, she listened attentively as I explained my study, and she agreed to an interview and to let me conduct research in her salon. On this day Charlie's husband was working with an electrician in the back of the salon to install new light fixtures. Although the salon was already comfortable and clean, they were remodeling to keep up with the upscale decor of their many competitors. Charlie's husband greeted me politely, but as I conducted the interview (which took more than two hours), he regularly cast disapproving glances our way, especially as Charlie recounted stories about her family life and became increasingly emotional. Her husband, visibly unhappy about his wife's sharing these personal stories, eavesdropped and interrupted us frequently by asking her various work-related questions. She would respond curtly, then return her full attention to the interview. Finally, he shouted, "When are you going to be done?" She retorted, "I don't know!" and continued to more or less ignore him. Sensing the rising tensions, I asked her whether she would like to complete the interview later. She replied passionately, "I have never been able to talk about my work like this. He can just do his work. I don't bother him to help me with doing nails—why does he bother me to help with his jobs?"

Charlie's response reveals several important dimensions of her experience as a nail salon owner. First, she clearly has power in the workplace to challenge her husband's authority, as she resisted his efforts to end the interview and force her to return to work. However, although she stood up to her husband, these attempts were visibly wearing as she tried to work with him while not completely acquiescing to his demands. Finally, the intensity and thoughtfulness of Charlie's responses indicate a strong desire to have her voice heard as part of this study, and she was extremely articulate in her account of coming to the United States as a wife and mother, becoming a successful manicurist and salon owner, and renegotiating her identity in the process. Although she embraced her work in the nail salon not merely as economic necessity but also as the fulfillment of her own dreams for greater freedom and mobility, she also critiqued the naïveté of these dreams and the conditions that undermine their realization.

Charlie was born in Inchon, South Korea, in 1964. As a child, she recalled, she was obsessed with ice cream and American movies, which fueled a strong "American fever" (miguk byung), a popular Korean expression describing a fervent desire to emigrate to the United States.[3] "Basically, I came here because I wanted to fulfill my dream," she explained. As Nadia Kim writes, many Koreans "had come to idealize 'America' through Hollywood movies and pro-U.S. ideology. Narratives abounded of 'America' rescuing Korea from a near inexorable fate (read: Communism, poverty)."[4] As with many South Koreans who emigrated to the United States beginning in the 1970s, Charlie was able to pursue her childhood dream of coming to the United States through a combination of local, national, and global factors. As I discussed in chapter 1, these included changes in U.S. immigration laws and close military, political, and economic ties between the United States and South Korea. In addition, as a woman, she felt that the United States offered greater freedom as well as better economic opportunities. However, like Charlie, many Korean immigrants who held these dreams also found themselves disappointed by the hardships of actual life upon arrival.

Charlie emigrated to New York City with her husband and ten-year-old son in 1993. Two months later she was working full time at a nail salon. Before they emigrated, she had not been employed, except for a part-time office job before she got married, and she confessed that she had no idea how hard she would have to work as a new immigrant in the United States, let alone what kind of work she would do. "I did not even know that I would work here, and I certainly did not think of doing this. I had never even seen nail salons before. After I came here and saw many Koreans working in the nail salon, I visited several salons and started." Thus, although she was surprised by the very idea of nail salons, let alone the prospect of working in one herself, the visible employment of other Korean women in nail salons normalized this work, and she was able to find employment through advertisements in a Korean-language newspaper.

In the beginning Charlie was excited about the prospect of working in a nail salon and expected the work to be fairly easy and enjoyable. "Also, the fact that most of the customers are Americans was challenging and attractive to me. I did not feel like doing work that deals with Koreans and thought it would be less interesting," she said. Contrary to widespread perceptions that immigrants want to remain within their own ethnic communities, like many other manicurists Charlie was drawn to her job in the nail salon because it offered connections to her new country and its people. However, her first days on the job quickly dispelled her excitement. Rather than fulfilling her dream of performing interesting work and developing friendships with Americans, the job and its demands shocked Charlie. "When I first got there, I started from the feet. I almost quit right there. I was so nervous. In the beginning it took about forty minutes to do the work that can be done in twenty minutes by a skillful worker. There was no nail school at that time, so I learned on the job. . . . I started from removing colors [old nail polish]. The owner lent me her hands and trained me, like the way to grip feet."

Many other manicurists shared similar feelings of surprise and even humiliation upon beginning nail salon work, especially doing pedicures. Joanne Shin recounted her intense negative feelings after her first day of nail salon work in 1999:

> I was so nervous doing nails in the beginning. I cried for the first time [when] I was doing a pedicure and the polish just wouldn't go on. I was so frustrated. It didn't look good to me, and I wondered how it must appear to the other person. . . . My roommate introduced me [to the nail salon]. I'd never imagined something like nail salons. . . . I really didn't like nail salons. It's not just about washing feet, but in Korea I didn't put on nail polish or take care of my own nails; maybe I would have taken it better if I was a type of girl who put on nail polish and things.

Despite these strong initial reactions, Joanne and most manicurists quickly learn to manage their feelings of aversion. Joanne said she had all but forgotten her early reactions and now enjoyed doing nails and earning a living from this work. "Honestly, I don't mind doing nails now . . . Thinking about nails alone, I don't like it, but I like doing nails because money comes out of it." The reformulation of her initial negative feelings is most dramatic regarding pedicures. "I don't mind doing feet now. I now like feet that are dirty because after I'm finished with the pedicure, the feet are clean and pretty. I feel good, as if I'm washing my own feet clean." Through the daily performance of this work, manicurists like Joanne internalize a service ideology that enables them to adjust to work that they previously found demeaning.

Like Charlie, these women have reformulated their emotional expectations regarding both nail salon work and their lives in the United States. Many downscale their expectations of friendships with customers and settle for cordial exchanges. Over time, rather than heavily investing in customer relations, many women concentrate on their ability to earn a living, their contributions to their children and families, their relations with their coworkers, and their sense of mastery in their own skills. As they become more proficient and build up savings, they turn their attention toward starting salons of their own.

PATHS TO ENTREPRENEURSHIP

After weathering the initial adjustment period, Charlie assessed her savings and the resources of her extended family and then began looking into the requirements for becoming a salon owner.

> I learned that there are two ways to get the resources. One is to start from an empty shop, filling it by myself; the other is to take over a shop from the former owner. Either way, I needed money. . . . I rented an empty shop, repaired some part of it, and started the business there. I needed everything, from table and chairs to small equipment and polishes. In total, I spent about $80,000. . . . Nowadays, it is much more expensive to open a salon. There are peak times and slow times. On average, my gross income is about $3,000 a week. I spend about 40 percent of the total income for salaries and rent and other costs. Also, since this is a partnership with my sister, we usually divide the rest of the income half and half.

Based on these figures and her habit of rarely closing the salon or taking vacations, Charlie's gross earnings can be estimated at roughly $156,000 a year, of which $62,400 go toward expenses, leaving $93,600, which she splits with her sister for a pretax take-home pay of approximately $46,800. These figures may seem impressive for an immigrant entrepreneur and indeed significantly exceed the earnings of many immigrant women. At the same time these figures reflect long and arduous hours, on average sixty hours a week, and do not include unpaid family labor by her husband, health care expenses, and other intermittent but consistent costs of running the business, such as new equipment and remodeling. Furthermore, Charlie's well-established salon is on the more profitable end of nail salon businesses, and many other owners see significantly lower returns.[5]

Like many Korean women, Charlie took a circuitous path to entrepreneurship. Eunju Lee documents three trajectories of Korean immigrant women who enter into small business ownership, and Charlie seems to embody the third category. The first group is comprised of women, mostly college-educated, independent-minded, and "informed partly by gender inequality in Korean society," who set their sights on entrepreneurship and actively pursue the goal of being their own boss. The second group is comprised of those who enter into ownership reluctantly and do so mainly because of their husband's low earnings; they regard their small business as a burden thrust upon them. In the third group are those women who do not initially plan to become owners but choose to do so once they arrive and realize that nail salon ownership is their best chance at upward mobility. They regard this work neither as the fulfillment of their dreams nor as a completely undesirable fate but simply as a realistic adjustment to the limited economic opportunities available to them as immigrants.[6] Consistent with Lee's findings, Charlie considers herself fortunate to be the co-owner of a successful salon in a "good neighborhood" (mostly white and middle class). However, the price of her economic success is high in terms of time, physical effort, and emotional expenditures both at work and at home.

RIDES AND LUNCHES: EMOTIONAL LABOR WITH COETHNICS

Like many salon owners, Charlie cited emotional management of her workers as one of the most difficult parts of her job. As with customers, the emotional labor required to maintain good relations with her workers is double edged. She genuinely cared about them but also found their complaints and demands stressful. The tasks of providing lunch and transportation for workers are forms of emotional labor that are particular to ethnic women entrepreneurs. These demands constitute forms of gendered work that are largely invisible but essential for maintaining loyal and reliable coethnic women workers, as a typical workday for Charlie reveals.

> I used to leave my home at about 8:30 in the morning, but now I leave a little bit earlier because I have to give a ride to others. Two workers live in this area, and the rest of them live in Queens. So I leave home at 8:15 and I go back to home at about 9:30 or 10:00 [P.M.]. . . . There are not many

people to work here because the Korean community in this neighborhood is very small so there is a problem of transportation of the workers if I lived in this area. I have thought of moving to this area [where the shop is located], but I might lose some workers by that [if I couldn't provide rides].

Charlie's practice of providing rides to her workers was common among Korean women nail salon owners. Many workers fear going into unfamiliar neighborhoods alone, because of real or perceived dangers. Many manicurists live in Queens, which at the time of my research was mainly serviced by the then–slow and overcrowded no. 7 subway train or the expensive Long Island Rail Road. While the car trip can become a valued part of the workday for women, when they can share concerns and get to know each other, it can also impose added emotional labor, as owners take on the roles not only of transporter but also of confidante and mediator.

I experienced this while riding home one day with a salon owner and two workers. Throughout the ninety-minute commute, the women exchanged humorous stories about customers, sang Korean pop songs together, and gave advice to a young worker about her boyfriend. By the end of the ride, it was clear to me how this daily ritual of commuting together can release tensions and foster strong friendships. At the same time I could see how it can add stress for the salon owner. As the owner later confirmed, car trips on other days are filled with frustration about stop-and-go traffic and complaints and conflicts between workers.

Given the significant burden of providing transportation, owners may turn to their husbands for assistance. However, sometimes the men are resistant, or the women, both owners and workers, feel uncomfortable with this arrangement. During my research I heard frequent stories about commuting relationships that developed into extramarital affairs. Mary Lee commented, "A lot of people who started a nail salon with their husband experienced break-up. This is why people close their shops and go somewhere else. Men who work in nail salons are more likely to be in contact with women. [A nail salon owner friend] also experienced this unfortunate happening. There were a lot of troubles of that sort." Whether they are as rampant as rumored, these suspicions of infidelity generated enough concern for some owners to avoid asking their husbands to give rides to their workers.

In other cases the desire to avoid providing transportation and other responsibilities of hiring coethnic workers led some salon owners to hire non-Korean workers. Mr. Lee, the co-owner of Downtown Nails, explained his preference for Latina workers: "Spanish workers are cheaper, and I don't have to worry about providing lunch or giving them rides, like I have to do with Koreans.[7] They don't make me tired—the Korean women make me so tired! They complain a lot, and they always ask for raises." Rather than deal with these emotional complexities, Mr. Lee turned to non-Korean immigrant workers to whom he felt little obligation, but he also lost out on the close relations that Charlie and other Korean women owners share with their workers.

Like the commute, lunchtime provides opportunities for collegiality for Charlie and her workers but also for additional work. On most days each of the Korean women brings a dish for a rotating potluck lunch in the backroom, where Charlie provides rice and a rice cooker, a small refrigerator, and small bowls and utensils, an arrangement replicated in many salons. Although on slow days this arrangement can provide a welcome break in the day and a time for camaraderie, it also exerts pressure on the women to do additional food preparation and engage in workplace socializing. In addition to providing meals at home, women assume the responsibility for stocking the refrigerator and shelves at work and for helping to maintain a clean and pleasant dining area. While these tasks are shared, they still add a sizable amount of work.

I experienced firsthand the mixed blessings of participating in this shared meal when in one salon the manicurists teased me that I needed to stop eating all their food and start cooking something to share with them. After overcoming my initial embarrassment, I was glad to do this and took it as a sign of being welcomed as an insider. Nonetheless, the task of preparing an appropriate dish to share for lunch undoubtedly complicated my fieldwork and gave me a glimpse into how participation in this communal meal can become a significant burden during an already busy week.

It is hard to imagine that nonimmigrant small business owners, men or women, would regularly assume the responsibilities of transporting

Figure 6.   The back room of a nail salon houses food and utensils for breaks and communal meals, which allow for camaraderie but also can create additional work.

workers to and from their business establishment as well as provide traditional ethnic food for lunch. For Korean immigrant women entrepreneurs like Charlie, however, these are expected parts of running their business. They are distinct to Asian women in nail salon work, but they also illuminate more generally how immigrant women entrepreneurs' work relations are both enriched and complicated by the simultaneous influences of gender and ethnicity. Likewise, the ways that nail salon owners negotiate the performance of emotional labor both at work and at home reveal complex intersections of gender and ethnicity in immigrant women's lives.

TRADE-OFFS BETWEEN WORK AND FAMILY

Hochschild describes how full-time working women continue to bear the brunt of the "second shift" of caring for children and doing housework.[8]

These dynamics are even more pronounced among Asian immigrant families, where traditional patriarchal relations are often resistant to the new economic roles for women and men that migration brings. Although Charlie can be viewed as a nail salon success story, she felt like a failure in her role as a mother and believed that her work extracted too high a toll in caring for her child and other domestic duties.

> Since I got here [to the United States], the problem that I failed most to solve was the children issue. I still feel sorry. . . . Just this morning, I was feeling guilty that I could not care more for my son because I had to work so hard. On the other hand, I was making excuses to myself that I could not help it since I had to support my family. But it is still a burden for me that I did not have time to care for him more [*she begins to cry*]. Because we had very little time to talk to one another, we became more distant. Although we tried to understand and know each other, it did not work that well, even though my son speaks Korean. It did not appear as a big problem at first, but little by little I could feel that we were not as close as before. We have lived here now for ten years. During those ten years, I felt like it would be just for a short time that my family was not as close as before. Now I realize that time was not a short time; it was very long.

Charlie described how the difficulties in her relationship with her son crept up over the years as her work absorbed more and more of her time and energy. Thus, like many immigrant parents, Charlie realized too late that she had missed out on her son's childhood.

In her book *Children of Global Migration*, Rhacel Parreñas documents the hardships experienced by Asian children whose parents must migrate abroad for work, in this case leaving children behind in the Philippines to find work in the United States or Europe.[9] Like the Filipina domestics in Parreñas's study, Charlie shows that even women who emigrate to the United States with their families must often leave their children at home to fend for themselves, even if the women are only commuting from Queens to Brooklyn. Charlie's son, contrary to the stereotype of academically successful Ivy League–bound Asian American students, struggled to complete high school and was neither in school nor employed. Charlie lamented:

Our home was in Queens. My son had to go to Manhattan to go to school, and I had to come to this salon [in Brooklyn]. So it was like a battle in the morning. Because I did not know much about the American educational system, and I was always busy running this shop, I had a hard time. I did not know what to do. . . . My son just graduated from high school. Actually, he did not graduate but took the GED. I thought as time passes by, he will naturally go to school and graduate. Now, looking back, I feel that I missed the time that I should have cared for and kept an eye on him, and it is too late now to get it back [starts crying].

Like many working mothers, Charlie agonized over her struggles to balance work, child-care, and homemaking responsibilities, but she shouldered the additional burdens of adjusting to a new culture and educational system. In contrast to the popular "model minority" stereotype of successful Asian entrepreneurs and their upwardly mobile children, Charlie and her son reveal a different scenario that increasingly is unfolding within Asian immigrant families. The term latchkey children has come into increasing use as children of Asian immigrants suffer from neglect as their parents work long hours and are unable to support them in school and careers. Lisa Sun-Hee Park finds in her study of children of Asian immigrant entrepreneurs that many of these children regard themselves as having missed out on a "normal childhood" and harbor feelings of resentment combined with strong pressure to repay their parents for their sacrifices.[10]

In addition, many of these children lack the will to work as hard as their parents in small businesses but at the same time are unable to gain access to mainstream educational institutions and professional occupations. This unfortunate convergence of factors has led some scholars to predict a trajectory of downward mobility or "second generation decline."[11] Sara Cho was a young manicurist who represented this trend. Although she graduated from a prestigious public high school and was accepted by the City University of New York system, she delayed college after her mother had a car accident and needed help running her salon. When I interviewed Sara, her original one-year deferral had stretched into its third year. While her divorced mother wanted Sara to take over as owner of the salon, she adamantly refused, explaining:

In the beginning I just worked part time to help my mom. Now I am
working full time so I should get a license, but that's like admitting that
I'm going to keep doing this. . . . I started working really young, fourteen
or fifteen. My mom just needed help, so I'd come in and do everything
except the nails—clean up, answer the phone, do the bookkeeping. My
mother had me watch the other workers to learn, and when I was sixteen,
I started doing the nails. I also would come in after school sometimes and
give the workers a ride home, but I couldn't do it everyday. . . . I haven't
even looked into it [getting a license] because I'm not going to be doing it
after this year. I plan to go to college and become an architect.

As a result of her refusal to see her nail salon employment as a long-term
proposition, despite having already worked there for several years, Sara
risked working without a proper license. While she dreamed of becoming
an architect, her confidence in her ability to enter and complete college
was eroding the longer she was away from school. Thus her caregiving
responsibilities for her mother, lack of financial and emotional support
from her father, and underground employment in the salon combined to
diminish her chances of upward mobility into a professional occupation.

Other nail salon owners' children may not experience the same kinds
of difficulties confronting Sara Cho or Charlie's son, but the women in this
study constantly worried about the negative effects that their work may
have on their children. Like Charlie, other women whom I interviewed
found out the hard way that entrepreneurship is an imperfect solution to
the demands of balancing work and family as an immigrant mother.

ENTREPRENEURSHIP AS A (FAILED?)
CHILD-CARE STRATEGY

Greater flexibility in negotiating child care as an important incentive for
entrepreneurship has virtually been overlooked in studies that presume
male ownership of immigrant small businesses. Many women in this
study identified the potential of having more time for their children as
their main reason for establishing their own business. At the same time
they were frustrated that the reality of entrepreneurship did not allow

them to balance work and family as freely as they envisioned. This was especially true for single or divorced mothers who bore the full responsibility for both caring for children and providing economic support. When asked about her motivations to become a salon owner, Jenny Park, a forty-eight-year-old single mother, responded: "I prayed to open a salon close to home when I first started in 1992. My daughter was beginning high school, and she was an adolescent. I wanted to be close to home and be around her. God answered my prayer and gave me 'Best Nails' two blocks away from home and right next to the train station. [My daughter] was able to stop by the store on her way back from school to home, since the nail salon was right next to the train station." As nail salon owners, women have the option of conducting child care at the work site or leaving the salon when necessary and attending to children's needs at home or school. The presence of children is less distracting and objectionable to the owner, workers, and customers in a woman-dominated service establishment such as the nail salons, in contrast to a high-traffic grocery store or a dry cleaner with dangerous machinery in constant operation. In addition, the nail salon is potentially more hospitable to the children themselves (although exposure to chemicals, which I discuss in chapter 6, remains a major health concern).

Susan Lee, the thirty-nine-year-old divorced owner of Crosstown Nails, used a second child-care strategy that also draws upon the flexibility of salon ownership—coming and going from the salon to attend to her son at home. She explained, "My son is nine years old, and I feel sorry for him. My mother stays home with him after school, but they have difficulty communicating. Lately, I try to leave the salon in the afternoon when it is slow and pick him up from school, and then I come back [to the salon] after five when it gets busy again." Because Susan's son was attending school, she needed greater freedom to leave the salon to provide him with transportation, as her elderly mother could not drive. Although it was not a perfect solution, as the owner she had the authority to manage her own schedule and workplace responsibilities to accommodate her mothering responsibilities.

Mr. and Mrs. Lee, the co-owners of Brooklyn Nails, also used their flexibility as owners to leave the salon to meet child-care needs when their children were young. They cited this as the reason they chose the location of their salon, as it was close to their home and their children's school. It was also the reason that Mrs. Lee hesitated to open their second salon on Long Island, where she would be far away and unable to return home easily. She recalled, "I waited to open the second salon until my children were old enough to take care of themselves. I wanted to be able to go home and greet them after school. Even though I couldn't do it everyday, it was enough to make sure they weren't getting into any trouble."

These women cited flexibility in meeting child-care needs as the main reason for becoming entrepreneurs, and they were indeed able to negotiate more fluid arrangements as salon owners than they would as workers or as owners of other kinds of business establishments. However, even this greater flexibility did not allow them to meet their child-care needs fully; as Charlie lamented, even as a salon owner, she had been unable to give her son the support he needed. In addition, although she was sympathetic to child-care issues, having struggled herself, Charlie acknowledged that she was unable to be as accommodating for her workers as she would like.

> When [my son] was a child, I was an employee of a nail salon. Because the salon was my workplace, I did not even think of bringing him there. . . . When there were problems in his school, I got phone calls and had to go to the school, but I had difficulties because I could not leave the salon during the busiest time. So I thought if I become an owner, I will be loose about children issues, which are hard to talk about to the owner. When I became an owner, when workers had some children's issues, I tried to adjust working hours for them. The time when I feel sorry the most is when workers who have babies cannot go back to home until late in the night. Even an hour is precious for a mother and baby, but it does not work as well as I wish. Then I feel so sorry for them.

Charlie's honest confession that she could not accommodate her worker's child-care needs demonstrates that even when owners wish to be responsive, the demands of running a small business often override commitment to families, their own as well as others'.

Work-family scholarship discusses how on-site child-care options can be a major factor in creating a "family responsive workplace" for professional women.[12] Such concerns have not been explored extensively for low-income women, especially immigrants. Instead, studies of immigrant families have focused mostly on other strategies for meeting child-care needs, such as reliance on extended family members or leaving children in their home countries to be cared for by relatives or by domestic workers, who are even lower on the rung in the global hierarchy of feminized jobs.[13] While these patterns are indeed prevalent, the ability to accommodate their workplaces to meet child-care needs, however imperfectly, remains an important factor in drawing immigrant women into entrepreneurial enterprises such as nail salons and reveals how family responsibilities intrinsically shape these women's work trajectories. Entrepreneurship can also provide some leverage in redistributing the gender division of labor in households with husbands, but again the gains are often partial and contested.

ASIAN PATRIARCHY AND IMMIGRANT WOMEN'S WORK

Immigration has wrought major changes in men's and women's traditional wage-earning and childrearing roles, yet patriarchal power in immigrant families has proved remarkably resistant to reorganization into more egalitarian arrangements. As Cecilia Menjivar notes in her study of Central American immigrants, "The dynamics of the local labor market, therefore, have facilitated these immigrant women's opportunities for work; they often work more hours and even earn more than men do. The consequences of this situation, however, reflect the women's vulnerability rather than their independence; it does not automatically benefit women and sometimes ends up reinforcing gender subordination in families."[14] Similarly, Asian immigrant women's labor force participation has not necessarily enabled them to renegotiate entrenched gender inequalities within their families and communities. In some cases paid work has heightened their vulnerabilities by adding the responsibilities of finding and performing low-wage, low-status jobs or running labor-intensive and potentially unstable small businesses.

Despite working long hours to manage their businesses, nail salon own-ers must continue to fulfill their expected gender roles as wives and primary caregivers to their children. In many cases husbands provide little help while imposing additional pressures and conflicts. Charlie commented:

> Most Korean guys were raised to think men rule the house. They think that they are not supposed to do housework so they are not willing to help their wives. . . . We argued a lot at the beginning. He complained about me as well because he thought I was not doing a good job as a wife. . . . I think this is a common problem for working women. First of all, there is less time to share with family. The only day that I don't open the shop is Sunday, but my husband and son are free on Saturday as well, while that is the busiest day for me.

Charlie illustrates hard-won yet tenuous steps toward a more egalitar-ian division of household and work-related responsibilities. In addition to having to juggle her child-care and work responsibilities, she had to negotiate with her husband about their respective contributions, adding another layer of stress and conflict to her daily balancing act.

Like Charlie, many Korean women in nail salons work full time yet shoulder the major responsibility for household tasks. According to Pyong Gap Min, they simultaneously "work exceptionally long hours, much longer than their American counterparts," and "undertake a greater share of housework than American working wives."[15] While most work out of economic necessity, they also gain a sense of accomplish-ment and autonomy. Even when they have positive feelings toward their work, many women feel torn between what Kim and Hurh describe as "the persistence of the traditional family ideology" and the demands of "a drastic new role, which the wives are forced to assume under the con-ditions of their immigrant life in the United States."[16] Thus these women may collude in preserving male privilege in the family, as they regard a strong father as important in maintaining control over children and preserving ties to ethnic culture.[17] At the same time, although nail salon entrepreneurship does not free women from patriarchal expectations and the consequences of violating them, it does afford spaces where they can subvert or redefine these expectations.

In Charlie's case, despite the widespread suspicions of the infidelity of husbands who provide rides and interact regularly with women manicurists, she pushed her husband to participate more in the business. In the end, however, Charlie and her husband maintained a traditional gendered division of labor in the workplace, where she performed the actual beauty work and handled customer and worker relations, while he took responsibility for maintenance and repairs. This traditional division of labor carried over to their household work. Although her husband had to make some accommodations because of her long working hours, Charlie explained that even these minor contributions were the result of many struggles: "He does help me [with housework] although I am not satisfied with it. Actually, his help is not enough for me, but he thinks he is helping me too much! When we first got to this country, he barely helped me. I took care of all the housework, from cleaning and cooking to taking care of the baby. But because I was so busy, I had to ask him to do it. Those requests often grew into arguments. . . . Now, we have gotten used to sharing the housework, and there is less work as my son grows up." Thus Charlie's work forced her husband to pick up certain household and child-care duties, but these changes came at a high price.

Gendered assumptions of a Korean wife's role as family caregiver and the husband's role as breadwinner are challenged by immigration, as the demand for feminized labor often means that immigrant women out-earn their immigrant husbands. As Yen Le Espiritu argues, "The recent growth of female-intensive industries—and the racist and sexist 'preference' for the labor of immigrant women—has enhanced women's employability over that of men and has changed their role to that of a coprovider, if not primary provider, for their families."[18] However, women's increased economic role does not necessarily translate into greater power and respect, inside or outside the family. Instead, the diminished economic status of men imposes additional stress on family relations. Thus many immigrant women are hesitant to challenge traditional roles, as they do not want to further undermine their husband's diminished status. These dynamics emerge in the following comments by a Korean man who was a nail salon industry representative. In drawing comparisons between Korean and Jewish women, he asserted that Korean nail salon owners have violated the proper order of gender relations in the family: "Korean women are different from Jewish women. If Korean woman becomes independent, she looks down on husband. Korean husband gets hurt, loses pride. Jewish women always respect their husband. Even if he does not make much money, they respect. They never quarrel in front of the children so children respect father—he is always king. So they keep family very good. We are worrying about this—Korean women don't keep family good." He then went on to describe several cases of Korean women who divorced after they opened a nail salon or who were experiencing marital conflicts, including domestic violence, which he again attributed to their lack of respect for their husbands. His comments reveal the background that constrains women's efforts to negotiate more egalitarian relationships. Fears that such efforts will lead to arguments, divorce, or violence temper the demands that women put on their husbands to change.

The expectation that Korean women should bolster their husband's sense of power and pride both at home and work can make the option of owning their own business in the women-dominated beauty service sector very appealing. Several women whom I interviewed cited the ability to operate their establishments without male support as a selling point for nail salon entrepreneurship. Sarah Kim, a forty-four-year-old owner of a salon in Manhattan, was married to a white construction worker, formerly a GI stationed in South Korea, but nonetheless offered insights about the dynamics of running a business with a Korean husband: "[My husband] knows nothing about business and can't help me at all. But even if I had a Korean husband who knew about running a business, I wouldn't want to do business with him. The nail salon is good for me because I can do everything myself. I don't need a man to help with lifting heavy things or watching out for thieves." The ability to run their businesses independently can be a bonus, in the case of married women who want to work separately from their husbands, and is a prerequisite in the case of single, separated, or divorced women who are sole providers.

While they continue to struggle with unequal gender relations at home and at work, nail salon owners for the most part enjoy greater freedom than their counterparts in other small businesses. Even when they are co-owners, women who work in dry cleaners or grocery stores often have to prepare meals, clean, and attend to their husbands in various ways. Pyong Gap Min discusses the "dual burden" of Korean women who work as unpaid family labor in their husband's establishment while continuing to fulfill domestic responsibilities at home.[19] In fieldwork at a Korean-owned grocery store, I observed how this dual burden is magnified for women who are serving both husbands and employees. The wife of the grocery store owner cooked meals in a small basement kitchen, not only for her husband but also for the entire staff of at least five workers, and then cleaned up afterward. She commented, "I cook and clean here in the store, and then I go home and cook and clean again." Although I discussed earlier how the responsibility of providing for employees' shared lunches adds to a nail salon owner's workload, it is much less than that imposed on women who work with their husbands in other kinds of small businesses. In contrast, the woman owner of a nail salon enjoys a privileged position among her workers, and the tasks of preparing and cleaning up after meals are shared.

While Charlie's relationship with her husband had become somewhat more egalitarian both at home and at work since she started work in the salon, she confided that the pressures of maintaining these arrangements wore on them both. Thus nail salon ownership created somewhat greater equity in family relations but demanded constant negotiations with her husband, child, and her own sense of identity. In short, women's entrepreneurship does not necessarily translate into diminished patriarchal power or into liberating identity shifts.

Like Charlie, other Asian immigrant women in this study experienced their lessened contributions to family life as a failure rather than a victory. Immigration lowered their standards and contributions to housework and child care, but many desired to give more attention to their families and homes. As one manicurist, Cathy Hong, said:

> A lot has changed. In Korea I cleaned the house everyday, but here I can't because I don't have time. . . . My husband does more housework than me; he does the laundry and cooking. He has more time than me since he comes home by dinner time. . . . My husband is more popular with the kids since he is a good listener; they probably don't like me since I yell at

them more, especially nowadays. Home, instead of being a cozy and comfortable feeling, it is more chaotic. So I get more agitated. My older daughter tells me that I've changed—she once commented, "Do you know that you've changed a lot?"

Cathy, Charlie, and others revealed that, for many immigrant women, less time spent on child care and housework can trigger a deep sense of loss at being unable to fulfill what many women still deeply feel are their primary roles—mother and homemaker. Thus, for these women, more equal sharing of household and childrearing with their husbands is not necessarily experienced as a gain so much as a concession. This finding is consistent with research on immigrant women from various ethnic groups, as well as native-born African American and other women of color, which shows that the prioritizing of work over household and family responsibilities is not necessarily experienced as liberation but as a loss.[20] At the same time these women do not simply cling to this desire to care for their children out of intrinsic attachment to traditional family values but because various systems of inequality operate to place their homes and families in vulnerable positions that require their constant and diligent attention.[21]

Whereas Charlie's experiences illuminate the ambivalent gains of married women with children in terms of trade-offs between work and family, Jinny's story highlights a different set of tensions that young single women encounter through immigration and employment in the nail service niche. Instead of establishing a small business as a means to improving their children's opportunities, younger immigrant women like Jinny Kim set their sights on their own economic advancement through manicuring work. Yet, while she prides herself on her skills as a nail artist, Jinny was very clear that this occupation was not one she would have chosen if other opportunities were available to her.

JINNY KIM—THE HIDDEN INJURIES
OF GENDER AND IMMIGRATION

Sennett and Cobb's classic study, *The Hidden Injuries of Class*, focuses on the ways that lower-class status fosters a sense of inadequacy and self-defeating behaviors.[22] Their study provides an interesting parallel to how gender and immigration can combine to undermine immigrant women's sense of self-worth and belonging. Many Korean manicurists like Jinny Kim resort to this work not so much out of choice as necessity, resulting in feelings of resentment and disillusionment, as this default pathway clearly falls short of their own immigrant dreams.

Despite her often gruff demeanor with customers, Jinny, the manager at Artistic Nails, a large and bustling nail salon in a predominantly black working-class neighborhood, had acquired a large following for her original hand-painted designs. An African American girl approached Jinny's station, and the child's mother announced that she was giving her daughter her first manicure as a birthday present. Rising to the occasion, Jinny gingerly cleaned and buffed the girl's tiny fingernails and polished them with expert strokes—but she was only getting started. The child's thumbnail as Jinny's canvas, she painted a perfect crescent moon, followed by a sun on the girl's index finger, then stars and planets of various shapes on her remaining digits. Customers gathered around and oohed and aahed at the designs, and the little girl muttered a shy but heartfelt thank you. Jinny beamed back an uncharacteristically effusive smile, then commented bittersweetly in Korean to me, "I couldn't stay in this job if I didn't get to do these original designs." Jinny's years of working in the salon clearly had left their mark. Her story reveals how nail salon work offers both an opening and a dead end for Asian immigrant women.

IMMIGRANT DREAMS MEET THE BAMBOO CEILING

Building upon the concept of the glass ceiling, which refers to the structural impediments that limit women and minorities' entrance into high-level professional jobs, the term *bamboo ceiling* has come to refer to the blocked mobility of Asians and Asian Americans into leadership positions in fields such as business, education, and government.[23] Jinny's case shows that for many new immigrants, the bamboo ceiling is based not only on race but also gender and immigration status. Furthermore, the bamboo ceiling is much lower for immigrant women of color, inhibiting incorporation even into entry-level positions.

Whereas Charlie viewed her emigration to the United States as the culmination of her childhood dreams, Jinny was much more cynical and pragmatic about coming to the United States to improve her economic situation. Upon arrival she planned to attend college, study accounting, and then work as a stockbroker. She found a part-time job in a nail salon to earn extra money during college, never expecting that this would become her full-time occupation.

> I was so stupid *[bitter laugh]*. When I was in Korea, I was working for a trading company. . . . I couldn't afford to finish college in Korea, and I wanted to study more so I came here. . . . I took accounting classes for two years, and I finished . . . but it was still hard for me to get a job and work with American people. I wanted to be a stockbroker, work on the stock exchange. I didn't know how difficult it was. I just dreamed. I thought it would be like all fancy and I would make money, a lot of money.

After earning her accounting degree, Jinny was unable to gain a position as a stockbroker and instead found a job in a small computer company in Manhattan, but she quickly became disillusioned as a result of exclusionary treatment by her mostly white, U.S.-born coworkers. She recounted, "The money was good, but I didn't like it. There were about seven workers. The problems started the first day. At lunch time they didn't ask me anything, and they all just went out together. So I was really alone. I just took a cup of coffee and when they came back, they didn't even say a thing, they just ignored me and, like, I don't know." Although Jinny does not explicitly identify her coworkers' behavior as racial discrimination, she suggests in her comments that such ongoing experiences of marginalization influenced her to leave and seek work in a Korean-owned company. "I thought about working for a bank, a Korean bank, but then I thought, 'That's so boring!' . . . Plus I get paid three times more money [in the nail salon] than in the bank so I just decided to work here." Thus, while she felt a Korean-owned company would be more hospitable, she was unhappy with the menial work and poor remuneration.

Jinny's experiences challenge the notion that educated Asians smoothly assimilate into U.S. work cultures without discrimination. Instead, like Jinny, many face barriers that influence them to seek jobs in ethnic-owned businesses or become self-employed, although these opportunities require hard work and do not always yield the expected returns.[24]

"WHAT OTHER WORK IS THERE?"

Faced with the prospects of working in an exclusionary environment in the mainstream U.S. labor market or in an unstimulating, low-paying job as a white-collar worker in a transnational or locally based Korean company, Jinny opted for a third choice—working in an ethnic-owned business within the gendered niche of beauty services. Asked why she made this decision, she shrugged and said, "The first reason is that I already knew how to do nails . . . and I thought, 'What other work is there?'" Given her previous negative experiences, she was not enthusiastic about exploring jobs in the mainstream white-collar labor market. Instead, as she had already gained a foothold in the nail industry working part time as a college student, it was easy for her to transition to full time.

Jinny's artistic ability and business sense led her to advance quickly to the position of manager. She said, "I didn't have to take a long time to learn everything because my owner, she really liked me. . . . Just three days I did pedicure. The owner said it took her two years, but just three days I did it! Then she just hired me as a manager even though I never worked manicure." Favorable relations with her coethnic employer at her first salon drew her back after her disappointing foray into the mainstream labor market.

Jinny's work trajectory can be seen as what Rhacel Parreñas refers to as "contradictory class mobility," where migration leads to higher wages but lower-status jobs in other countries.[25] Consistent with this pattern, Jinny moved down the socioeconomic ladder in terms of job prestige but significantly improved her actual earnings by working in the low-status, but for her better-paying, niche of beauty services. Many Asian immigrant women like Jinny start off with ambitious career plans but are derailed by the reality of educational challenges, legal barriers, and workplace discrimination. They enter low-status nail salon work as a short-term means of supporting their ambitions, but once they become acclimated to this work, staying on indefinitely becomes an easy path. Thus they follow on the heels of generations of immigrant women with professional aspirations who entered into low-status work such as domestic service as a temporary job but ended up staying long term.[26]

Like Charlie, Jinny was initially averse to the job, but staying on became the path of least resistance once she crossed the hurdle of entering into this work. She was able to take this step only after overcoming negative perceptions instilled by her teacher in South Korea, who had studied in the United States. "She thought it was like a dirty job, a low job. . . . [My teacher told me,] 'Well, you're really going to have a hard time. If you find a new job, just don't go to the nail salon.'" Despite her teacher's disparaging words, Jinny realized that nail salon work was her best employment alternative, given her limited choices.

Although Jinny clearly recounted exclusionary treatment in other jobs as one of her main reasons for going into nail salon work, when asked why she and so many other Korean women work in this niche, she instead referenced stereotypes of Asian women as naturally good at service work. When I asked why so many Korean women work in nail salons, Jinny asserted, "I think it's a natural endowment. Korean women have talented hands. Really, it's true. And Korean women are really strong, stronger than Korean men. To live in this country, you have to be strong." Rather than acknowledging their subordinated group position as Asian immigrant women, Jinny appealed to essentialized group characteristics, overlooking that Koreans have carved out this niche as a response to blocked pathways into professional employment. In addition, she and other Korean women maintain a discourse of individual strengths and "not wanting to be a loser" as driving their investment in nail salon work. Thus even though she recounted exclusionary treatment in other jobs, this did not translate into a critique of U.S. society or the mechanisms of the global service economy. In her account of her difficulties, she also downplayed the perils of undocumented immigration status and the limitations that this imposes on her employment possibilities, both inside and outside the nail salon niche.

NAIL SALONS AND IMMIGRATION STATUS

As an undocumented worker, Jinny gives a face to those who live in this precarious position during a period when illegal immigrants attract hostility and blame for many of the country's economic and social ills. In choosing to focus on Jinny's case, I recognize the danger of feeding misperceptions of Asian manicurists and of immigrants in general as conniving law breakers. At the same time Jinny's story is worth telling as it reveals important and often misunderstood aspects of nail salon work, as well as of immigration more broadly. Firsthand accounts like hers of the everyday realities of living and working as an undocumented immigrant can bring much-needed clarity and compassion into current immigration debates.

Determining the number of Asian manicurists working with undocumented status is difficult, but various studies show that the number and impact of undocumented immigrants in the United States is generally much less than suggested by the level of public animosity. This in no way minimizes the many social costs, the fears of deportation and harassment, or the need for pathways to decriminalization and legal status. Instead, it demonstrates how the targeting of illegal immigrants as the cause of U.S. economic problems is out of sync with the widespread reliance on their labor. As the historian Mae Ngai writes, "Undocumented immigrants are at once welcome and unwelcome: they are woven into the economic fabric of the nation, but as labor that is cheap and disposable."[27] Thus, while the presence of large numbers of undocumented, unlicensed laborers in any industry is undesirable for workers, business owners, and customers, as well as for U.S. society, it is also misguided to hold these individuals solely responsible for their status without considering the many factors that stem from and contribute to their illegality.

Given the constant state of fear in which many undocumented immigrants live, I was not surprised that many women declined to discuss their immigration status. In Jinny's case, although she did not fill in the details, she recounted a difficult and still unresolved immigration saga. Jinny followed the not-uncommon trajectory of coming to the United States on a student visa, finding sponsorship for work, and then leaving that job and overstaying. Because she was not planning to make a career as a manicurist, initially she did not get a license and was able to find a position without one, "but three years later, I needed it so I went to the nail school to apply. . . . I went to school just for that [to gain a license]." Many nail schools sponsor I-20 and M-1 student visas for foreign nationals enrolled in their programs.[28] However, the students must be able to pay for these programs and enroll for at least twenty hours per week, which can be difficult for new immigrants, especially those with jobs. Even if they are able to afford these programs, it is increasingly difficult to move from undocumented to documented status, and efforts to do so can make a worker vulnerable to criminal proceedings and deportation.[29] Like Jinny, many start but are unable to complete the process. She said that her situation was "not bad for now," as she could continue working without a license at her current salon while waiting for avenues to legal status to open. She added, "They [her former employers] didn't care [that she doesn't have a license]. She [the current owner] doesn't care. Actually, she cares so she was trying to find the way for me." However, while some employers may or may not care, many others—customers, state officials, politicians, and pundits—care vehemently whether women like Jinny are properly documented and have mobilized harsh sanctions against those who are not.

Like Jinny, many women end up finding and staying in nail salon work because it is one of only a few ways for them to find employment. Many seek proper work authorization and legal immigration status after already being employed for some time in a salon. Thus working in ethnic-owned small businesses like nail salons can serve as an entry point into the labor force and a vehicle for gaining legal immigration status, but it is by no means a guarantee.

As U.S. immigration policies become more exclusionary and legal entry becomes ever more difficult, more Asian immigrants seek to gain entry through neighboring countries. In Jinny's case she first emigrated to Mexico and then to New York. "Before I came to New York I went to Mexico. I took Spanish classes for two semesters." While Jinny explained her reason for going to Mexico as wanting to learn Spanish, secondary migration through Latin America is one strategy for Asian immigrants seeking to come to the United States. The anthropologist Kyeyoung Park documented this account of a Korean immigrant woman, Mrs. Chung, who crossed the border from Tijuana: "The group of four Koreans and one other person crawled into the tunnel and waited there from 6 A.M. to 6 P.M. Then they boarded a farm truck carrying vegetables and fruit and crawled behind the seat to a space under the produce. After an hour they arrived in San Diego and were moved to a van. In the next hour they were transferred to seven different trucks. Finally, Mrs. Chung was dropped near Koreatown in Los Angeles. There she had to pay the rest of her fee."[30] Although Jinny did not have to suffer such extreme hardship in crossing the border, she lived with the fear of living and working without legal documentation.

Although the problem of "illegal immigration" is often framed around Latin America, significant numbers of Asian immigrants, like Jinny, also struggle with the economic, legal, and social marginalization of undocumented status in the face of strong nativist sentiments. As Juan Perea writes, "The targets of today's nativism wear Mexican, Central American and Asian faces."[31] Like undocumented Latinas, Asians who lack legal status also perform a delicate balancing act wherein they recognize the precariousness of their situation but also find ways to live with it. When he visited Los Angeles in 1997, Hector Silva, the mayor of San Salvador, noted that while he had expected to find "an impoverished, fearful community of Salvadorans," what he found, to his surprise, was that "many have set down roots, have become citizens and are taking an active part in the lives of their communities."[32] Similarly, like Jinny, undocumented Asians struggle with the fears and limitations of their status while also contributing to society and remaining hopeful that, with patience and hard work, they will be able to change their status. Unfortunately, this hopefulness is increasingly hard to maintain, and can even be misguided, in the face of harsh policies and rhetoric regarding illegal immigrants.

RACIALIZED SEXUAL HARASSMENT
OF ASIAN WOMEN

Whether they have official licenses and immigration papers or not, the marginal status of manicurists, combined with racialized and sexualized stereotypes of Asian women, make them easy targets for sexual harassment. Men are increasingly frequenting nail salons, which adds complexity to the dynamics of physical intimacy and emotional management that manicurists must perform. Asian women, especially those with more traditional values, often find service interactions with men uncomfortable, as they violate these women's ideas of appropriate gender relations. When I asked Jinny what the most difficult thing about her work was, she responded: "I don't like to [serve men]. Sometime when I finish the manicure, I have to massage their hands and I don't like that. I don't like that feeling. I hate it. . . . [Some men come here] just because they want to hold a woman's hand. Yeah, sometimes I feel that's what they like to do." When I asked her how she handles these situations, she said, "I don't say anything, I just ignore it." She then described one instance in which a man kept rubbing her hand and making suggestive comments about going home with him. "I just told him he can go right away, because in front of my store, there always is a police car." While Jinny herself did not attribute such forward behavior by men to her Asian ethnicity, other respondents saw such encounters as stemming from widespread perceptions of Asian women as sexually available. Sarah Kim commented, "Some think that we're easy, like bar girls. They've seen movies, or some may have been GIs in Korea and visited the camptowns." Such presumptions increase the vulnerability of these women to both subtle and overt forms of what Sumi K. Cho calls "racialized sexual harassment," which she defines as a "particular set of injuries" that make Asian and other women of color vulnerable to sexual advances in the workplace. Cho documents how the converging racial and sexual stereotypes of Asian women as the passive and submissive model minority on the one hand, and, on the other, as exotic and erotic "Suzie Wongs," combine to fuel harassers' beliefs that the women will be receptive to, or at least not reject, their advances.[33] Consistent with Cho's analysis, the intersections of intimate body labor performed by sexualized and racialized Asian women, especially those

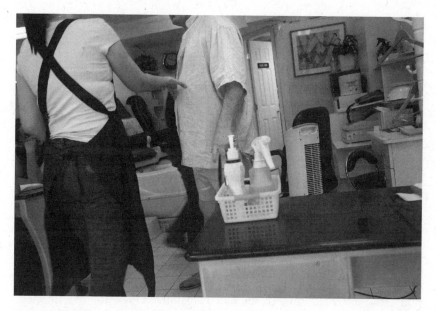

Figure 7. A man argues with a manicurist over a back waxing. Intimate body labor like this can lead to instances of racialized sexual harassment toward Asian women.

lacking legal immigration status, heightens nail salon workers' vulnerability to sexual harassment and leaves them little recourse to combat it.

In my research I came across two salons that regularly refused services to men. As I discuss in later chapters, this is mostly because of the fear of crime, but the sexual politics of serving men is also a contributing factor. One salon owner, Cara Park, said that she sees a higher turnover of manicurists when her business has many male customers. "Even though most men are good customers, if a worker has one bad experience, she feels really bad and doesn't want to come back. Most Korean women never touched another man's hand except their husband's." Consistent with this owner's description of most men as "good customers," the customer interactions with men that I observed were for the most part cordial and respectful. However, I observed several incidents where men's interactions with Korean manicurists exhibited clearly sexualized overtones. In one case I witnessed an older white man in business attire jokingly yet provocatively ask a manicurist at Uptown Nails, "Don't you want to marry me? I bet I'm richer and better looking than your husband." In another instance I observed a young black man who came into Downtown Nails and insisted on being attended to by one particularly attractive young manicurist. When the owner explained that the manicurist was in the middle of a time-consuming job and attempted to steer him toward another manicurist, a middle-aged woman, he looked scornfully at the second manicurist and retorted, "I can do better at another salon," and left abruptly.

These incidents suggest that some men who patronize nail salons harbor perceptions of Asian women as sexual objects.[34] Studies of sexual harassment have demonstrated how sexual harassment is pervasive in a range of occupations and undermines women's professional advancement and psychological well-being.[35] The converging forces of gender, race, immigration status and low-wage work on the body foster an environment in nail salons that can incite harassers while making it difficult for workers to rebuff or discourage these unwanted advances. Even Jinny, who forthrightly confronted women customers in various situations, told me that although she hated sexualized encounters with men, she tried simply to ignore their unwanted advances.

Thus racialized sexual harassment casts a shadow over the already challenging nature of body labor in nail salons. Although the majority of men who patronize nail salons are respectful, the few that engage in sexual harassment, even in the form of "playful" innuendo, make it necessary for women to keep up their guard. The demands of working in the beauty service sector, particularly the expectation of physical and emotional attentiveness, can increase susceptibility. When Asian women manicurists like Jinny encounter male customers, they must not only manage their own feelings and those of the customer, but they must do so within a public discourse that infuses this encounter with charged racial and sexual stereotypes.

NEITHER HERE NOR THERE—CAUGHT
BETWEEN WORLDS

Jinny's sense of satisfaction with nail salon work and immigrant life was further diminished by openly racist and derogatory remarks that enforced her sense of marginalization in U.S. society.

Sometimes I feel like crying, but I never do, because I don't want to cry. I want to be a winner. . . . Sometimes I get bad customers. "OK, I'm an immigrant—you're an immigrant, too! You know American history?" . . . In my mind I can [say this to them], but I can't say that out loud. So I just ignore them. . . . Sometimes they curse me—"fucking Chinese girl" and things like "you go back to your country." But I can deal with it. . . . "OK, no problem. Thank you so much." That's it. . . . At first I tried everything, and I called the police the first year. But now I'm used to doing it, so I just ignore them. . . . When I'm really angry, I don't think anything. I just get away and get a pack of cigarettes and smoke about three straight. Then it's OK. . . . When I meet my Korean friends we drink. We never stop drinking until two or three o'clock, because nobody wants to stop. I want to stop.

As I discuss in later chapters, other manicurists report similarly blatant racial epithets while working in a nail salon. Despite her assertion that she just ignored these incidents, Jinny was visibly upset when sharing them and revealed how she often internalized stress from work and channeled it into unhealthy behaviors such as excessive smoking and drinking. The owner of the salon where Jinny worked told me that she was concerned about Jinny's "rough friends," as well as about her physical and emotional health, and had tried to get Jinny to go to a Korean church, but Jinny did not want to go.

Jinny's limited prospects for the future also added to her concerns. Whereas an earlier generation of Korean women saw working as a manicurist as a short phase until they opened their own salon, Jinny saw this as an unlikely possibility for her. She was well aware of the current challenges of starting a salon, including growing start-up costs, intense competition and increasing rates of business failures. "I've heard that now 80 percent of the owners are Korean, but ten or fifteen years later it will be about 20 to 25 percent. It is because of competition. Here, there are about five Korean nail salons. Last winter a Chinese nail salon opened up there, near here. The price is much lower than us and they do nails very good. So why come here?" Thus Jinny did not think that she could sustain a successful business over the long run; in this she was similar to many nail salon workers who have given up aspirations of becoming owners. Jenny Park, a manicurist and owner in Brooklyn, commented:

I want to mention that not all Korean women who open nail salons are successful. Many nail salons that are opened are maintained and nothing more. A person like me has a lot of experience but nowadays, a lot of women who have only a few years of experience open up stores because they don't want to work for someone else. They want to be seen as 'the boss.' The inside story is that they open up stores without generating any profit. They are satisfied if they are able to take home their salary.

Given the relatively small differential in earnings between ownership and employment in many small salons, this desire to be the boss is increasingly outweighed by the uncertainty of nail salon entrepreneurship. Thus the pursuit of economic mobility and a sense of belonging in the host country through entrepreneurship is no longer viable for many Korean immigrant women.[36]

Because she saw the nail salon niche as virtually saturated, Jinny instead nurtured hopes of one day opening a liquor store. "When I'm about forty-five or fifty year old, I'm gonna open up my own liquor store because I love to drink. I'm just kidding, but I am considering a liquor store. I don't want to do this [nail] business for a long time. Less than ten years. . . . Because now I have no choice. This is the best way, so I can do it. But if I have more money, I'm not going to do it." Whether Jinny will be able to start her own liquor store, however, is debatable. Such an enterprise requires a large capital outlay, and the ongoing management requires much assistance, which Jinny lacked as a single woman without family or business partners. Thus, while she nursed dreams of owning her own business, she accepted the current reality of working in a job that did not fulfill her career goals, imposed many daily hardships, and aggravated a sense of alienation in her new country.

Jinny told me that after living for almost ten years in the United States, she would find it difficult to return to Korea. At the same time she often felt like an outsider in both mainstream U.S. culture and the Korean American community: "Koreans don't think this job is a proud job. They are embarrassed about it. Me, never, but most of them, especially older women, they think cleaning someone else's feet is really embarrassing." While Jinny claimed that she did not share these negative feelings toward nail salon work, her story suggests otherwise. Far from her dream of a high-status position in finance, Jinny's job carried little cachet in any of her social worlds.

WHAT DO WOMEN GAIN AND LOSE THROUGH NAIL SALON WORK?

Charlie's and Jinny's stories provide complex answers to the question of what women gain and lose through immigration and, in particular, through work in a low-status gendered ethnic niche like nail salons. Employment and self-employment in the nail salon industry has enabled many Asian immigrant women like Charlie and Jinny to overcome barriers in the mainstream labor market by carving out their own opportunities. Furthermore, this work provides some flexibility to balance the simultaneous demands of work, family, and community responsibilities. At the same time these women's experiences reveal deep cracks in the ideology of Asian immigrants' assimilation and upward mobility.

Like other gender and migration researchers, I believe that immigration brings only modest gains to women's individual autonomy, power in the family, and ideologies of gender equality, despite their increased economic contributions. These women's "failures" to transform patriarchal relations reflect their subordination not only as women but also as racialized foreigners employed in a low-status occupation. Although women do contribute to maintaining traditional family values and relations, it would be a mistake to argue that these arrangements persist simply because women themselves internalize and reproduce them through their "natural" maternal or feminine feelings. Historical and global forces have shaped perceptions of Asian immigrant women as more docile and hardworking than their male counterparts, thereby giving the women access to more economic opportunities and often thrusting them into the role of primary wage earners. While they must rise to fill this economic role, women are not given additional material or ideological resources, as their husbands, community, and government often fail to support their multiple responsibilities.

CONCLUSION

Acknowledging the mixed gains of nail salon entrepreneurship and employment does not discount the many contributions that Korean immigrant women have made through this work, nor does it validate model minority Asian success narratives. Rather, it captures the tensions and compromises women make in their lives as they perform this work. After I presented the findings of this chapter at a university seminar, a Korean graduate student approached me and said that my presentation ran counter to her observations. Asserting that the Korean women she knows who are employed in salons "feel that they are helping people and do not feel like they are discriminated against," she said they would be upset by my characterization of this work as demeaning. I responded by agreeing that most Korean manicurists do indeed take great pride in their work, even as they acknowledge the hardships associated with it. At the same time failure to acknowledge the dynamics of exclusion that shape their work does not mean that these dynamics do not operate. For most people, showing up for work every day would be a difficult task if they focused solely on the exploitative nature of their jobs. Instead, most workers find a way to see their work as gratifying in one way or another, be it through positive customer interactions or through a sense of pride in being able to support themselves and their families. Even women like Jinny, who clearly recounted experiences of exclusion that led her to nail salon employment, still cited their skillfulness and enjoyment of the work as reasons they "chose" this work, even as they made these choices within very circumscribed conditions.

While later chapters explore the embodied dimensions of this work, in this chapter I have emphasized the dynamics of emotional management, including the complex feelings that owners and manicurists hold about their transplanted lives and the ways that they manage these feelings both at work and at home. This vantage point sheds new light on a persistent question in the study of gender and immigration—how do the processes of immigration transform women's lives, and how do women experience these changes? Rather than feeling liberated from domestic duties through nail salon work, married women with children like

Charlie are forced to shift their expenditures of emotional labor from caring for their families to caring for their customers. Simultaneously, these
women continue to bear the emotional burden of the domestic responsibilities that they must leave unattended. Single women like Jinny can
feel stuck in jobs that they feel are beneath them, but are constrained in
finding other employment. Furthermore, like Jinny, in their private lives
they can feel isolated from both the Korean American community and
mainstream American society. A sense of personal insecurity and social
alienation in their new country can be heightened by undocumented
immigration status and demeaning racialized and sexualized interactions. Stereotypes of Asian women as sexually available leave these
women vulnerable to sexual harassment, undermining their feelings
about their work as a source of economic and personal power. Negative
perceptions of nail salon employment in the ethnic community further
undercut the potential empowering aspects of the work. These factors
combine to impose high levels of stress that can foster unhealthy health
and social behaviors, such as excessive smoking and drinking and with-
drawal from social contact.

Charlie's and Jinny's experiences dramatize the complexities of living and working as immigrant women employed in the U.S. beauty
service sector. While their experiences are clearly shaped by gender, gender alone cannot account for the multiple dimensions of their work and
identities. Rather, gendered processes are refracted through race, class,
and immigrant status, generating experiences and feelings about these
experiences that are not universal to all women. Instead, they are specific to these women's locations as Asians, immigrants, and employers
or service workers who perform body labor. The next chapter shifts from
these emotional and embodied vantage points of nail salon owners and
manicurists to those of their customers.

Three Hooked on Nails

You kind of become a slave to it. You start coming, you have to keep coming to keep up your nails, because once you see how nice they look, you
don't want them to be the other way. You get hooked—it's an addiction.

Alexandra, customer, Exclusive Nails

[I design my own nails] because I don't like looking like anyone else. My
nails say "me." They're the first thing people notice about me.

Jamilla, customer, Downtown Nails

I'm looking down at the sidewalk, mesmerized by the women's feet. One of
them is wearing open-toed sandals, the toenails painted pink. I remember
the smell of nail polish, the way it wrinkled if you put the second coat on too
soon, the satiny brushing of sheer pantyhose against the skin, the way the
toes felt, pushed toward the opening in the shoe by the whole weight of the
body. The woman with painted toes shifts from one foot to the other. I can
feel her shoes, on my own feet. The smell of nail polish has made me hungry.

Margaret Atwood, *The Handmaid's Tale*

What is the hunger that drives women to polish their nails? Is it hunger
for beauty, power, and romantic love? Or are these cravings substitutes
for a deeper hunger for meaning and recognition? What is it about manicured nails that simultaneously feeds and deprives women's desires?
How do different women hunger for different things, even in the common pursuit of beautiful nails? In Margaret Atwood's dystopian novel

Figure 8. Pedicures and other pampering services often become an important part of women's self-care and feminine identity.

the sight of polished nails stirs in the narrator a fierce longing for the freedoms she once possessed in a formerly democratic society. Forced by ruling Christian fundamentalists into a role based solely on her reproductive functions, she must now dress like a nun without any accoutrements of bodily care, even hand lotion. In an interesting, albeit imperfect, role reversal, she gazes enviously at the painted toes of a Japanese tourist who wishes to take her picture. Atwood composed this fictional scene before the widespread emergence of Asian-owned nail salons, and a Japanese woman on a sightseeing tour is not interchangeable with a Korean immigrant service worker. Nonetheless, the anomaly of a white woman's hungering after an Asian woman's painted toes rightly serves as a powerful and unsettling image of a society radically different from that of the United States today.

The value of this fictional snapshot is that it provides an opportunity to reflect upon the present and disrupts the contemporary social landscape, wherein Asian women are not coveted for their polished nails but are more likely to be polishing another woman's feet. Atwood viscerally captures the potent appeal of manicured nails, even, or perhaps especially, in circumstances where women lack basic resources and opportunities. Like Atwood's handmaid, many women hunger for manicured nails not as an optional dessert but as staple food for their sense of self.

Manicured nails and women's intense hungering for them serve as a point of entry to examine competing constructions of beauty and what these reveal about women's lives. Why do so many diverse women get their nails done, and what are the differences and commonalities in the meanings that they give to their nails? What are the boundaries of acceptable nails; how are these boundaries defined, policed, and challenged; and what are the consequences of transgression? While nearly all women in this study acknowledged desire for feminine beauty as underlying their purchase of manicures, their notions of what constitutes beauty, and beautiful nails, contrasted sharply. Gendered constructions of beauty and beauty services are overlaid with racial and class meanings but are not simply reducible to race and class positions. Instead, women of similar social backgrounds may sport similar nails but ascribe very different meanings to them, while women whose nails appear quite dissimilar may be linked by shared desires.

At the same time, while diverse women can choose whether and how to manicure their nails, the meanings that they give their own nails compete with the meanings imposed by others. In this chapter I explore how women regard their nails as expressing everything from individuality and self-sufficiency to professionalism and relational commitments. However, a narrow discourse of acceptable and unacceptable displays of the female body often overrides women's self-definitions. Women's choices of nail styles and services reflect the social construction of beauty, which is not based on natural or biological traits but upon socially conditioned tastes that are deeply entrenched in gender, race, and class differences.

These differences in manicuring self-presentations, similar to conspicuous displays in matters such as food, leisure activities, and other types of cultural consumption, serve to legitimate and reinforce social prestige along the lines of "good" and "bad" taste. As Pierre Bourdieu writes in *Distinction: A Social Critique of the Judgment of Taste*, "art and cultural consumption are predisposed, consciously and deliberately or not, to fulfill a social function of legitimating social differences."[1] Bourdieu's notion of habitus, which refers to "the conditionings associated with a particular class of conditions of existence," illuminates the ways that seemingly superfluous displays (such as women's nails) in fact speak volumes about differing social positions.[2] Thus variation in women's manicuring practices does not simply represent personal tastes but reflects embodied distinctions associated with the customers' habitus. While Bourdieu focuses on class distinctions, women's habitus, as enacted in their nail styles, also draw heavily upon race and gender, as I demonstrate in this chapter. By applying an intersectional analysis to Bourdieu's concept of habitus, this study broadens it to include multivalent influences in addition to class and focuses attention on the array of service providers—from chefs to golf caddies to masseuses and manicurists—that is necessary to maintain displays of embodied distinction.

In focusing on how customers negotiate the meanings of beauty from their particular habitus, or set of aesthetic dispositions associated with their social position, I examine six customers and compare them with each other and with additional cases. These customers are not meant to represent all women who frequent nail salons, nor is it my intention to generalize about their experiences. Rather, these profiles draw out themes and contrasts that emerged at particular sites and that illuminate the situational forces that shape these sites. The first two customers— Alexandra and Jamilla—highlight competing constructions of "good" and "bad" beauty across racial and class lines and how these categories are defined in opposition to each other. Theresa and Brianna's manicures reflected their identities as mothers and the contrasting ways that society validates or fails to validate them in this position. Ella and Cheryl prioritized the meaning of the manicure in the workplace and illustrate the mechanisms of racial and class differentiation that operate through bodily presentations. Finally, I examine how women's relationships with men, and the social institutions that define these relationships, influence women's manicuring practices.

These women demonstrate that nail salon customers are neither simply victims of an exploitative, patriarchal beauty culture, nor are they fully self-determining actors. Although they do assert individuality in manicuring their nails according to their personal preferences, women's manicuring practices emerge within larger social contexts and ideologies. The following accounts begin with customers' own explanations of their manicuring practices and then explore dimensions of these practices that women themselves may not acknowledge.

MANICURING RACIALIZED
AND CLASSED FEMININITIES

In her acclaimed book, *Black Sexual Politics*, Patricia Hill Collins writes, "All women engage an ideology that deems middle-class, heterosexual, White femininity as normative. . . . Moreover, these standards of female beauty have no meaning without the visible presence of Black women and others who fail to measure up." She further asserts that dichotomous framings of beautiful and ugly solidify into categories of normative versus marginalized feminine beauty based on hierarchies of race, class, and sexuality. These categories are read through specific embodied traits— mainly, skin color, hair texture, body type, and facial features.[3] To this list I add nails as an important and neglected dimension that shapes notions of feminine beauty. Regardless of the intentions of the women wearing them, French manicures and pastel colors signal white, middle-class, heteronormative feminine beauty, whereas sculptured airbrushed nails are markers of black, poor, sexually deviant, marginalized femininity. In short, women's nails "whiten" or "blacken" them, as deeply entrenched social divisions impose meanings upon their embodied self-presentations.

While emphasizing the black-white division, Collins argues that other women of color also occupy subordinated positions in this hierarchy of racialized beauty. Similarly, Julie Bettie finds in her study of Chicana and white high school girls in California that hairstyles, clothes, and makeup, along with the color of nail polish, are building blocks for the performance of different forms of femininities—which she refers to as "dissident" versus "mainstream." Bettie identifies the "importance of colors as a tool of distinction," wherein "las chicas" preferred dark colors and "preps" wore lighter colors.[4] Her findings, that certain colors are read as class and racial markers, are similar to my findings with regard not only to the color but the design, length, and shape of nails.

The following profiles of two nail salon customers—Alexandra and Jamilla—contrast these two women across the binary of white middle-class and black lower-class femininities. This binary is problematic and incomplete, but it persists as a hegemonic framework that pervades other women's experiences and shapes the parameters of racialized beauty. While women like Alexandra and Jamilla strive to express their identities through their nails, their own meanings serve only as the top coat, layered over a much thicker social hierarchy of racialized, classed, and gendered bodies.

Alexandra

> I have to look a certain way and so I have to get my nails done. I cannot walk around with a big line of bare nail up here without paint because people are going to notice. And even though I feel like I am driven, and I have a lot of things to do, even when I don't really have time, somehow I have to make the time to get my nails done. When you have long nails, you cannot keep long nails naturally. See, it is a social thing. Our society sucks. It is coming to this—long nails are nice and pretty, but realistically you cannot have long nails without a little help.

As Alexandra, a twenty-seven-year-old white teacher at a private elementary school and regular customer at Exclusive Nails, elaborated on her beauty practices, a complex picture emerged of a woman who critiques but ultimately acquiesces to feminine beauty norms. She confessed that she was "hooked" on manicures, and she invested substantial time and money in maintaining both her pastel French nails and her overall coiffed appearance. At the same time Alexandra criticized society for demanding that she have long beautiful nails—and for judging her negatively when she failed to meet these standards. However, while clearly articulating this analysis, she did not alter her regular practice of manicuring her nails. By referring to herself as a beauty "slave" with an addiction to beautiful nails, Alexandra framed herself as a victim of the beauty industry and the ideology that supports it, but she also said she chose to do her nails because they make her feel good. What can we make of these seeming contradictions?

On the one hand, we could take a hard view that Alexandra is simply a hypocrite who does not practice what she preaches, but then we would still need to dig deeper and ask why she doesn't. Is she unwilling, or unable, to act on her critical awareness and actively resist beauty dictates? Is she insufficiently empowered to deal with the real consequences of a fall from beauty's grace? Or does she reap the benefits of appearing to conform while strategically carving out her own agenda for her nails and her overall bodily display? I was not able to ask Alexandra these questions directly, nor would her own answers necessarily tell the whole story. Instead of probing more into her own beauty beliefs, I drew inferences from her comments about other women's nails, particularly those who did not fit her standards of acceptability.

Although she did not mention the concept of the beauty myth explicitly, Alexandra reiterated many of its main themes in her tirade against a society that pressures her to invest time, material resources, and psychic energy in maintaining her appearance, at the expense of other activities that she was "driven" to do. While she was well versed in the critique of beauty, women like Alexandra not only continue to play, and win, at the beauty game, but they also become enforcers of its rules, thereby excluding other women from the ranks of the beautiful. In order to attract positive attention from both men and women in both personal and professional contexts, Alexandra conformed to narrow rules of femininity for her own nails and imposed these on other women. When asked if she ever got nail extensions or designs, Alexandra shook her head vehemently.

> You look gaudy, maybe cheap or something, and I think you also look like you're wasting money out of stupidity. The kind of nails I get are seen as more practical, they fit with my image—neat, but not long hair, simple stylish clothes. I think if you're paying to have them done, your nails should bring you positive attention, not negative. And there is also that other part, that other people are saying, "Oh, your nails look so good. They look so nice." That feels good too. . . . Men and women notice them.

I'm sure they would notice if I didn't do them . . . because they look really nasty after working with chalk all day long. . . . When you see people with those dragged nails and rises, it looks kind of crazy. . . . If I do a simple design, I would like it, that would be nice and I could live with that, but I don't want to go too far.

While she conformed to mainstream beauty standards, Alexandra was neither a simple "cultural dupe" who unconsciously reproduced dominant ideologies nor was she a true believer in the value of beauty.[5] Instead, she calculated what kind of nails would bring her the kind of attention that she desired, and she chose accordingly. It was, however, a circumscribed choice. She was acutely aware of the negative repercussions of making the wrong choice, either by having nails that look uncared for, voiced in her concerns about her nails' being covered with chalk dust, or about appearing "cheap" and "stupid" if she were to wear ostentatious nails.

While Alexandra herself did not explicitly attribute long airbrushed nails to black working-class women, she clearly positioned herself and her own tastes as distinct and in opposition to those that "look kind of crazy." Although she did not name race and class, her concerns about going "too far" with her nails established clear boundaries of normative femininity and hinted at the lines along which these boundaries are transgressed. Alexandra moaned that "society sucks" when it comes to images and standards for women's beauty, but she did not resist this ideology in her own beauty practices. Furthermore, she created divisions with those who followed different beauty conventions.

Similarly, other white women in the study refrained from naming long elaborate nails as racial and class signifiers but at the same time clearly disassociated themselves from these beauty practices and the women who engage in them. In response to a question about what kind of women get extensions and designs, most white middle-class women in the study coded their language in a subtext that suggested, but did not name, race. For example, when one customer, Sylvia, explained her distaste for nail art, she stated that the women who like it are "flashy women, I think people who like to be noticed," indirectly referencing a racialized subtext of women of color as flamboyant. Other women emphasized factors such as age and skin color, but not race explicitly, as measures of appropriateness. For example, Margaret said, "I choose colors according to my skin, something which doesn't make me look stupid, like I'm trying to look like a young kid." Thus she couched her comments about color and skin as not being about race but instead as a "stupid" denial of age.

The women who spoke most directly about nails as racial and class markers were neither white middle-class women who embraced normative femininity nor black working-class women who embodied its antithesis but instead women who occupied a place in-between. Van, an Asian American college student and the daughter of working-class Vietnamese immigrants, spoke to the racial and class associations of elaborate nails in terms of her own marginalized social position. "Once I went and got an airbrush—just because I wanted to try it—and my parents freaked. They said they didn't want me looking like I was, like, low class. . . . Yeah, well, I guess they see more of the black girls wearing it, the black and Hispanic girls, and that's what they don't like. But I also think they just don't like them 'cause they think they're too flashy and they don't look clean or something." While Van explicitly acknowledged the racial and class meaning of nails, she still invoked coded descriptions such as "flashy" and a lack of cleanliness to explain the marginalization of these forms of femininity.

Likewise, Jacqueline, a second-generation Italian American hairdresser in her late thirties, spoke from a semimarginal location as a white woman who came from a working-class immigrant family and community. She identified closely with her parents' status as immigrants, which she said motivated her to learn to speak Italian fluently and visit her homeland and connect with relatives. Her experience as a beauty service worker further molded her perspective. Unlike other white women in this study, she openly commented on the racial meaning of nails:

> African Americans are a big supporter of the acrylic nails and the airbrushing. Frankly, I give them credit for getting them done because it looks good—they take pride in their nails, and they have an artistic outlook. You have to be confident and secure in yourself to have really outrageous nails. It takes a certain kind of personality, very creative and artistic. I know

because when I have the acrylics done, people will look at me like they're too bold, too bright, too long. Maybe college and high school kids get them done, but your regular housewives will get more mature nails.

Jacqueline expressed admiration for women with artistic nails as expressing self-confidence and creativity and framed these as positive attributes of African American women. At the same time she reproduced a cultural framework of excluding these women from the normative category of "regular housewives." Like Margaret, she also invoked age to soften racial undertones, saying that ornate nail styles are acceptable for "kids" but not for women desiring more "mature" nails.[6]

Most women danced around explicit references to race and, to a lesser degree, class, instead emphasizing such characteristics as age, cleanliness, or "flashiness" to judge nail styles. In contrast to these veiled allusions, the racial and class politics of nails confront African American working-class women like Jamilla head-on, as their nail styles stigmatize their bodies as deviant and even ugly, according to standards of mainstream femininity.

Jamilla

Jamilla, a twenty-six-year-old African American restaurant worker, part-time student, and regular customer at Downtown Nails, proudly displayed her inch-and-a-half nails adorned with segments of the New York City skyline in bold black and framed by an orange and yellow sunset. "I draw a new design for Mr. Lee each time I go. That's why I go to him—he does hand painting, not just airbrushing on some decals or someone else's design. . . . I spend between $50 and $60 every two weeks. In the summer time I spend more because of the pedicures, say, $150 to $170 a month. It's worth it." Jamilla, who took pride in her original nails, elaborated on her personal aesthetics in designing her own nails. "It all depends on my mood. Like this design makes me feel like I'm on top of the city, like it can't bring me down." I commented, "You've literally got the city at your fingertips." She laughed loudly and replied: "Yeah, no one's gonna mess with you when you got nails like this." These nails allowed for original self-expression and imbued her with a sense of power, as she asserted that no one would "mess with" a woman with nails like hers. Given her job as a server, I asked her if managers or customers ever complained about her nails. She responded, "When they do, I just move on." Thus her unique nail styles took precedence over conforming to mainstream social norms, even to keep her job.

Whereas Alexandra tailored her nail style to fit into normative standards of feminine beauty, both in her personal relations and professional life, Jamilla flaunted her one-of-a-kind hand-painted designs, even in the face of social disapproval. However, beneath the appearance of profoundly different nail aesthetics, these women may have far more in common, as their tastes reflect their respective social worlds. While her nails may have disqualified Jamilla from the white middle-class beauty norms to which Alexandra conformed, Jamilla can be seen as a winner on a separate beauty stage, one that reflects the habitus of her racial and class location. When I asked Jamilla why she invested so much in her nails, she replied, "I have big hands for a female. I never had those long, thin ladylike fingers. My father used to say my hands were bigger than his. I want long nails because they make my hands look more feminine." As Collins writes, "One benchmark of hegemonic femininity is that women *not* be like men."[7] Unlike Alexandra, whose nail aesthetics reflected her concern with appearing to be the right kind of woman, neither disheveled nor gaudy, Jamilla's nails guarded against her being seen as masculine and thus not a woman at all.

Contrary to Alexandra's portrayal of women with elaborate nails as aberrant, Jamilla shows that her nails make sense within her own social context. Whereas Alexandra's manicures were mostly a solitary experience, Jamilla's time in the nail salon involved socializing and bonding with other women. "My mother started me out going in there when I was a junior in high school. She saw all these nail salons, and she just decided we should go get them done and—end of story. . . . I pledged a sorority and for my initiation I had to cut them—they knew that was the real test for me! I really thought about if it was worth it, but I did it." As a hazing ritual, Jamilla's sorority sisters put her to the ultimate loyalty test of cutting her nails, thereby backwardly reinforcing their shared investment in similar artistic nail styles. Thus, while drawing disdain from white middle-class women such as Alexandra, Jamilla's nails attracted admiration and solidified ties with women in her own community.

While she emphasized the quality of her nails as a unique form of self-expression, Jamilla situated this self within her black working class habitus and the need to balance toughness, self-sufficiency, and creative expression in order to achieve her ideals of femininity. She was living in an apartment with her parents and her younger sister, struggling to complete a bachelor's degree while she worked nearly full time at various restaurant jobs. Jamilla knew the odds were against her, but she maintained high hopes for her future, along with strict regimens that included the care of her nails. "I go in, and they take the polish off and check for loose, cracked areas and treat for fungus. My nails grow out really uneven. Mr. Lee tortures me by ripping up the old acrylic. He's the owner and I'm really finicky so I only go to him—I expect perfection." Thus she invested both a significant amount of money and physical effort in order to maintain them. Sadly, the very nails that Jamilla tended with such diligence can mark her in the social world outside her own neighborhood as unemployable and, ultimately, unfeminine.

The poignancy of Jamilla's refusal to change her nails emerges in contrast to other black working-class women who acquiesce to trimming both their nails and their own bodily aesthetics in their search for upward mobility. Serena, a twenty-four-year-old African American mother, part-time student, and package clerk, also regularly patronized Downtown Nails. While she wore nail extensions and designs, she scaled them down because she knew they were an impediment to more prestigious jobs.

> I keep them practical. Nothing too outrageous, [like] lime green and purple and hot, hot pink. I get browns, light pinks and neutral colors. For designs I get florals or tropicals, like a palm tree. I don't go too overboard. Where I work, the customers look at my hands, and it doesn't look right or appropriate if they're really long and wild. I was always told—like in books about preparing for job interviews—that first appearances are important, and they'll look at your hair, your clothes, and your nails. . . . I've been thinking of doing some job interviews for the MTA [Metropolitan Transportation Authority] or maybe on Wall Street, and I can't go in

with, say, all-black nails. . . . So if they see my hands, I want them to think they look good. If your hands have warts or are fungus-y or ashy, they may think, "I wonder what her house looks like."

Serena recognized that her hands and the nails that adorn them send strong messages to potential employers, serving as a proxy by which they may evaluate other parts of her life, such as how she keeps her home. While she saw her nails as not outrageous, she nonetheless conceded that she would have to adjust her nail styles further to find better work.

Similarly, Alia, a twenty-two-year-old African American woman who was working as a supermarket cashier but aspired to go to nursing school, attested to the need to subjugate her own nail aesthetics for occupational mobility. "I've thought about it—if I become a nurse, I can't have long nails. They would have to be a little shorter, but I would still paint them. I would just have to wear gloves because the paint might chip, and you have to be sanitary. If they really had a problem, I guess I would just go and have a plain manicure." For women like Jamilla, Serena, and Alia, their manicuring choices carry consequences for either constraining or facilitating their movement into other social positions.

If these women are aware of the negative consequences in the job market of having nails that fall outside conventional beauty standards, why don't they just get rid of them? One white middle-class colleague, in providing me with feedback on this chapter, shared her initial feelings of frustration in reading about Jamilla and the ways that she seemed to sabotage herself by insisting on a body presentation that hampered her job prospects. "But then it hit me: I left a job because I couldn't wear jeans to work, so how is that so different than leaving a job because they won't let you wear your nails the way you like them?" Her insight reveals underlying similarities in women's accommodations, or lack thereof, of their embodied self-presentations to their work demands. However, the consequences of their success or failure in achieving their respective standards of beauty diverge sharply. Across jobs, women alter their bodily displays, but untenable standards can serve as reason to leave. Thus, while it would be easy to surmise that these black working-class women with elaborate nails have little in common with white middle-class women like Alexandra, not only in the appearance of their nails but in the meanings attached to them, this interpretation would belie their common strivings for feminine beauty. At the same time they conform to different standards and face different consequences for nonconformity. In Alexandra's case her beauty choices involved feeling good or bad about herself, attracting positive or negative attention, and challenging or acquiescing to dominant standards of beauty. For Jamilla the stakes were much higher. While her nails may have earned her respect and admiration within her community, they stigmatized her within the dominant culture, leading to potential loss of employment and blocked mobility out of urban poverty.

In determining what kinds of nails constitute beauty, women must negotiate different standards—those of their own communities, those of particular institutions, such as the family and the workplace, those of the dominant white culture, as well as their own standards. As Lynn Chancer writes in *Reconcilable Differences*, "The woman of color must contend not only with the bad woman/good woman dichotomy, which itself historically was at once racialized and gendered, but also with the maddeningly mixed cultural messages regarding what constitutes beauty, anyway, for a woman who is not white. . . . As a woman, she has in common with all women being differentially valued on the basis of looks, on the basis of beauty. But beauty by whose standards?"[8] Determinations of what constitutes beauty thus reference specific social contexts. When Alexandra conforms to the beauty standards of her white middle-class position, she achieves the status of "good beauty," whereas Jamilla's adherence to the beauty aesthetics of her black working-class background are more likely to earn her approbation for "bad beauty." Therefore, rather than assuming universal categories of ugly and beautiful, it is crucial to recognize that women face different definitions of beauty in different contexts and according to different identities. In particular, women who claim differently racialized and classed identities as mothers confront shifting boundaries of acceptable and unacceptable beauty practices, as illustrated by the cases of Theresa and Brianna.

MANICURING GOOD AND BAD MOTHERS

When a woman walks into a nail salon, she is not simply a woman getting her nails done but a woman of a particular social status in a particular social context. For women who are mothers, this identity serves as a master status, a prism through which others view their appearance and their actions. At the same time discourses about women's worth as mothers are refracted through race and class, with poor black women and middle-class white women encountering different responses as they become mothers.[9] As Karen McCormack argues, "Motherhood continues to be venerated when the mothers are middle and upper class, married and white: the mothering done by poor, nonwhite women, however, is systematically devalued."[10] The legal scholar Dorothy Roberts adds that the denigration of poor black women as mothers has resulted in their subjection to punitive state policies ranging from sterilization to imprisonment, because "society does not view these women as suitable mothers in the first place."[11] Women's nails, and their bodily presentations more broadly, then become fodder for how society judges them as good or bad mothers.

Theresa

"When you don't get your nails done, it kind of can make you feel down and depressed. When you get them done, it boosts your ego up a little bit," said Theresa, a thirty-five-year-old white middle-class married mother of two small children. She was wearing designer jeans and open-toed sandals as she slid into the manicuring chair at Exclusive Nails with a mixture of anticipation and guilt. She had hired a babysitter to tend her infant daughter and toddler son while she stole away for her limited dose of "Theresa time"—a significant chunk of which she invested in maintaining her nails. While she saw her nail salon visits as an escape from her homemaking responsibilities, it was an imperfect one, as she conformed her nail styles to the demands that awaited her outside the salon:

> Right now, because I have two small children I don't grow them that long. It is hard—cooking, cleaning, taking care of kids—I can't have them

long. . . . I like getting my nails done. Just getting your hands to look better, you feel better. After being home with two small kids, you just want to pick yourself up. It gives you a little boost and energy. . . . I like very simple and tasteful designs. Maybe I'll do it a little slanted with a little diamond. I am not very into bright colors, sometimes you can do a marbling thing on your nails, but that is too much.

"Why is it too much?" I inquired. She hesitated and replied thoughtfully, "Hmm, maybe, that it is too youthful." For Theresa long elaborately designed nails were not only impractical, given her caregiving and housekeeping responsibilities, but they were incongruous with her image of herself as a homemaker. Instead, they signified youth and the accompanying freedoms that her current life did not allow. She sheepishly acknowledged that she comes to the nail salon for "purely selfish reasons" and as "an escape" and "boost" from the demands of full-time mothering.

But why was Theresa in such need of these boosts, and when she did not make it to the salon, was it really the appearance of her nails that made her feel depressed? What was missing in her life that a weekly visit to the nail salon fulfilled or at least assuaged? Theresa said she spends approximately $50 a month on her nails. When I asked her how this compared with what she spent on other beauty services, she laughed gruffly, saying, "Is there any other beauty service? Not for me—this is the treat of the month." For Theresa to miss her manicure is to forgo the only indulgence that she regularly allows herself. Furthermore, it preserved one of few remaining ties to her former life, as she used to visit the same nail salon as a working professional. "I was working in an investment bank, so I had to be very professional," she said. "So, it is good to have a little grooming. I think it helps you feel more confident at work. . . . I guess I could do them at home, but I would rather have somebody else do it. You get a little carried away at home sometimes. You have accidents. You cut a little too much and ones are not even, one nail is square when one is round. It just does not work. Who needs that at the end of a hard day?" Where Theresa's manicures once signaled a sense of confidence in the world of finance, they now assuaged her lack of status in her homemaking role and helped her avoid the additional frustration of botching her own nails.

In addition to providing a respite from homemaking responsibilities, manicured nails, for Theresa and other women in similar circumstances, provide a way of maintaining some small connection to their former identities in high-earning careers. Her somewhat apologetic remarks suggest that, as a full-time homemaker, she regarded paying for manicures as an undeserved treat, whereas she formerly was able to justify her manicures by saying forthrightly, "I had to be very professional." Thus Theresa's hunger for the ego boost of a professional manicure, once the pampered privilege of wealthy women of an earlier generation, instead reflected the contemporary context of women's constrained work-family choices.[12] Theresa fell into the category of women who are "opting out," a contested term that refers to leaving the labor force to pursue full-time motherhood. While researchers have challenged the assertion that women are leaving professional jobs in droves to stay at home to raise children, the real or imagined conflicts that women like Theresa face about staying home versus working have generated a media and cultural blitz.[13] The oppositional framework of the "mommy wars" saturated public discourse for a time, couching these choices as a cat fight between individual women and ignoring the complex factors that affect women's participation in the labor force as well as their negotiations of family commitments.[14]

Ambivalence about leaving the paid workforce is heightened for women who are pushed to do so by external forces. Danielle, a forty-year-old graphic designer, lost her job "when everything crashed after 9–11" and was staying home with her two children. However, she was clearly dissatisfied with the situation—"I love my kids, but I never wanted to do the stay-at-home-mom thing"—and she relied on her manicures to bolster her as she searched for a new job. She confessed, "It's a self-esteem thing. I lost my job a few months ago so I've been having them done a lot. I don't have a job so I might as well have nice nails, right?" Danielle, dressed in sweatpants and with her hair pulled back in a ponytail, felt compelled to explain her appearance: "I rushed out [to the salon] the minute my husband walked in the door because I was about to lose it."

Like Theresa, Danielle revealed that she sees the nail salon as a haven from the demands of children, but she also views her nails instrumentally as a vehicle to help her improve her job situation. When I asked her if she ever had nail extensions or designs, she scoffed, "I'm looking for a job plus I have a baby. They're fun, but people won't take you seriously. They wouldn't be appropriate for going on a job interview. I used to bite my nails. I'm going on job interviews, and they notice that kind of thing. I don't want to give that impression so I make sure my nails look nice." In her jobless state Danielle's nails were both an emotional balm and a perceived edge in her job search—and they prevented her from undermining a professional appearance by biting her nails.

In the nail salon women like Theresa and Danielle find comfort and escape from the often untenable choices they face between pursuing their careers and caring for their families. Their manicuring habits are not simply personal indulgences. Instead, they are outgrowths of women's still unequal and precarious positions in the job market and the culture wars that impose unattainable standards on mothers. In this context the nails of white middle-class women and the procurement of manicuring services substitute for the security, stimulation, and respect that are often lacking both in paid jobs and unpaid work as mothers. For black working-class women, manicures and motherhood are also entangled, although around very different choices and constraints, as Brianna illustrates.

Brianna

While Brianna and other black working-class mothers similarly situate their nails and their visits to nail salons as extensions of their identities as both mothers and workers, they encounter a starkly different cultural discourse regarding these roles. These women's nails, like their status as mothers, are not seen as indicators of their middle-class work and family situations; rather, their nails mark them as failed women in the arenas of beauty, work, and reproduction. Women like Brianna resist these pathologizing judgments and strive to reclaim their manicuring practices in ways that support more positive definitions of their femininity.

Brianna, a thirty-two-year-old who identified as black and Puerto Rican, came to Artistic Nails to show off her child while proudly asserting her identity as a mother and a member of the community. In the salon she shared moments of connection with other women, who provided emotional and practical support: "Oooh, bring that baby boy over here. You go ahead and do your nails, sugar, I'll hold him. He's a handsome devil!" Brianna handed over her fourteen-month-old son to an older woman seated in the waiting area. Later, when I asked her who the woman was, Brianna said she didn't know her name but that she was a friend of her grandmother's.

As several women cooed over the child and he squirmed and laughed, Brianna smiled and settled in for her manicure. "When you tired of holding him, just put him in the stroller. And don't give him no candy!" she instructed. Brianna, the baby, and the customers all appeared perfectly comfortable with these spontaneous caregiving arrangements. While she was not personally close to any of these women, Brianna was a resident of this neighborhood in Queens for most of her life, until very recently.

> Right now I live in Manhattan. I just moved, like less than a month ago. I come here because my grandmother still lives around here. It's really funny because I won this apartment in a lottery. It's in a nice building, but they did a lottery, like twenty apartments below affordable income housing, and I actually won. I just wanted to get the baby out of this neighborhood. . . . I just wanted to get out of the area and I put my name on this list, I went for it, and I actually won it! It's a nice neighborhood but it's not affordable to me. I have to still come back here to where I know. Like, say, my family and people are still here. So I make a day of it and come and do everything. Then I'll probably drop in [at] my grandmother's later and whatever. And I still come out to do nails here.

Brianna worked at the customer service desk of a limo company, a job she had recently obtained after a year of relying on government support. She was raising her son, Danton, as a single mother with the help of her grandmother. While she maintained a relationship with Danton's father, Tariq, they did not live together and saw each other intermittently. Tariq worked as a waiter and also liked to get his nails done, so they occasionally arranged to meet at the nail salon. Brianna explained, "Yeah, I come with Tariq . . . because we don't see each other a lot, and we want to catch up. And that's about it."

Brianna may not have been able to provide her child with the guarantees of a stable family, home, or health care, but in the world within the nail salon she was not merely an unwanted statistic of black and Latina single motherhood and recent welfare dependency. Instead, she could experience the joy of having her nails done among women who understood and cared about her, and she gained both practical and emotional support for her dream of completing her college degree and providing a better life for her son. She said, "I have about thirty-six credit hours in college. I never finished, though. The baby came and da da da, you know how it goes. . . . I really want to go back now. Yeah, I will. I will. I'll do nights or something. I know it can be done . . . . [I am] just trying to get into my neighborhood, get good doctors for him and stuff." Despite Brianna's determination, it seemed unlikely that she would be able to complete her college education anytime soon. While she was lucky and secured a decent apartment, she was unsure whether she would be able to afford even the subsidized rent. Furthermore, her new neighborhood lacked the familiarity and practical support provided by her grandmother and friends.

Whereas Jamilla viewed her long original nails as "saying 'me,'" Brianna asserted the opposite, insisting that such elaborate nails do *not* represent her sense of self. "In summer, I like the French manicure, lighter colors. I'd be reading a magazine like *Jane,* and I see they have on hot pink or something, and so then I'll have extra pink. . . . I don't like designs. They're cheesy to me. . . . I used to do the acrylics. I found out that wasn't really me. I didn't really like it. . . . Then I had the baby and stuff. So I didn't want long nails. It wasn't me." In contrast to their self-definitions, Brianna and Jamilla were likely to be placed in the same category as black working-class women, although they had very different identities, not to mention very different tastes in nails. In fact, despite their race and class differences, Brianna arguably had more in common with Theresa, who also eschewed long designer nails as inconsistent with her homemaking and childrearing responsibilities. Both can be seen as conforming to the ideology of what Sharon Hays calls "intensive mothering," the belief that mothers should be the primary caregivers of their children and that they should unconditionally invest their economic and emotional resources in raising them.[15] Thus mothers are told that they must simultaneously invest in motherhood as their primary responsibility while also supporting the consumer needs of their families through paid work. Both Theresa and Brianna felt frustrated by their inability to measure up to this impossible standard, yet these two women confronted divergent consequences for their inability to live up to it. Whereas Theresa may have felt guilty about her manicuring habit, her social status protected her from approbation, even when she walked away from her caregiving duties to indulge herself. Furthermore, she had the financial resources to secure child care during her momentary escape. While she was conflicted about sacrificing her career for her children, she was given the benefit of the doubt that she is a good mother, no matter how or how often she gets her nails done.

Brianna, on the other hand, had to be on guard lest any behavior trigger the always ready accusation of bad motherhood that low-income single black mothers face. Although she no longer received welfare payments, Brianna confronted the social stigma of supposedly irresponsible motherhood because she was not married and could not fully support herself and her son. In this already stigmatized identity, Brianna's manicuring practices are easily appropriated by others as evidence that she is undeserving and negligent.[16] McCormack's study shows that women like Brianna are subject to such accusations not only by disgruntled white middle-class taxpayers who feel that they are footing the bill for such indulgences but by members of their own communities. McCormack cites comments by Joan Clark, a black mother of two, who saw spending money on oneself as the mark of a bad mother. "Some people that get it [welfare] don't use it on their kids. . . . They buy themselves clothes, make themselves look nice, don't do nothin' for the kids."[17] While I did not observe such criticisms directed against Brianna, I did overhear black women in this salon make disparaging remarks about other mothers and their spending practices. One middle-aged black woman, commenting on a young mother who had brought her daughter in for a manicure, looked askance and muttered, "Better to buy the child some books." Young black mothers thus face a host of negative judgments both from inside and outside their communities. In Brianna's case, coming to the

Figure 9. Visits to nail art salons are often a communal affair, as customers often bring their children and arrive with friends.

nail salon served as a way for her to reconnect to her community, especially around her identity as a new mother. However, salon interactions did not necessarily validate or support her mothering or beauty practices, even by members of her own community. Nonetheless, getting her nails done helped Brianna feel good about herself, as she asserted, "I mean it works for me. It just makes me feel good."

While fostering a sense of self-worth is an important function that should not be underestimated, nice nails alone will not help Brianna to raise her child, afford her rent, complete her education, or influence her partner to commit to a more stable relationship. At the same time her nail salon visits gave her time to socialize with other women, especially those who, like her grandmother, provided tangible support in the form of child care. The nail salon also periodically served as a venue in which to spend time together with her child and his father. As Elaine Bell Kaplan writes, many black single mothers experience a "poverty of relationships." In this context the nail salon serves as a meager but still important resource to ameliorate the isolation of "relationship-poor" women.[18] In contrast to Theresa, who saw her visits to the nail salon as an escape from domestic life, for Brianna the nail salon served as a partial substitute for family ties and social supports that were missing in Manhattan.

MANICURING PROFESSIONAL IDENTITIES

Just as Theresa and Brianna conformed their manicuring practices to their identities as mothers, employed women manicure their nails according to workplace cultures. Paid work enables these women to afford regular manicures, and some employers regard the professional manicure as a staple of a professional appearance. Cheryl, a secretary from an Italian working-class background, and Ella, a black physical therapist of Jamaican descent, were recent arrivals on the manicuring scene. These women took their manicures seriously as a duty more than a treat.

Cheryl

"I think almost everyone in New York gets them done—at least anyone with a decent job who cares about how she looks. It's not like my boss would ever say anything if I didn't do them, but I think it's one of these things that lets people know you take your job seriously," said Cheryl, a twenty-eight-year-old white woman employed as a secretary in a Realtor's office in Manhattan. Cheryl, who frequented Uptown Nails on her lunch hour, viewed her regular manicure as part of the code of appearance in her workplace. "Sometimes I choose colors to match with what I'm wearing, but there's really a pretty limited range of acceptable colors—from pinks to reds, and not even really bright reds. It's like makeup—you're expected to wear it, but you can't overdo it." In their study of appearance standards in the workplace, Dellinger and Williams found, "Appropriate makeup use is strongly linked to assumptions of health, heterosexuality, and credibility in the workplace. In turn, these qualities are associated with professional success."[19] As with makeup, nail styles focus attention not just on gender but on race and class in shaping whether women's bodies are read in the workplace as productive or incompetent.

In explaining her manicuring practices, Cheryl did not reference abstract notions of feminine beauty but rather specific appearance expectations for women in the traditional female occupation of secretary. A question about nail tips and designs elicited a telling response, as she grimaced, "Oh, that. That stuff is the exact opposite. I don't know how those women get any work done. There's no way you could type or even answer the phone with those nails." Like Alexandra, whom I profiled earlier in this chapter, Cheryl disapproved of women who transgress the boundaries that she had drawn around acceptable nail aesthetics. But rather than looking down on such nail styles as unfashionably gaudy, she disparaged them as violations of workplace protocols and productivity.

While Cheryl appeared to be staunchly middle class in her dress, speech, and mannerisms, her middle-class status was tenuous, both in terms of her family of origin and her education and occupational status. She described herself as "from a typical Italian family, big, hardworking" and somewhat reluctantly acknowledged that she "only graduated from community college." Rather than assuming middle-class privilege, she had to prove her membership, and her nails served a dual purpose in this enterprise. First, they helped her project a professional appearance, as she conformed to normative gender, class, and racial self-presentations. Second, the actual experience of purchasing nail care services augmented her sense of class privilege, as she acknowledged: "What can I say? It's decadent. It's a luxury item, kind of like eating Godiva chocolates. But it makes me feel good, I like getting pampered. I guess I could do them myself—I'm pretty good at putting the polish on, but there's something about someone else doing it that makes it feel even better."

Cheryl balanced this desire for a pampering experience with a practical attitude of bargain shopping. She calculated a trade-off, luxury status versus cost and efficiency, and Korean nail salons won out. "I always go to the Koreans. The beauty salons charge twice as much, and they don't do as good a job. It's not worth paying extra just for the status of getting them done at some ritzy salon." Asked whether she regarded Korean-operated salons as lower status, she responded, "Well, it's just that it's just not such a scene here, you know, 'see and be seen' and all that. It's more like 'run in for a quick nail job and run back to work.'" Thus, although she relished the pampering aspects, Cheryl did not seek a posh retreat so much as a practical and professional enhancement that solidified her foothold in the white middle class. By purchasing manicuring services, Cheryl both gained nice nails and positioned herself on the socioeconomic ladder above women who cannot procure these services, as well as above the women who perform them. Other women, like Ella, also accommodate their nails to their workplace but grudgingly so.

Ella

Ella, a twenty-six-year-old physical therapist who identifies as both Jamaican and African American (she emigrated when she was five and grew up in New York), shared similarities with Cheryl in selecting nail styles that augmented her professional identity. Both women fell between the poles of normative and marginalized femininities. Cheryl, as a white woman of working-class background, and Ella, as a black middle-class immigrant, both chose nail styles that met standards of mainstream feminine beauty. However, Ella acknowledged that she could never fully buy her way in to this privileged category, and at the same time, by even trying, she experienced conflicts of racial allegiance and authenticity.

Ella's pastel nails matched well with her crisp Capri pants and tailored white cotton blouse. She had recently moved to Long Island with her fiancé, who taught high school there, but she patronized Convenient Nails, which was near the health center where she worked. She explained, "I usually keep it basic, either French manicure, pedicures, or just the solid color. . . . Because it's for my job, I use my nails. So I don't feel the need to be all glamorous, the patients wouldn't go for that, but just so they are clean." Thus, like Cheryl, she viewed her nails as a workplace asset that projected professionalism, and she similarly prioritized low cost and convenience but with some semblance of pampering service. She calculated, "Well, spas, you get the all-you-want treatment for like hours and hours and hours. You only have to experience that once, but, yeah, it's more indulgent. But if you are paying $10 or $15 for a pedicure, I think this is awesome, too, versus 180 bucks for a massage. So I think, for the price, it's reasonable."

In addition, Ella shared Cheryl's concerns about proving her status as a middle-class professional, but whereas Cheryl's status anxieties derived from her working-class background, Ella's concerns stemmed from race. "Sometimes when I walk in to see a patient, they'll give me this surprised look, and then they'll say something like, 'Oh, you look so young,' like that was the reason they were surprised to see me." When I asked her to elaborate on the real reason for the patient's surprise, she rolled her eyes at me, saying, "I think you can figure it out." Thus she saw her race as an unspoken but obvious source of difference that undermined her professional credentials in the eyes of certain patients. As she was already sometimes treated suspiciously on account of her race, she was careful not to mark herself with nails that would further undermine her legitimacy. When I asked her what kind of women she thought wore long designer nails, she unhesitatingly attributed differences in nail styles to race: "Because I am from a black community and that's where I'm mostly around. I see black people with them on, but in the workplace I see Italian women with them on, I see white women with them on, but it's funny I don't see a lot of Asian women with them on, the ones who give most of the service. But I see Italian women, I see black, I see, you know, white, but I would say people think they're a black thing." Although she herself saw many different kinds of women wearing these nails, she noted their strong association with black women. Ella in fact admired artistic nails and wore them herself in high school and college: "I see people's nails and I'm like, 'Wow, Wow.' But I can't wear them like that." Thus she opted for more conservative nail styles, not out of personal taste but as a concession to the expectations of her workplace and her position as a black woman within it.

Ella is one of many black professionals who have gained inroads into the middle class through education (she has a master's degree), suburban residence (she lives on Long Island), and occupational status (she is a physical therapist) but continue to experience overt and covert racism, both on and off the job. In a society that has grudgingly accepted blacks into the professional mainstream, she had to constantly walk a fine line to distance herself from stigmatized black women like Jamilla and Bri-anna. Although she was a Jamaican immigrant, Ella's ethnic identity was superseded by her skin color, which placed her in a common racial cat-egory with other blacks, regardless of national origin or class position.[20] In this social context, where race is an ever-present prism through which other dimensions of identity are refracted, nails can become potent signi-fiers of racial identity, as well as reflect racialized notions of class. Ella had certain experiences in common with Cheryl, who also chose her nail style to deflect any questions about her professional status, but unlike Ella's race, Cheryl's class background was not immediately recogniz-able through her physical appearance. Therefore Cheryl did not have to prove her class status from the outset and was more concerned that she would be found out as a impostor. Her performance of beauty, as embod-ied in her nails, was coded in racial and class terms that augmented her sense of belonging in the white-collar world of a Manhattan Realtor's office. On the other hand, Ella's nails served as a tipping point that could nudge her customers into questioning her professional status, thereby influencing her to choose traditionally feminine nail styles.

Ella and Cheryl's cases illustrate that gender alone does not deter-mine the presentations of women's bodies in the workplace, but specific racial and class performances of gender shape women's embodied prac-tices, as enacted through their manicures. Women of various racial and class locations steer clear of more elaborate nail styles, not simply out of personal taste but because these styles can stigmatize them. Gendered self-presentations mark women not only as beautiful or ugly but also as qualified or unemployable in the workforce.

OF NAILS AND MEN

Most women in this study rejected the idea that they do their nails for male attention in general or for the approval of a particular man. Instead, the women insisted that they do their nails for themselves, even when the men in their lives disapprove of manicures. However, while the women denied or downplayed their desire to please men as a motivation for doing their nails, women across racial and class lines end up subjecting their bodies to examination and control by both individual men and male-dominated institutions.

Vicki was a twenty-one-year-old single African American college student who was majoring in criminology. She asserted, "I like the curved tips—I think they're sexy. . . . My boyfriend likes them, but I don't do them for him, I do them for myself." This assertion of "doing my nails for myself" emerged as a refrain of many women in the study, but a refrain that often unraveled upon closer investigation. Raven, a twenty-two-year-old immigrant from Jamaica, lived in New York City for two years and was then studying for her GED while she worked as a salesperson at Home Depot. She was single and had a seven-year-old son. The following exchange reveals her initial resistance to her boyfriend's insistence that she cut her nails and her eventual acquiescence to the combined pressures of his complaints and the expectations of her workplace.

Why do you get your nails done?
Because I like when my nails match my outfit. That's mostly why I really get my nails done—it's pretty. . . . [I do them] mostly for myself, because my boyfriend don't like nails. He always says I should get rid of these.

What do you say to him?
No! I like my nails!

Why doesn't he like them?
Because he thinks I can't do anything with them. Because when I'm driving I can't turn the wheel and stuff like that.

So he doesn't mind the way they look?
No, he just thinks I can't do anything. These are about two inches. I used to have them longer than these. I cut them back, mainly because of my work, and I can't do stuff with it when it's so long. So I cut it to where I can use it, and he's okay with it.

Although Raven acknowledged adjusting her nails to her workplace demands and to her boyfriend's criticisms, she continued to assert that her manicuring choices were dictated purely by her personal tastes. Even after we had this conversation, she reiterated her original assertion that she chooses her own nail styles, saying, "I just come in here and I be looking at what they do and the designs up there. . . . That's a nice design up there. I just pick what I like."

Similarly, Brianna asserted that she did not acquiesce to anyone, whether her friends or her boyfriend, where her nails were concerned, but her actions contradicted this. Whereas some women, like Jamilla, assert their independence through original nail designs, Brianna resisted pressure to have longer nails and opted for more conservative nail styles, saying, "I have friends do curly things, that's wild. That's the biggest thing they do, but it's not for me. I keep saying, 'I'm not into that, but I know it's hot.'" In choosing demure nails even though she knew others would consider her "hotter" if she wore fancier styles, she demonstrated strength and individuality in her manicuring practices. These qualities were also evident in her resolve to create a better life for her and her child, with or without a male partner. At the same time her self-sufficiency, while admirable, did not preclude her longing for male attention and support, in particular, for a more committed relationship with her child's father, Tariq—and she conformed her manicuring practices toward this end. Brianna mentioned that Tariq liked to get his nails done, and sometimes she met him so they could get their nails done together but at his convenience rather than hers. I glimpsed the dynamics in their relationship when I asked her if he would be interested in being interviewed, and she became excited about helping to set up the interview. "I'll try to get ahold of him tonight. Like I said, I can't promise. I may not get him if he's serving somewhere, then I can't get him. But I will try to get to you before you go back and let you know. And I say my place in Manhattan because he can come an hour before he goes to work. You guys can just sit and talk, and he can walk right down to the job. That's how I'm trying to lock him into it." While I appreciated her efforts, I sensed that something other than her desire to help me with my research was driving her enthusiasm. The interview seemed to serve as bait for her to get Tariq to come to her apartment for a rare or even first-time visit. In the end I did not interview Tariq, but Brianna's excitement about arranging this meeting revealed her persistent efforts to integrate him into her life and her willingness to invoke all possible weapons, including her nail salon visits, in what seemed a losing battle. Working-class black women like Brianna and Vicki thus exhibit contradictions in their nail practices. While they assert control over their own bodies through their choice of nails, at the same time the appearance and care of their nails, and hence their bodies, are clearly up for negotiation within their significant relationships.

These tensions between individual agency and social control of women's bodies emerge in race- and class-specific ways. Some middle-class white women's manicuring choices, as well as their overall physical appearance, derive from their relationships with male partners and their social positions. These women's nails enhance their status, not by augmenting their own professional accomplishments but by signaling their attachment to a high-status husband or boyfriend. Wendy, a former fashion designer in her late thirties who identified herself as a Jewish American stay-at-home mom with two kids, got her nails done especially for events related to her husband's work. She explained, "My husband has a social position—he's an art dealer—so we do a lot of entertaining, and the people are very well tended. When I accompany him, I look better and feel better if my nails are done. I feel more grown-up." However, despite this acknowledgment, she reiterated the "doing it for myself" refrain, saying, "I come in here just to be quiet—no phone calls, no kids screaming, no obligation to communicate. . . . Even though I don't work, I want to look pulled together. . . . It makes me feel good." Like Alexandra, Wendy saw her time in the nail salon as time for herself, but she also regarded her nails as a professional asset, not for her but for her husband. Thus, like African American working-class women such as Brianna and Vicki, Wendy saw her nails as an investment in her relationship but in her case as the wife of a man in a prestigious occupation.

For single white middle-class women, nails can be an important asset in attracting the attention of potential partners. Beverly, who was in her midthirties and single, was a real estate broker of Polish Irish descent. Her office was near Uptown Nails. Asked why she had her nails done, she responded without hesitation: "Men love nails. I was walking down the street, and some guy shouted out, 'Hey, your nails look great!' I mean, I didn't know him from Adam, but it makes you feel great when people look at your nails and make comments about them." For Beverly, as well as other women in the study, nails are as important or even more important than their hair for their physical appearance. She confessed, "I definitely spend more time on my nails than my hair. Someone gave me a gift certificate to get my hair done at Saks, and I've been holding on to it since September. I just don't make the time in the same way." Manicured nails, similar to stylish and well-kept hair, signal a brand of femininity that elevates a woman's status vis-à-vis her attractiveness to men.[21] Whether they use a manicure as a vehicle to draw male attention or to validate the companionship of a high-status man in the eyes of onlookers, Beverly and other women hew to the belief that "men love nails," and it is a strong force behind their manicuring practices, although many go out of their way to deny this.

Nails can also serve as symbolic markers of milestones that solidify significant relationships with men. Sylvia was a fifty-six-year-old homemaker of Italian descent who worked part time as a housekeeper. When I asked about her most positive experience of having her nails done, she responded, "The best was when I got married—my nails were really nice." For Sylvia nice nails were not merely a minor detail in her wedding but something in which she invested a great deal of effort to guarantee top form. She recalled wistfully, "When I got married, my nails were twice as long as this. I wanted them that way, and I went every week to my girl who was doing my nails. So I got married when I had really pretty nails." In addition to paying close attention to her nails for her wedding, she felt proprietary about the woman who was doing them, to whom she referred as "my girl." Sylvia continues to pride herself on her nails and said that she had been having them done for most of her adult life. Although she cleaned houses, she did not see herself as defined by this work but did it just "to have some money for myself." She added, "I clean houses, but that doesn't mean I have to have rough hands." Instead of focusing on her work, she emphasized that she had been married for nearly thirty years; her husband was a construction foreman, and they raised two children and sent them to college. Thus she constructed her nails not only as cementing her position within a normative heterosexual partnership and family but also as enabling her to distance herself from the low status of her job. In addition to solidifying these roles, her nails were an investment in claiming normative femininity based on her appearance, as revealed in the following conversation:.

> If I have short nails, my hands look fat. Short and fat. If my nails are lon-ger, my hands look, well, not fat. This time, these are not my own nails. One broke, so I cut them all. . . . But I don't like fake nails. I would not put on fake nails so that I can't grow my own nails.

> *Didn't you say those are fake nails?*
> These are not my nails, but they are not fake, they're just wraps.

In Sylvia's mind her nail wraps did not constitute fake nails, which she denigrated as indicators of marginalized femininity. Instead, her choice of nails provided insurance against the feared label of "short and fat." Unlike women who associate their manicures with their professional identities, Sylvia used her nails to dissociate from low-status work. Instead, she focused attention on her ability to meet her idea of accept-able appearance standards, not only for herself but consistent with her identity as a wife and mother.

It would be easy but erroneous to conclude that, regardless of what they tell themselves, women really manicure their nails for men and male approval. Concluding that they use manicured nails just as a lure for men, however, oversimplifies the complex ways that women use their nails to define themselves in relationships with men and within a male-dominated culture. These women are acutely aware that a wom-an's value is still heavily influenced by whether she is in a traditional heterosexual partnership, especially one sanctioned by marriage, and her appearance serves as a measure of her worthiness in this pairing. At the same time many women are able to carve out the care of their nails as a pleasurable and rewarding activity. Although potentially empower-ing to individual women, these practices cannot escape the influence of male-dominated institutions, in particular, the family and the workplace, as well as relationships with individual men. All these influences exert some control over the time and money the women invest in their nails and the meanings of the nails themselves.

Interestingly, many men have told me that they "could care less" about how women's nails look, and some even resent the resources their partners spend on their nails. One man said to me, "I guess I really need to read your book because I really don't get this thing women have about their nails." This sense of cluelessness does not mean, however, that men do not influence or benefit from women's investment in these practices, as nice nails cater to the notion that women's bodies garner value through their attractiveness and availability to men.

BEYOND THE BEAUTY MYTH—
AN INTERSECTIONAL CRITIQUE

In the introduction to this book, I criticized scholars of beauty culture by highlighting their neglect of the experiences of beauty service workers and the ways that consumers contribute to unequal and exploitative working conditions in the beauty service industry. While I will expand upon these arguments later, here I want to engage with beauty scholars on their own terms, by framing manicuring practices as complex negotiations in which women respond to the dictates of normative and marginalized forms of feminine beauty. Further, I argue that women situate their manicuring practices not within abstract notions of beauty but in reference to specific relationships and institutional settings and their racial and class contexts. In analyzing case studies of women and their manicures in this chapter, I examined and synthesized three theoretical frameworks: beauty as an oppressive versus empowering force; beauty in specific historical and institutional contexts; and hierarchies of beauty defined by race, class, and other forms of difference.

The first framework juxtaposes competing arguments about beauty as coercion versus power. One side of this debate positions beauty as oppressive, constraining women's economic advancement and emotional and physical health. The other side regards beauty as a tool of resistance in which physical attractiveness and the rituals involved in it can be celebratory and transformative aspects of women's lives.[22] Rather than taking sides in this debate or accepting its either/or terms, I see it as highlighting the ongoing tensions in women's definitions of their nails, the social constraints on their manicuring practices, and the ways that they accept, reject, and redefine these constraints. Jamilla's case shows that women who are marginalized according to race and class can use their nails to claim control of their bodies and define their own positive body aesthetics. These efforts, however, can also undermine their social acceptance, particularly in workplaces that privilege conformity to mainstream ideals of femininity. Black working-class women like Jamilla thus face a double bind—living in marked bodies and drawing further stigma through their efforts to reclaim their bodies. Alexandra, on the other hand, confronts a different dilemma. While norms of femininity confer a higher status on her conventionally attractive white middle-class looks, her acquiescence to these norms causes dissonance in her own critique of beauty culture. Both Jamilla and Alexandra thus demonstrate that beauty can be simultaneously empowering and oppressive, although these tensions unfold in particular ways depending on women's very different social positions.

A second theoretical framework addresses the specific social and historical contexts in which beauty is constructed, as well as the limited agency of women in negotiating various institutional settings.[23] As Debra Gimlin in her book *Body Work* asserts, "The meanings of the body are neither free-floating in culture nor created solely by individuals, but are embedded in those institutions where culture and individual effort meet."[24] The case studies in this chapter dramatize her point by situating women's beauty practices not only within particular salons but within social institutions and ideologies, particularly those related to work and family. These contexts of salon interactions in turn are shaped by specific occupational standards, consumer culture, ideologies of the family, and structures of gender, racial, and class inequality. At the same time women do not simply absorb the beauty dictates of the dominant culture or of particular communities and organizational settings. Instead, women manipulate beauty ideology to compensate for perceived deficiencies in themselves (from "short and fat" to "flashy" to "like a man") and to negotiate the multiple contexts that constitute their lives. For example, Cheryl invoked the manicure to consolidate her position in the white middle class, despite her working-class background, modest education, and occupational status as a secretary. Ella's demure manicure added credibility to her position as a physical therapist and distanced her from negative racial constructions. Sylvia used her nails to shift emphasis onto her identity as a wife and mother and to deemphasize her work as a house cleaner. Thus these women support Huisman and Hondagneu-Sotelo's assertion that women's appearances are "both individual achievements and collective identities" and are "simultaneously shaped by their orientations to past habits, future possibilities and emergent events."[25] These multiple reference points, rather than a search for beauty in and of itself, frame their manicuring practices and their outcomes.

In addition, women's achievements of beauty, on both the individual and collective level, do not reference generic institutional and historical contexts but instead reflect specific racial, class, and sexual locations within these contexts. Thus a third theoretical framework situates beauty within social systems that rank certain forms of femininity above others.[26] Much of this literature focuses on black and white women as embodying beauty constructions that are both mutually exclusive and interdependent. As Sarah Banet-Weiser asserts, "The nonwhite body functions as a specter—the marked other—against which the ideal female citizen is defined."[27] Whereas her study focuses on spectacles of women's bodies, such as the Miss America pageant, this chapter looked at routine beauty practices and their social meanings.

When applied to the study of manicures, an integration of these three frameworks illuminates how women of diverse racial and class backgrounds are both empowered and constrained by their nails but in different ways and with different repercussions. When white middle-class women, such as Alexandra, choose conventionally attractive nail styles, they reap personal rewards such as positive social attention and greater self-confidence. Simultaneously, they reinforce their own already privileged racial and class positions within hierarchies of feminine beauty. In contrast, working-class black women, like Jamilla, whose nails reflect the standards of their own racial and class communities, express originality and enjoy bonding with other women through shared nail aesthetics. At the same time their nails can be coded as racial and class markers that further relegate them to a category of deviant, inferior femininity. Some working-class black women, like Serena and Alia, conform, often reluctantly, to dominant feminine styles, in an attempt to leverage their nails toward socioeconomic mobility. However, this can alienate them from their own cultural identities while still not conferring the social rewards of whiteness.

Figure 10.   Black women challenge narrow norms of feminine beauty with hand-painted nail designs, but these nails can also stigmatize them as deviant in the eyes of mainstream society.

Bourdieu's work illuminates the ways that distinctions in everyday tastes, as in notions of beauty, are shaped by social locations. While he focuses particularly on class, his concept of habitus can be enlarged to address how gender and race also influence embodied self-presentations and their role in reproducing social hierarchies. Reciprocally, bodily displays such as nail styles then become markers of a customer's habitus. Thus manicuring practices represent multilayered social processes in which women's bodies reflect multiple forms of difference and inequality.

CONCLUSION

Nails, and beauty more broadly, dangle a seductive yet powerful promise, if not of redemption, at least of respite, from the complex pressures that women face in their daily lives. Is it any wonder that so many women, and so many different women, seek out manicuring services on a regular basis? As the women in this study show, the rewards of beauty can include everything from higher self-esteem, attractiveness to romantic partners, stress relief, and bonding with other women, to career advancement and increased mobility. In seeking to maximize these social rewards, women manipulate beauty to enhance their status not simply as women but as women whose social positions are defined by race, sexuality, and social class.

While many studies of beauty emphasize the rising standards for women's appearance as driving women's obsession with their appearance, the narratives in this chapter demonstrate that other factors may be equally or even more important. These include women's entrance into the paid workforce and the disposable income and expectations for professional attire that this generates; the increasing demands placed on women who are mothers and a lack of social supports for this role; the pressure of being defined by heterosexual unions even as these unions are increasingly unstable; and the boundaries of acceptable and unacceptable femininities that frame these processes.

In sum, women's nails grow out of their bodies but also out of the social relations and circumstances in which these bodies are embedded. However, women of different racial and class positions confront different constraints in asserting their own beauty and beauty practices. Rather than being an end in and of itself, nice nails and beauty more broadly are vehicles, albeit flawed and unreliable vehicles, to claim power in work, family, and relationships. Beautiful nails can serve as a form of anxiety management in a historical moment in which asserting one's own definition of womanhood can be a fraught enterprise. At the same time definitions of what it means to be a woman, and what it means to be beautiful, are highly contested and evoke varied responses from women, not the least of which is how they wear their nails.

The high stakes that women have in their nails are then transferred to their relations with the providers of these services. The chapters that follow explore the ways that manicuring interactions become charged with racial meanings, as these encounters embody not only women's investment in their appearance but also their different understandings of the rules of this exchange and the forces that govern it.

Four "I Just Put Koreans and Nails Together"

NAIL SPAS AND THE MODEL MINORITY

Having them done is a pleasure, a luxury. Doing them myself is tedious, having them done is a treat. It's the whole idea of going and having something nice done for myself. If I do them myself, it's just routine upkeep of my body—like washing your hair or keeping your clothes clean. . . . They do it all day long so they are better at it. The Koreans are usually very good at the massages. . . . I just put Koreans and nails together.

Kathy, Uptown Nails customer

Let me tell you about you. You come in here with your fingernails gleaming and outstretched; you've just had them done next door at ajumma's beauty salon. My mother is jealous of your nails, not because she likes them, but because you have the time to do them.

Ishle Park, "Anatomy of a Fish Store"

Customer satisfaction in upscale nail spas depends not only on the attractive appearance of their nails but also the enjoyment derived from being pampered, and customers regard Korean women as particularly skillful in this enterprise. Body labor transforms a hygienic process, otherwise equated with washing hair or clothes, into a richly rewarding physical and emotional experience—that is, when it meets customers' expectations. When it fails to do so, the physical and emotional intimacy of this exchange produces an equal and opposite negative reaction. Appropriate performance of this form of "pampering body labor" involves extensive physical care, along with attention to the emotional needs of customers, including engaged conversations.

The manicure takes on additional complexities when considered from the other side of the table. The poet Ishle Park depicts a Korean immigrant woman who is eyeing her customer's manicured nails. In this case the Korean woman is not the manicurist herself but the proprietor of a neighboring fish store. Nonetheless, this *ajumma* (literally, "aunt" but used generally to address middle-aged Korean women) expresses jealousy toward women who receive manicures, not necessarily because of their appearance but because they can indulge in this kind of self-care. The poem resonates with women working in nail salons, like Jean Hwang, an owner in Brooklyn, who noted, "Grooming one's feet and nails is unimaginable in Korea. It made me think how Americans enjoy themselves. With twenty dollars they treat themselves and enjoy themselves. I was jealous. . . . I don't think we have that leisure. We've experienced and are still living very rigorous lives." These women chafe at the differences between themselves and their customers that are manifested in the unequal treatment of their bodies and feelings.

In upscale nail spas the manicure is not simply an economic transaction. It is also a symbolic exchange that involves the buying and selling of deference and attentiveness. In accommodating the various demands of body labor, Asian immigrant women rewrite their own identities to conform to a pampering service demeanor and to the "model minority" stereotype. Customers may profess a belief in Asians as "honorary whites," but in their face-to-face interactions they do not necessarily hold Asians in high esteem.[1] Thus the appearance of cordial intimate relations belies underlying tensions, as the gendered practices of pampering body labor uphold the race and class privilege of customers and enforce the subservience of manicurists.

The hit television sitcom *Seinfeld* provides a humorous yet revealing representation of Asian manicurists' interactions with white middle- and upper-class customers. Elaine, a regular at a Korean-owned nail salon, becomes suspicious that the conversations among the Korean-speaking manicurists include references to her that are less than admiring. To her dismay she learns that the manicurists are in fact calling her a princess and ridiculing her self-importance. Although she is upset, Elaine does not want to find another nail salon, as she sees her Korean manicurists as the best.[2] Thus she must negotiate conflicted feelings, because she regards highly the actual physical manicure but is upset by the lack of emotional attentiveness.

In capturing Elaine's quandary, the *Seinfeld* episode underscores the complexities of the manicure for customers who patronize upscale nail spas—it is not enough that their bodies get pampered; they often want their feelings massaged as well. Conditioned by the stereotypical framing of Asians as the hardworking and accommodating model minority, many customers, like Elaine, come to Asian-owned nail salons expecting both a high-quality manicure and a subservient demeanor. They are often surprised and offended when instead they get "attitude." Their reactions to the manicuring exchange invoke not only gendered notions of beauty but also racial perceptions of Asians as the providers of these services.

This exchange is illuminated by Michel Foucault's influential work on the production of "docile bodies" through disciplinary practices.[3] Nail salons serve as sites that discipline certain women's bodies to conform to beauty regimens while disciplining other women's bodies to provide the services necessary for these regimens. Feminist scholars have recognized Foucault's many contributions to illuminating the body as a locus for the exercise of power, but have criticized his neglect of gender. Sandra Bartky asks, "Where is the account of the disciplinary practices that engender the 'docile bodies' of women, bodies more docile than the bodies of men?"[4] However, feminist scholars have overlooked how women's bodies are not only disciplined to be more docile than men's but also that some women's bodies are rendered more docile than others based on race, class, and other forms of difference. By bringing Foucault's scholarship on disciplinary technologies of the body into dialogue with feminist intersectional approaches to gendered work, this chapter examines how the performance of pampering body labor disciplines the bodies of Asian manicurists into docile service to other women's bodies. Interactions in nail spas such as Uptown and Exclusive Nails illuminate the general patterns of pampering service in nail spas as well as the ways

Figure 11.   Nail spas offer pampering body labor to mostly white middle-class and upper-class customers in upscale neighborhoods.

that individual actors challenge and renegotiate these exchanges and how particular conditions support or undermine this resistance.

GENDER AND THE MODEL MINORITY

Service interactions between Korean service providers and white middle-class customers reinforce the model minority stereotype, described by Eric Fong, by which "Asian Americans either do not face any discrimination relative to other racial minority groups or, if they did, they have overcome them."[5] This stereotype permeates public discourse and has been thoroughly critiqued in academic circles. Rather than a single stereotype, the model minority references a constellation of factors that frame Asians not only as a laudable racial group but as proof that the United States is open and egalitarian. The core characteristics used to describe the model minority include hard work, laudable family values, economic self-sufficiency, noncontentious politics, academic achievement, and entrepreneurial success. Thus it is not simply that Asian Americans are praiseworthy but that this praise is premised on their smooth assimilation into productive but passive citizens who validate the vision of an open meritocratic U.S. society. Academic scholarship has complicated this one-dimensional stereotype, arguing that it is far from a positive representation of Asian Americans. Instead, the stereotype enforces simplistic and idealized views not only of Asian Americans but of other racial groups and, more broadly, of race relations in the United States. As Dana Takagi writes: "The concept of the model minority was born in the midst of the tumultuous racial change of the 1960s. Against the backdrop of rioting in black ghettos, the 'long hot summers' of the late 1960s, and mass public demonstrations for civil rights, Asian-Americans appeared to be a relatively quiescent minority. . . . Angered by black criticism of the 'white establishment,' some whites pointed to Asian-American achievement as evidence that racial minorities could get ahead in America, if only they would 'try.'"[6] The designation of one group as the "model" thus enforces a hierarchy in which other minorities are judged as lacking. While ostensibly lauding Asian Americans, this framework chastises other racial and ethnic minorities, particularly blacks, for not following in Asians' footsteps. By emphasizing the success of Asians and their commonalities with whites, the model minority concept serves the dual purpose of holding Asian Americans up as an example for other people of color while also defending the existing U.S. racial order.

The bestowing of honorary white status on Asians simultaneously denigrates other racial and ethnic groups while reinforcing white privilege—and both purposes are enacted through body politics. As David Palumbo-Liu writes, "The image of the Asian in America performs certain ideological functions that serve to secure certain racial and national identities for both Asians and whites," and these ideologies emphasize the "correlation of the raced body and the national psyche."[7] He asserts that views of racialized Asian bodies, and foreign bodies more generally, as desirable or undesirable emerge as part of a larger project through which nonwhite immigrants and their descendants are welcomed into or excluded from the American nation based on their willingness to support U.S. capitalism and its expansion.

The embrace of Asians as the model minority thereby is premised simultaneously on their embodied demonstration of economic productivity and smooth assimilation into mainstream cultural norms, and it is quickly withdrawn when these conditions are not met. Laudatory views of Asians can be invoked to discredit the claims of other minority groups and then revoked when Asians emerge as a potential threat to whites. In addition to the fickle and contradictory ways that it is applied, the model minority framing of all Asian immigrants and their children as economically successful and upwardly mobile is itself a fiction, as the category of Asian American encompasses heterogeneous groups and experiences ranging from Hong Kong financiers to Hmong refugees to Amerasian adoptees.[8]

How does gender matter in shaping the ideology of the Asian model minority, and what new dimensions does a gender analysis illuminate about this racial framework? The focus on the gendered work processes of body labor expands the study of the model minority beyond a U.S.-centric focus on racialized representations to focus attention on workplace interactions shaped by the restructuring forces of global capitalism. Specifically, a gendered analysis of Asian women's work in nail salons reveals new embodied and emotional dimensions of how Asian Americans are constructed as a deserving group based on their willingness to perform deferent and subservient work. As Yen Le Espiritu argues: "Because of their racial ambiguity, Asian Americans have been constructed historically to be both 'like black' and 'like white,' as well as *neither* black *nor* white. Similarly, Asian women have been both hyperfeminized and masculinized, and Asian men have been both hypermasculinized and feminized. And in social class and cultural terms, Asian Americans have been cast as the 'unassimilable alien,' and the 'model minority' (Okihiro 1994).[9] Their ambiguous, middling positions maintain systems of privilege and power but also threaten and destabilize these constructs of hierarchies."[10]

Drawing on Espiritu's analysis, I bring a gender perspective to the critique of the ideology of the Asian model minority as an erroneous and politically motivated myth. Specifically, nail salons uncover forms of interaction that reproduce racialized, classed, and gendered discourses of the

Asian model minority, through representations but even more so through material embodied exchanges. Customers, owners, and workers all participate in this reproduction, even as they offer limited forms of resistance.

MANICURING THE MODEL MINORITY

The model minority stereotype of Asians, and Koreans in particular, as successful, servile, and industrious takes on specifically gendered dimensions in the niche of nail services. Pampering body labor intersects with racial discourses in ways that valorize the work ethic of Korean and other Asian immigrants and construct a specifically gendered version of this discourse. The comments and behavior of customers demonstrate that while many adhere ideologically to the laudatory view of Asians as the model minority, their interactions with Asian women belie this rhetoric.

Like many customers in this study, Kathy, the white personal trainer whom I quoted earlier in this chapter, attributed a particular skillfulness in service, especially in the giving of massages, to Asian women, even elevating this understanding to the level of urban lore:

I assume they're Korean. That's interesting—I wonder how I first came to know they are Korean. I think it's one of those urban myth kind of things you just pick up on it when you're living in New York. . . . Like the delis—everyone says, "I'm going to the Korean deli." Now that I think about it, they could be Chinese or Japanese or Vietnamese, but I just heard the people who did the nail salons were Korean, and then I see someone who looks Korean enough, so I just assume they're Korean. It's like if I had a massage and the person doing it were tall and blond and blue-eyed, I would just assume they were Swedish. . . . [The stereotype of Koreans is] willing to work very hard, interested in their children's education. Like, a friend of my husband's [is] Korean, and his parents worked for thirty years in a Dunkin' Donuts and sent their kid to Columbia. That kind of captures it. . . . [Regarding nail salons] I agree that they work hard.

Kathy frames Korean women's skillfulness in manicures as similar to equating "Swedish" with massage. However, Swedish massage is a type of massage characterized by specific techniques rather than simply an ethnic designation. In contrast, Kathy references cultural stereotypes, not specific techniques, to explain why she regards manicuring work as the distinct purview of Korean women. Ignoring the forces of immigration, racialization, and economic restructuring, she holds to a simplistic gendered version of the model minority stereotype that essentializes Korean women, or women who look "Korean enough," as possessing intrinsic manicuring skills.

Similarly, many white middle-class respondents explain Asian women's clustering in nail salon work by invoking their natural ability and innate sense of service. Thus gendered Orientalist tropes of Asian women's inborn affinity for body services naturalizes their work in nail salons as somehow deriving from inherent biological or cultural traits.[11] As this customer described it, having an Asian manicurist imbues these services with an exoticized quality that enhances their appeal: "The quality of the massage here is much better. I like to go to the Japanese beauty salons for the same reason, they do shiatsu on your head, it's amazing. Culturally, there are things Asians can bring to [this] service that I don't think others are as sensitive to. . . . This [American] culture doesn't understand a service. It's not subservience or being a doormat. It's just the level to which you are willing to accommodate the needs of another, to go out of your way." Thus Orientalist framings reinforce the notion that Asian women not only are well suited to this work but that they enjoy it.

According to the sociologist Christine Williams, this belief that people end up in certain jobs because they like them is a distinctly "middle-class conceit." In her study of retail employees in toy stores, she debunks the myth that workers select their jobs based on their interests, skills, or preferences—"In the world of low-wage retail work, no one assumes that people choose their occupations or that their jobs reflect who they are."[12] However, with regard to Asian women in nail salon work, the assumption that they somehow choose this work because they like it and are good at it is strangely persistent. Yet customers do not apply this same logic of natural affinity to other racial and ethnic women in nail salons. For example, Barbara, an Uptown Nails customer, commented, "I think it's because they [Asian women] specialize in making the manicure a nice experience, but they also seem to enjoy it and know what they are doing. I used to have my hair, facial, and nails all done at the same place; it was women from Russia or Poland. But they didn't really want to do manicures." Thus Barbara regards women from Eastern Europe as quickly moving in and out of the salon industry because they are not well suited to it. In contrast, her racial construction of Asian women in nail salons positions them not simply as having expertise in this work but as finding the work enjoyable and something they "want to do."

Consistent with Barbara's observations, many Russian immigrant women initially worked in the nail salon niche but then moved into other work. However, contrary to Barbara's assertion that they simply do not enjoy it, the explanation for Russian women's departure does not lie solely in their individual proclivities for this work or lack thereof. A trade magazine article suggests one explanation: although Russian immigrants dominated nail salons before the 1970s, "their education level suggests that once they mastered English, they moved on to other opportunities."[13] While this explanation is somewhat plausible, it fails to address why Korean women, many of whom also have high levels of education and similar mastery of English, have not been able to move on to other opportunities.

Furthermore, although Russians dominated the niche at one point, the association of Russian women and manicurist did not become a wide-spread cultural stereotype. Why not? The answer lies not only in individual human capital, such as language ability or education, but in racial categorization. Once they acquire basic language fluency, Russians and other recent immigrants from Eastern Europe are able to quickly assimilate as whites—not as "honorary whites" or as a "model minority" but simply as whites. Even with heavily accented English, this racial status then gives them greater ability to enter into the U.S. mainstream and gain access to wider employment opportunities.[14] In contrast, Koreans and other Asian immigrants, even those who conform to the stereotype of the upwardly mobile, hardworking model minority, still occupy a marginalized status in which nail salon work remains among the best of the options available to them.

These racial and gender constructions of Asian women as gentle, hardworking, and eager to please normalize their position as willing and able providers of service to higher-status groups. This gendered version of the model minority further disciplines other racial and ethnic women who do not meet the same standards of industrious deferential service. Elizabeth, a social worker in her midfifties whose Russian parents fled the former Soviet Union, lauded the industriousness of Koreans while chiding other groups, particularly blacks, for their supposed animosity toward Koreans. Referring to the boycotts of Korean grocery stores in the early 1990s (see chapter 5), she said: "You know, I'm a Russian Jew—so I have a special feeling toward people coming and trying to make a new life in a new country. To attack people based on their ethnicity because they're trying to earn a living—they [blacks] could have done that too [started small businesses] . . . . I admire the ability of you Koreans to pull together group resources, to help each other. I'm always open to people who work hard and take care of themselves."[15] Interestingly, many of the white respondents in the study who invoked a sense of affinity with Koreans were Jewish. Thus Jews, who may be considered white but also have a history of oppression, as well as fairly recent immigration, may feel a sense of connection with Asian immigrants that mainstream whites do not necessarily share. In addition, customers like Elizabeth not only emphasize similarities between Asian immigrants and their own Russian Jewish ancestors but also chastise blacks, whom they regard as unfairly blaming Koreans for blacks' own lack of resourcefulness. Thus Elizabeth attributes the paucity of black women in the ranks of nail salon owners (and owners of other small business enterprises) to African Americans' own failures, rather than questioning whether Elizabeth or her friends would patronize these businesses if they were black owned. In the post–civil rights era, the employment of blacks in service jobs can evoke feelings of guilt or fear on the part of white customers. Thus white customers' enthusiasm for Asian manicurists not only reproduces gendered model minority constructions of Asians but also enforces less desirable views of black and other minority women.

These racial constructions also draw distinctions and hierarchies among different Asian ethnicities. In contrast to the black working-class customers in chapter 5 who tended to lump Koreans into a broad category of Asians or "Orientals," most middle-class white customers specifically identified the nail salons as Korean owned and attached favorable ethnic-specific meanings to Koreans as opposed to other Asians. Clara, a high school teacher in her early forties, identified most nail salons in her affluent neighborhood as specifically Korean run and invoked the model minority framework to describe them:

> I know they're Korean. Different ethnic groups go into different fields—the Chinese have laundries, the Koreans have produce stands and nail salons. . . . I know the stereotypes about hardworking students and close families. Although I took an aerobics class with this young woman who was doing research about the boycott of the Korean stores. She was an ultra, ultra-liberal. . . . Anyway, she completely disabused me of those success story stereotypes—but then again, she got her BA from Harvard, and I think she was going to Yale, and now she's teaching college somewhere.

While Clara claims that she has been disabused of the narrow "success story stereotype" of Koreans, in the end this encounter validates her belief in the model minority. In her mind the Korean American aerobics student's attendance at Ivy League institutions stands out more than the woman's arguments refuting the stereotype.

While these ethnic-specific views of Koreans are significant, overall they feed into generalized model minority views of Asian Americans as a group. Some customers, particularly the descendants of white ethnic immigrants such as Jews, assert a sense of affinity with Asians while still asserting their own white privilege. Ignoring the historically and culturally heterogeneous experiences that shape Asian Americans as a diverse racial group, the model minority stereotype lumps them all together into a single collective autobiography. In this monolithic story line the much-touted upward mobility of the second generation deflects attention from the difficulties confronted by the first generation, as well as from inequalities in U.S. society.

Gendered service interactions in upscale nail spas reflect large-scale social forces, but these forces are often concealed behind racial and gender stereotypes of Asian women as naturally doting and deprecatory. In line with customers' expectations, upscale nail spas place great importance on physical and emotional attentiveness as crucial components of the service interaction. Rarely do customers, or manicurists themselves, recognize the influence of discrimination or other structural barriers as pushing these women into this niche. Even less do customers acknowledge how they benefit from and participate in the truncated opportunity structures that relegate Asian women to working as their manicurists. In nail spas such as Uptown and Exclusive Nails, the gendered expectations of beauty service work combine with the racial stereotype of the model minority to produce a style of pampering body labor that is not natural but imposed.

UPTOWN NAILS

The concentrated faces of six Korean immigrant women sitting in a row of small manicuring tables are visible from the right side of the storefront window beneath the neon cursive letters spelling out "Uptown Nails." The women are identically attired in matching pink smocks and white pants resembling the uniforms of dental assistants and deftly wield emery boards, cuticle pushers, quick-dry sprays, and assorted polishes. From the left side of the window the customers sitting across the manicure tables are visible—five professionally dressed white women and one white man in suit and tie—all with their hands languidly extended before them in a posture suggestive of concert pianists or praying mantises.

"Tuesday is my salon day," explained Gwen, who was in her eighties and regularly patronized this salon. Her statement was not an exaggeration, as her regular visits were nearly half-day affairs. Dropped off by her professionally dressed daughter in the morning, Gwen would remain for two or three hours before being picked up by a private home healthcare provider. During her stay in the salon this customer received, in addition to a manicure and a pedicure, various caregiving services that were taken for granted yet unremunerated. Removing Gwen's shoes and knee-high panty hose and helping her climb up to the thronelike pedicure chair required two manicurists. For the next hour these women stooped at Gwen's feet, preparing a fragrant foot bath, massaging her arthritic feet and legs, clipping her cracked yellow toenails, placing cotton balls between her toes, polishing her nails in pastel pink, sliding on brown paper slippers to prevent smudges, and escorting her as she walked ducklike to the manicuring station. These elaborate processes were then repeated on her hands.

While the degree of care that Gwen demands is beyond what the average customer receives, she nonetheless illustrates the intense emotional and physical attention that is common in pampering body labor. Gwen usually needed to go to the bathroom at least twice during her visits, requiring at least two manicurists to virtually lift her out of her chair and walk her gingerly to the restroom. After settling her at the drying table, manicurists brought her a magazine and cup of coffee. On one occasion Gwen drifted off to sleep and began to slump sideways in her chair. A manicurist spotted her and carefully slid Gwen's chair next to the wall to prevent her from falling. When she awakened, Gwen prattled happily about the weather, the comings and goings of her children and grandchildren, and her various ailments and medications. The manicurists attended to her smilingly as they indulged her in conversation. "Your grandson is graduating from college already!" "Are you wearing a new dress?" While they were clearly fond of her, the exacting toll of her visits was evident. As Gwen approached the front door one day, Stacey, the manager, sighed and asked, "OK, who wants the 'famous grandmother' today?"

Steeped in the discourse of Asians as the model minority, many middle- and upper-class whites like Gwen extol the virtues of their manicurists and exhibit comfort with and even a measure of gratitude toward them. At the same time the customers are mostly oblivious to the hardships involved in manicuring work and are even less aware of the ways that they participate in the maintenance of subtle and not-so-subtle practices of privilege and subordination. For example, Gwen appreciated the care she received at Uptown Nails but seemed blind to the demands she placed on the women who provided this care. Instead, she claimed, "We have fun together. I like to talk, keep it lively. Some of them don't understand, which can be frustrating, but I know they try hard. They are very kind, hardworking people and they are very good at what they do. . . . I think this is a good job for them. I've heard some of them even get rich doing this." Glossing over the demanding work that her manicurists performed before her eyes, or rather at her feet and on her hands, Gwen described this as a good, "fun" job and a vehicle for upward mobility. Overlooking the physical and emotional effort of the women who perform this work, she suggested instead that she accommodates them by tolerating their limited language ability.

When her caregiver arrived, Gwen thanked her manicurists for their help and left what seemed like a generous tip. But what did this tip cover? How much would it cost to pay her home-care provider for the two hours of assistance that her manicurists provide for free as an extension of their manicuring services? How much pay would her daughter forgo if she had to take a morning off from work to care for her mother herself or assist her at the nail salon? None of these hidden costs was reflected in the price of Gwen's mani-pedi. Instead, the physical and emotional care conferred in addition to the actual nail services was invisible, as was the toll of this work on the women who do it.

DISCREPANCIES IN THE VALUATION OF BODY LABOR

The disjuncture in the valuing of a manicure by customers versus the work invested by manicurists often shows up in the customers' assessment of tips. Sheila, a white woman in her late twenties who works in advertising, saw herself as a generous and appreciative customer, especially toward Esther, whom Sheila saw often. A seasoned Korean manicurist who had worked at Uptown Nails for nearly ten years, Esther was in high demand for her relaxing and invigorating hand massages. She energetically kneaded, stroked, and pushed pressure points, finishing off the massage by holding each of Sheila's hands between her own and alternately rubbing, slapping, and gently pounding them with a flare that had wooed many a customer into a regular nail salon habit. Sheila appreciated Esther's efforts and said, "I think I'm a good tipper. I usually tip 20 percent regardless, just like in a restaurant." After she left, Esther commented, "I can't believe she thinks she's a good tipper. We should get more than what they tip at a restaurant. This takes more skill, and we are making them look pretty, not just putting food on the table like a waitress. I don't expect her to tip a lot because she looks like she doesn't make much money, but I can't believe she thinks she's a good tipper."

Clearly, two different standards for tipping, and for assessing the value of a service, were operating in this exchange. Sheila calculated what she regarded as a big tip, in accordance with the protocols of other service occupations, such as waiting tables. Esther, on the other hand, made a different assessment based on the unique nature of *this* service and the particular skills and effort it entails. From her perspective a manicure is not comparable to serving food. In terms of the benefit to the customer, it enables the highly valued accomplishment of looking pretty. In terms of the output by the manicurist, it requires more skill, not only in the physical manicure itself but in attending to the feelings of customers.

Many customers did show appreciation for Esther's hard work. Margie, a white accountant in her midthirties who was single, squeezed Esther's hand at the end of a hand massage and said, "I swear, I couldn't stay in my job without this!" Esther reciprocated with a warm, somewhat shy, smile. This customer's compliment acknowledged the benefits she received but did not take into account the wear and tear on Esther's own hands. In chapter 6, I address the occupational health risks involved in manicuring work in more detail, but these include exposure to toxic chemicals, allergies, rashes, carpal tunnel syndrome, and repetitive strain injury. These common health complaints of long-time manicurists like Esther, let alone the effort it takes for manicurists to discipline their own bodies to perform this work, rarely appear on the radar of customers.

DISCIPLINARY TECHNOLOGIES OF BODY LABOR

From the gentle removal of undernail dirt to the careful trimming of cuticles and buffing of calluses to the massaging of hands and feet, Korean manicurists literally rub up against their customers, who are mostly white middle-class and upper-class women.[16] In their efforts to pamper other women's bodies, the manicurists must discipline their own. Like many manicurists at upscale salons, thirty-four-year-old Judy Cha, who emigrated in 1993, told me that attentive body labor was not something that came naturally to her. Instead, her ability to conform to the pampering service expectations of her elite clientele was hard won over time. Furthermore, these were not simply voluntary adaptations but were dictated by the feeling and body rules of her workplace. She explained:

> Three years ago we didn't give a lot of massages but now customers ask more and more. It makes me weak and really tired . . . I guess because I don't have the right training to do it in a way that doesn't tire my body. Some manicurists give massage all the time to get tips, but sometimes I don't even ask [clients if they want a massage] if I'm tired. Owners keep asking you to ask them, but on days I'm not feeling well, I don't ask. . . . One of my biggest fears working in the salon is, what if I don't understand what the customer is saying? They don't really talk in detail, just say, "How is the weather?" But in order to have a deeper relationship, I need to get past that and to improve my English. It makes it very stressful.

Judy had learned not only to give manicures and massages but also to attend to customers' emotions, especially by engaging in conversation to make customers feel comfortable and relaxed. Learning to perform body labor thus includes both physical and emotional dimensions and the integration of the two.

The physical dimensions of pampering body labor encompass a range of service practices, including the use of high-end salon products and equipment, massages, and creation of a soothing and relaxing atmosphere, as well as management of the workers' own bodies as they perform these services. The attention devoted to creating a pampering environment at Uptown Nails is impressive and included hot cotton towels, bowls of warm soaking solution, and calming background music. The salon also offered specialized services, such as hot stone massages, lactol and paraffin wax soaks, aromatherapy, and skin refiners. The salon boasted high-end equipment, such as special drying tables with ultraviolet lights and pedicure chairs with hydrotherapy and massage features. These are big-ticket investments— high-end equipment costs thousands of dollars—and they are indicative of the substantial capital outlay that is necessary to open and sustain an upscale salon. However, while the products and tools are important, the effective delivery

Figure 12. In addition to offering pampering services, nail spas invest in expensive equipment such as spa pedicure chairs.

of pampering body labor depends mainly upon the performance of the manicurist herself.

Manicurists' efforts to adapt their bodies to this work are evident in their changed comportment during break times. During lulls in customer flows, manicurists often slip off their shoes and assume relaxed postures. Some women comfortably assume squatting positions, knees together, feet apart, while others sit casually with one leg bent and the foot tucked under the opposite thigh. The moment a customer walks in, however, they immediately assume upright positions. These dynamics are certainly not unique to nail salons, as it is not uncommon for service workers in a range of industries to adopt what Erving Goffman calls "frontstage" and "backstage" bodily self-presentations, relaxing when customers are not around, then snapping to attention when someone appears.[17] However, when a customer walks in, manicurists quickly both abandon their off-duty postures and avoid any bodily arrangements that suggest premodernity and ethnic otherness. Furthermore, they do not choose their postures—these are mandated by customers' expectations and labor management practices in the salons. For example, Grace Lee, a new worker and recent immigrant who was employed at Uptown Nails, prepared for a pedicure by assuming a squatting position at her customer's feet. Stacey, the manager, slid a stool over to Grace and chastised her, saying, "It doesn't look good to squat. Sit on this." At another salon I heard one owner hiss, "Don't take your shoes off while you're with a customer," after spying a manicurist who had slipped her shoes off under the table. Nail salon owners and managers thus pick up on cues from their customers' embodied norms and then impose these bodily controls on workers.

THE BODY POLITICS OF FOOD

Practices of bodily control not only target manicurists' physical postures but extend to the management of the foods, particularly the strong-smelling ethnic dishes, that the manicurists eat. Cara Park, the owner of a nail spa in Brooklyn, actively discouraged certain pungent Korean foods in her salon, especially kimchi, the Korean national dish of pickled cabbage with hot red pepper. "We don't eat kimchi or other smelly foods here because the customers don't like it—they think we're low class if our food and breath smells." Whereas this owner imposed an explicit policy prohibiting certain foods, other salon owners implemented indirect measures to control workers' meals and the body odors they produced. Esther, the manicurist at Uptown Nails, told me, "In another salon where I worked the owner gave us gum after meals. Once I heard her say to a manicurist that she should go brush her teeth. We all brought different dishes and shared our meals, and sometimes [the owner] would look unhappy and make comments that something had a strong smell."

Manicurists themselves also regulate their food at work so as not to offend customers. Nancy at Uptown Nails expounded on the politics of smell, acknowledging customers' concerns but countering that while she vigilantly regulated her food-induced ethnic body odors, her customers were oblivious to their own emissions. "They [customers] are very sensitive about the smell of Korean foods. I know kimchi has a strong smell even for those that are used to it, so I understand that we shouldn't eat it right before sitting so close to someone for a manicure. . . . But those people don't realize that they also have a strong American smell." When I asked her to elaborate on what constitutes an "American smell," she reacted with surprise:

> You don't know the American smell? It's not exactly like milk, it's sort of like milk and grease together [laughs]. I remember the first time I arrived here from Korea at JFK, and I walked off the plane and it was like—aigu [wow]! I could tell we were in America because of the way the people smelled, but they don't think they smell. One time I went into the waxing room, and there was a woman lying down for a bikini wax. She must have just eaten a hamburger and French fries for lunch and she smelled so bad, but she didn't seem to notice or care.

Nancy's comments reveal her understanding that she must control her own body odors while not reacting to her customers'. Although certain practices are imposed by management, the workers internalize these expectations and conform to them, as they recognize that the embodied protocols of service work are one-sidedly focused on regulating foreign bodies.

What do the micropolitics of smell reveal about the performance of body labor by Asian immigrant women? As the American studies professor Robert Lee writes in his book *Orientals*, "Food habits, customs, and rules are central symbolic structures through which societies articulate identity; you are, symbolically at least, what you eat."[18] Evaluations of food smells—from both the food itself and the clothes or breath of those who have eaten it--are thus culturally relative and context specific, yet they carry great weight in everyday interactions. It could be argued that avoiding emitting unpleasant body odors is simply good manners. However, pleasant and unpleasant are subjective categories. Nearly a century after the large wave of Italian immigrants moved into lower Manhattan, the strong smell of garlic on the breath of customers at high-end restaurants in Little Italy is no longer a signal of low class and ethnic otherness but rather of gourmet dining. In contrast, the strong smell of garlic in Korean food and on those who have consumed it often elicits strong negative reactions.

Exhortations to abstain from eating strong-smelling ethnic foods emerge in the social context of the nail salons, not simply as proper etiquette pointers from Miss Manners or Emily Post but rather as labor management practices. The regulation of body odor through the control of ethnic food consumption in nail salons does not arise simply out of individual adjustments to new cultural norms but as a by-product of body-service work. Immigrant manicurists learn to conform their bodies to white middle-class American expectations because the manicurists' jobs demand this. These demands are communicated both through the direct labor control of owners and managers and through the indirect disapproval of customers. Such disapproval also is directed at manicurists' uses of language.

THE LANGUAGE OF SERVICE

"Your nails look awesome!" Angela Shin, a perky twenty-seven-year-old receptionist at Uptown Nails, would tell customers, peppering her speech with colloquial phrases such as "How's it going?" and "Why don't you hang out and read some magazines?" While somewhat comical, her conversational style succeeded at putting customers at ease, even though her actual language ability was less advanced than that of some of the other Korean women who worked in the salon. Angela's conversational ability was the hard-earned outcome of an intensive "accent reduction" class, a cottage-industry that has sprung up to serve recent immigrants. Later, when I interviewed her, I was surprised that her seeming fluency was mostly artifice, as she did not understand when I ventured outside the vocabulary of salon services and asked her questions in English that were related to my research.

While a friendly, chatty receptionist can certainly be an asset in a business predicated on making customers feel good, Angela's conversational practices reveal more than just a talkative personality. They reflect the communicative demands of what Robin Leidner in her book *Fast Food, Fast Talk* refers to as "interactive service work."[19] While Leidner notes a general expectation of pleasant conversation in service interactions, this dimension of service work is heightened when the service provider and customer do not speak the same language. Korean manicurists thus must learn two new languages—basic English and the language of pampering service. More important than general fluency are the particular language skills related to the provision of nail services that manicurists must also learn. Customers expect conversational attentiveness, owners and managers dictate it, and manicurists develop skills to provide it.

Despite the manicurists' efforts, many customers complain, not only about the manicurists' limited English ability but also their communication among themselves in Korean. Like Elaine in the *Seinfeld* episode, many white middle-class customers have strong reactions to their manicurists' practice of speaking in Korean and are suspicious that clients are the topic of these conversations. Customers are often unaware of the demands that they impose on their manicurists for proper and unaccented English and attentive conversation. In addition, clients often become upset when they perceive that service providers are intentionally ignoring their requests or talking about them. Many express feelings like those to which this customer attested: "To tell you the truth, I don't think they really listen, they just do what they want to do. It's not because they don't understand me." Thus some white middle-class customers interpret the lack of response to their service requests, as well as the Korean women's use of their native language, as signs of willfulness, manipulation, or subversion, and in some cases the customers are right.

EVERYDAY RESISTANCE TO BODY LABOR

Even to maximize their earnings or job security, manicurists are not solely committed to meeting customers' needs. Instead, they balance meeting customers' demands with maintaining a sense of dignity in accommodating this work. While the manicurists may recognize the value of English fluency as a way of conforming to model minority expectations in their work, they also develop ways of resisting what they see as excessive demands. The ambivalence that some Korean manicurists express toward improving their language ability hints at the benefits that accrue from the inability or perceived inability to understand English. While most manicurists are intent on improving their language ability and want to communicate effectively with customers, some, like Sandy, avoided conversations and requests as a way of rejecting the role of subservient model minority member. Unfortunately, this strategy often was double edged, as it both shielded against and increased tensions with customers. Upon completion of her manicure, a customer frowned disapprovingly at the color and asked Sandy, "Since it's not dry yet, do you think you can just change the color?" Refusing to pick up on the obvious cues of a dissatisfied customer, Sandy responded, "Oh, dry, you want dry, go over there," pointing to the dryers against the opposite wall and briskly escorting the customer from her seat. In addition to buffering Sandy from dissatisfied or derogatory comments and allowing her to respond in kind, her language strategies enable her to have a modicum of control over the work she performs. However, these strategies also undercut her ability to earn higher tips and acquire skills that could enable her to move into other kinds of work, let alone to feel more at ease in her new country.

Unlike Sandy, most manicurists recognize customers' high expectations with regard to standards for communication, and they largely conform to these expectations. At the same time they find ways to subvert these demands, and language can serve as an effective, albeit limited, tool of resistance. The ability to communicate in Korean makes their working conditions more tolerable and serves as a form of resistance to cultural domination. Nancy, who was usually easygoing and soft-spoken, had raised hackles as she recounted an instance of talking about a customer as a means of retribution for the woman's insensitive comments:

> Once I was with a customer, and she hadn't said anything to me, not even, "Hi, how are you?" but all of a sudden she asks me, "Is it true that you eat dogs in Korea?" I didn't know what to say, so I just acted like I didn't understand her. Later, when she was drying, I told Esther what she had said. So right in front of her, Esther says in Korean, "Yes, we eat dogs but only raw!" You know how funny Esther can be, she went on and on. I was laughing so hard I can't remember everything she said, something like we only eat the fat ones that are other people's pets! I know it's not right, but I have to admit, I really enjoyed making fun of her.

Whether the customer's question about eating dogs indicates derision or insensitivity, it taps into a familiar motif that placed Nancy in the position of having to defend her culture. The title of Jessica Hagedorn's novel *Dogeaters* illustrates the pejorative ways that the consumption of dog meat in particular has been used as a way of denigrating Asian cultures.[20] Such comments call into question the acceptance of Asians as a model minority. With Esther's help and their ability to talk about the customer, Nancy used humor and camaraderie to neutralize the sting of the customer's query. Thus manicurists use language practices both to fend off work requests and to release negative feelings aroused by insensitive or upsetting customer comments. However, these uses of language as resistance are largely symbolic. They help to vent frustrations, but they do not fundamentally challenge relations of power and privilege. Customers' discomfort with manicurists' speaking to each other in Korean signals clients' recognition of this act as subversive, whether intentional or not. In some cases manicurists use Korean to talk about customers, but more often they are simply communicating about work-related issues or conversing with coworkers. These practices allow them to reestablish a sense of identity independent of their work, but they carry a high cost.

Some would argue that speaking in another language in front of others who do not understand it is simply rude and should be discouraged in all situations. However, this understanding of rudeness is unevenly applied in different contexts. Many English speakers regularly use English in front of those who do not understand it, adopting an "English-only" mentality even in foreign countries or communities that speak another language.[21] Acknowledging these tendencies, Jiwon Cho, a manicurist at another upscale nail salon in Manhattan, voiced sympathy for the customers and urged her colleagues to learn English and abstain from speaking in Korean. She said:

> When you don't understand and speak English, your job becomes so pitiful. I didn't realize this in the beginning. For example, if a nervous and difficult customer comes, there is no one who can take care of that customer. When she complains about something, even though it might be a very simple and basic problem, since no one understands, the customer leaves very upset. . . . Some customers tell me, "Before making money, learn

English." In the beginning I thought that it was just a friendly advice, but then as time went on I realized that they really meant what they said. . . . They are frustrated, and they look down on us. I get angry when they say these things, but sometimes I wonder if they are right. If a foreigner was living in Korea and did not speak Korean, I would pity them and look down on them, too.

While Jiwon conjectured that she too would harbor negative feelings toward foreigners in her country who do not learn the native language, the reality is that many foreigners go to South Korea for business or travel and never learn a word of Korean yet usually are treated well or at least are not denigrated. In fact, many U.S. citizens, even when they are visiting or working in another country, expect that others should speak English, rather than that Americans should make an effort to learn the culture and language of the country they are visiting.[22] Given these language dynamics, manicurists like Jiwon are more likely to see themselves as pitiful for resorting to the use of Korean rather than questioning the customers' strong reactions to hearing a foreign language.

Similarly, manicurists who remain in nail salon work for the long term mostly conform to customer demands in terms of embodied expectations. At the same time, as with language, the manicurists engage in limited acts of embodied resistance that may ameliorate but do not change the demands of pampering body labor. At Uptown Nails one form that this takes is poking fun at customers' serious investment in their nails. One day, close to Halloween, I entered the salon during a slow time to find the manicurists festively, and somewhat conspiratorially, painting each other's nails the colors of M&M candies. They revealed that they also painted hearts on their nails around Valentine's Day and green clovers for St. Patrick's Day. In their gleefulness they seemed aware that they were doing something mildly subversive by bestowing on each other a semblance of the pampering treatment that they usually reserve for their customers. At the same time they were doting on each other in a way that undermined the seriousness of the enterprise and instead made it both playful and somewhat ridiculous. However, when the women left the salon at the end of the day, they had removed the candy-colored polish from their nails. Thus these seeds of resistance did not flower into any sustained collective consciousness or action inside, let alone outside, the salon.

Resistance to body labor is further undermined by manicurists' identification with the needs and status of their customers, wherein they claim status by association with their customers' racial and class privilege. Some manicurists gain satisfaction and a vicarious sense of status by performing skillful work for customers of a higher social position and earning their appreciation. For example, as the owner of an upscale salon in Manhattan, Lisa Park has a well-established clientele and is in high demand. She is the only manicurist at the salon who schedules appointments, and these are reserved for elaborate silk or linen wraps. The painstaking process of layering nails with thin strands of delicate fabric to strengthen, lengthen, and smooth them can take well over an hour and generally costs more than $50. After Lisa completed a flawless silk wrap one day, her regular customer exclaimed, "Lisa, you're the best in the city!" and supplemented her appreciation with an exceptionally generous $20 tip. Lisa beamed and proudly displayed her $20 to her workers and customers. Later, when asked about her relationship with this high-tipping customer, Lisa did not acknowledge any particular fondness for her, saying, "I think maybe she's a lawyer. Anyway, she's a very rich and high [status] person, and she only trusts me, so I feel good." Even when they do not become personally close to their customers, some owners and manicurists, like Lisa, enjoy helping their well-heeled clients to look good, in addition to realizing the monetary rewards that may accrue as a result. In many salons the more skillful manicurists perform difficult and expensive procedures and mainly attend to regular patrons, thus putting themselves in a position to receive the biggest tips and most appreciation.

Manicurists thus exhibit a range of responses to the demands of pampering body labor. Some internalize the service ethic and identify with the higher status of their customers, at times deriving a sense of status by association. Others engage in strategic acquiescence, outwardly fulfilling service expectations but inwardly rejecting positions of subservience. Finally, some manicurists are able to engage in subtle forms of resistance, by talking about customers or refusing to perform certain tasks. These responses demonstrate their assertion of agency but also reveal the circumscribed parameters in which the manicurists exercise resistance. At another upscale salon, Exclusive Nails, customers and service providers were able to express genuine caring and connection, but underlying power relations persisted.

EXCLUSIVE NAILS: THE LIMITS OF PERSONAL TIES

Charlie, the owner of Exclusive Nails (see chapter 2), is a generous and proud woman who regarded her relations with customers as based not on servility or economic necessity but on friendship. Her position as owner, the prosperity of her salon, as well as the receptivity of her customers allowed her to validate this more empowering framing of her work. At the same time this alternative framework was subject to cracks, as even a well-liked and successful owner like Charlie is not immune to the demands that she acquiesce to a position of subservience as she supplies pampering body labor. Despite the absence of overt discrimination or exploitation, inequalities persist, as does the discourse of the model minority and the expectations that accompany it.

As she had with many of her customers, Charlie had developed a special relationship with Patti, a hospital social worker and chronic nail biter. These two women had forged a relationship as customer and manicurist that was mutually supportive and humanizing, and they attempted to rewrite the dynamics of service as a story of genuine friendship. However, this alternative narrative did not hold up against structural forces that overrode the terms of their connection. Patti, who was plagued by her nail biting habit, did not take for granted the care that she received. "I always get very anxious and this is my habit. I don't smoke or overeat, I don't drink or do drugs, but I bite my nails. . . . So, it is important that [the manicurists] take care of me. They would hurt me unless they are very careful. See? You see what I did to my nails. You see the bottom of the thumb? . . . I would not go anywhere else. It is nice here compared to other places where they are not as careful and they do not care. . . . I trust her [Charlie]." Patti frames the intensive body labor that she receives at Exclusive Nails not as a commercialized exchange or as an exercise in racial and class privilege but as a relationship with another woman based on trust, intimacy, and reciprocity. She was eager to help Charlie with English-language documents and often stepped in as an intermediary with new or disgruntled customers. Poignantly, Patti told me, "There have been times when the only way I celebrated my birthday was to come here to get a manicure from Charlie."

In return, Charlie expressed appreciation for Patti and also referred to her as a friend. At the same time Charlie acknowledged the multiple challenges of negotiating their relationship within the constraints of their roles as customer and service provider. Charlie said of Patti, "She is my friend, we help each other. . . . Really, her nails are in terrible shape—I have to be so careful not to hurt her because all the skin under the nail is exposed." As Charlie acknowledged, although she appreciated Patti's patronage and various forms of assistance, working on her gnawed nails was highly stressful. Despite both women's insistence that they were friends, ultimately, the work of maintaining their relationship fell on Charlie. Patti often refers to Charlie as her "therapist," which attests to the level of emotional labor that Charlie invested. I noticed that if Charlie was working on another customer when Patti arrived, she hurried to finish or asked another manicurist to take over so that she could attend to Patti promptly. On one occasion Patti had waited for a few minutes, then apologetically but impatiently pointed to her watch, pressuring Charlie to finish quickly. These interactions do not suggest the equal footing of friends but rather the dictates of a generous but nonetheless demanding customer toward a beholden service provider. Furthermore, while Charlie and Patti were able to forge some semblance of a friendship within the salon, this relationship did not extend into their lives outside the service setting. When I asked Charlie whether they ever saw each other outside the salon, she took the question literally—"Oh, yes, she always waves when she walks by."

All this is not to say that the kind of genuinely caring service relationship that Charlie and Patti had nurtured is not meaningful or worth developing. What it does say is that while these positive microinteractions can take the sting out of the subservience associated with body labor, they do not fundamentally alter the terms of these exchanges and the relative status and power of the actors involved. These relationships coexist with systemic inequalities, including the hierarchies of service provision and the racial discourses of white privilege and the Asian model minority. They do not erase them. Furthermore, these embodied and emotional dimensions of service provision shape particular patterns of assimilation.

EMOTIONAL AND EMBODIED ASSIMILATION

Through the performance of pampering body labor, immigrant women service providers like Charlie undergo processes of emotional and embodied assimilation in order to conform to customers' expectations, the protocols of their workplace, and racial and gender stereotypes of Asian Americans. I ran into Charlie one day as she was leaving a gourmet deli with a bag of groceries and a bouquet of rainbow tulips. Pointing to the flowers, I asked if she was going to visit someone, and unlike many immigrant women, who might feel self-conscious or indulgent about such a purchase, she answered unapologetically, "No, I just bought them for myself." Charlie often brought fresh-cut flowers into the salon, earning customers' approving comments, and it appears that the attention she put into pampering body labor had rubbed off on the ways she now pampered herself. As a successful nail salon owner, Charlie rewarded herself for a hard day's work in quintessentially American style—through the conspicuous consumption of high-end goods. These small purchases reveal that the day-in, day-out work of conforming to the physical and emotional register of customers reconfigures manicurists' own identities in small but unalterable increments. The performance of pampering body labor fosters emotional and embodied forms of assimilation that draw upon both the racial rhetoric of Asians as the model minority and the gendered framing of Asian women as attentive to service and aesthetics. These frameworks extend beyond the nail salon into other areas of women's lives.

At the same time Charlie had not yet internalized the service expectations of her customers to the point that she herself would purchase the same kind of high-end manicures that she so expertly provided. When I asked her about this, she curtly replied, "No, that's what I do for work." In other words, although Charlie had absorbed certain elements of the ethic of pampering self-care, she drew the line at actually shifting from the seat of the beauty service provider to that of the consumer. Her assimilation into the ethos of pampering body labor redefined her identity and relationships in ways that complemented but did not alter her social position as a manicurist and nail salon owner performing pampering body labor. In the end she conformed to the discourse of the model minority and to the gendered norms of spa-level beauty service.

Sadly, even with this high level of assimilation, Charlie is still viewed and treated by many customers as someone outside the American mainstream. In the following exchange, Alexandra, a regular customer, revealed both her high standards for body labor as well as her sense of privilege over Charlie as a provider of these services. When I asked Alexandra what improvements she might like to see at the salon, she first directed her comments to me, then made a revealing shift in tone as she addressed Charlie in broken English:

> Make it more like a spa. Have aromatherapy when you get a pedicure. It is not that expensive, and you can do probably forty-fifty pedicures and use that one same bottle before you run out. I don't think it is going to be a lot of added cost. . . . They are going to remodel the place which they really need. The place is so outdated. [She notices that Charlie is listening and directs her next comments to her, conspicuously switching her tone and grammar.] People come in and see old decoration, they think old store, dirty, not good. So they are more likely to leave. When you have fresh new appearance, people think fresh new look, good stuff!

Later, when I asked Charlie, who had lived in the United States for more than ten years by then and was quite conversant in English, how she felt about Alexandra's way of speaking to her, she shrugged and said, "They all do it. Maybe they think they are making it easier for us to understand, but it shows how they think we are stupid."

Alexandra was not intentionally disrespectful of Charlie or the other Korean women in the salon—on the contrary, she prided herself on her knowledge and appreciation of Korean culture and she proudly shared how she taught a unit on the "Asian model minority" in her social studies class. Nonetheless, her social position as a white middle-class customer gave her the prerogative to make recommendations to the salon owner about how to run her business and to do so in language that replicated stereotypical notions of Asians as foreigners who cannot speak English. Far from elevating Charlie to a position as an equal, or even as a member of a model minority group, Alexandra spoke to Charlie as if chastising a child. In so doing, she exercised her own racial and class privilege while diminishing Charlie's social position. Even as a successful, highly assimilated salon owner, Charlie was vulnerable to such service exchanges, which reveal to her that customers like Alexandra "think we are stupid." In addition, such exchanges undermine claims that Asians have triumphed over discrimination and exclusion.

CONCLUSION

Manicuring exchanges in Asian-owned nail spas serving mostly middle- and upper-class whites call into question the "model minority" representation of passive and industrious Asians who easily assimilate into the mainstream and enjoy high socioeconomic and racial status comparable to whites'. Instead, interactions in upscale nail spas reveal that derogatory stereotypes and unequal power continue to infuse these exchanges. The mundane exchanges in Asian-owned nail salons demonstrate that racialized representations, combined with gendered stereotypes of Asian women as subservient and well suited to detailed handiwork, naturalize their concentration in this work. Different patterns of service emerge at different sites, refuting the one-dimensional stereotype. The dominant, albeit not exclusive, pattern in nail spas serving white middle- and upper-class customers is one in which gendered work practices, as enacted through pampering body services, reinforce existing racial and class hierarchies.

At upscale salons such as Uptown Nails, the servicing of some women's bodies entails the disciplining of other women's bodies. Manicurists not only must enact embodied practices directly associated with the manicure, such as clipping, polishing, touching, and massaging, but they also must regulate their own bodily comportment and contact, including the ways they sit and the foods they eat. In responding to customers' feelings about these embodied exchanges, manicurists must learn to speak not one, but two new languages. First, they must acquire basic English-language fluency, and second, they must develop fluency in the language of complimenting, coddling, and capitulating to their customers' needs. Language skills are an essential element of the emotional management involved in body labor, but language skills can also carry the price of increased vulnerability to negative comments and excessive customer demands. At the same time manicurists can use their language skills to resist these demands and unsettle customers by conversing in Korean. However, such subtle acts of resistance carry costs in terms of negative responses from owners and customers, and they do not fundamentally alter the power dynamics of these exchanges.

At Exclusive Nails the manicurists engaged in fewer of these attempts at resistance because relations with customers were genuinely more authentic and therefore required less ostentatious displays of deference. However, this did not mean that the inequalities in these relations disappeared. Just because women are genuinely nice to each other and treat each other with dignity does not change the vast differences in their lives and resources. At the same time the real measures of caring and respect expressed between them are not insignificant. They enable women who work in these salons to maintain their self-respect while doing this work. However, the modicum of genuine connection that they forge can easily disappear in the face of customer dissatisfaction or insensitivity, or simply the pressures of a busy day.

The forms of emotional and embodied assimilation that Asian manicurists undergo in performing gendered service work ultimately reinforce dominant racial and gender framings of Asian women as docile, subservient, and well suited to detailed work. At the same time, while the structures of the global service economy channel Asian immigrants into this niche, these women are not mere cogs in the machine of global capitalism. They make choices and give meaning to this work, either by embracing their customers and the work itself or by asserting limits on how they perform it. Nonetheless, as Carol Wolkowitz writes in her book

Bodies at Work, such "intra-psychic" forms of resistance rarely challenge the "emotional order" of organizations but instead "enable individual workers to distance themselves psychologically without necessarily encouraging more collective efforts directed towards transformation rather than survival."[23] Similarly, customers are not bound to the enacting of scripts of pampering and privilege but can rewrite them, in either more oppressive or more egalitarian ways.

Some customers actively resist the idea that nail salon interactions reflect prejudices and social inequalities, insisting that their relations with their manicurists are affectionate and mutual. One customer approached me in a salon and asserted, "I really care about these women, and I think I can say the same for them. How can you not feel something for someone who has done your nails for years?" Indeed, strong emotional bonds between manicurists and customers are not uncommon. However, these bonds do not negate the often invisible inequalities of race, class, and immigrant status that shape body labor. Instead, intimate emotional and embodied contact coexists with and can even further entrench divisions between women. Thus the act of women serving women, even and especially when the purchase of pampering body labor is involved, is not a recipe for forging alliances so much as for reinscribing differences.

Five

Black People "Have Not Been the Ones Who Get Pampered"

NAIL ART SALONS AND BLACK-KOREAN RELATIONS

Black people on a whole have not been the ones who get pampered. There was a time when only white people could do this. So in that sense, I do feel something for the Koreans because there is more access to it now. I can just cruise in on a Saturday morning and get my hands and feet done.

Alexis, African American customer at Downtown Nails

I had seen television broadcasts of the L.A. riots so I was afraid to go to black areas like Brooklyn or the Bronx. But after working there, I found that they were very friendly and I'm not afraid of them anymore. I've learned that whites are more picky and demanding in fact, I'm more afraid of whites now than blacks.

Jade, nail technician

The "black-Korean conflict" reifies both "African" Americans and "Korean" Americans and the conflict itself. In so doing, the inter-ethnic conflict becomes a ready made explanation for diverse phenomena and diverts our attention from other events and explanations.

Nancy Abelmann and John Lie, *Blue Dreams*

After being refused a manicure at Bloomie's Nails in Manhattan as the salon was about to close, rapper Foxy Brown, a regular customer, kicked and hit two nail salon workers on August 27, 2004. She eventually pleaded guilty to misdemeanor assault charges. According to the *New*

York Times, prosecutors charged the rapper, whose legal name is Inga Marchand, with assaulting the manager, Sun Ji Song, "causing 'bruising and swelling to the face, as well as substantial pain.'" They said the salon's employees ran out to Marchand's car and stood in front of it to block her. At one point, they said, Marchand slugged one of the workers with a cell phone.[1]

This account of an altercation between a black customer and a Korean nail salon manager would be almost comical if it did not so easily trip ready-made story lines of racial tensions between blacks and Koreans. Whereas chapter 4 showed how privileged white customers receiving pampering at the hands of Asian manicurists reinforce the rhetoric of the model minority, this chapter addresses how depictions of high-profile run-ins such as this resuscitate discourses of entrenched black-Korean conflict.

As the political scientist Claire Jean Kim asserts, "Black-Korean conflict has become part of American urban mythology."[2] This mythology has been fueled by media representation and cultural production related to events such as the contentious 1990 boycott of the Korean-owned Red Apple market in Brooklyn and the massive looting and burning of more than two thousand Korean-owned small businesses in Los Angeles in 1992. Most notably, the rap artist Ice Cube, in his controversial hit song "Black Korea," protested Korean merchants' suspicious treatment of black customers and threatened to burn down their stores. This song became a lightning rod for tensions between African American and Korean American communities in the lead-up to the Los Angeles riots. Korean American leaders, disturbed by his call for boycotts and the burning of Korean-owned businesses in black neighborhoods, strongly criticized Ice Cube and organized their own boycott of the album.[3] These tensions emerged as part of a constellation of events referred to in popular media and academic discourse as "black-Korean conflict," a phrase that emphasizes entrenched and widespread animosity between these two groups.

"Black Korea," while a significant cultural representation of contemporary racial politics, overlooks more nuanced and mundane dimensions of black-Korean relations. Likewise, the Foxy Brown incident gives the impression that such conflict pervades not only Korean-owned grocery and retail stores, but also service establishments such as nail salons. However, such depictions run counter to the experiences of customers such as Alexis, who credits Korean-owned nail salons with providing her with a formerly inaccessible service. In this chapter I address these gaps, showing how Korean and black women both reproduce and rewrite the representations of conflict and exploitation that frame their interactions. The ideology of the model minority situates Asian immigrants as above blacks and close to whites in social status, but many black women reject this racial hierarchy and see themselves as superior because they do not engage in such subservient work. In addition, they regard themselves as having higher status because they speak English and are U.S. citizens. Just as relations in nail spas challenge the monolithic model minority framework of Asians as easily assimilating and enjoying socioeconomic and racial status comparable to whites', nail art salons challenge the notion of endemic "black-Korean conflict." I do not dismiss the existence of conflict between these groups, but I do seek to explain variations in the contexts and factors that fuel or mediate tensions.

The concept of "expressive body labor" identifies a style of service provision that emerges at Downtown and Artistic Nails and other nail art salons situated in predominantly (but not exclusively) black working-class neighborhoods. This form of body labor prioritizes nails as a form of self-expression for black customers. In addition, it recognizes the importance of expressing respect and fairness toward black clientele. Expressive body labor focuses less on pampering and more on creating aesthetic nail designs while exhibiting community respect and reciprocity in the process.

Whereas I argued in chapter 4 that gendered practices of pampering body labor reinforce racial privilege, here I assert that the expressive style of body labor can foster common gender identifications that challenge totalizing frameworks of racial conflict. The gendered processes of expressive body labor to some degree "deracialize" these Korean-owned businesses and their relations with black customers. However, while this form of body labor can create spaces in which gender solidarity can emerge between Korean manicurists and owners and black clientele,

Figure 13. Nail art salons provide expressive body labor that prioritizes original designs and respectful relations with the predominantly black working-class communities they serve.

numerous variables shape whether these possibilities are acted upon and the degree to which they can be sustained.

In this chapter I examine the current scholarship on black-Korean relations and apply an intersectional analysis of the multiple dimensions of body labor to enrich this research. Next, I describe the general patterns of service provision in nail art salons serving black working-class customers and show how they both disrupt and reproduce dominant frameworks of conflictual relations between these groups. Fieldwork in two salons, Downtown and Artistic Nails, both located in predominantly working-class black neighborhoods, highlights how gender commonalities emerge only as highly contingent articulations enacted at specific sites. I conclude the chapter with a discussion of the lessons that these sites offer, both for the study of black-Korean relations and for understanding the complex ways that the gendered practices of body labor shape and are shaped by racial difference and socioeconomic inequality.

GENDERING BLACK-KOREAN RELATIONS

Race matters, but not exclusively, in relations between immigrant entrepreneurs and minority customers in urban settings. However, in the case of black-Korean relations, racial and ethnic differences often are viewed through a one-dimensional framework that presupposes conflict and excludes other dimensions of social relations, particularly gender and class. As Abelmann and Lie argue, complex events such as the Los Angeles civil uprising of 1992 are reduced to the narrow rubric of "black-Korean conflict," as if members of these two groups are destined to square off in a racial politics of entrenched animosity. Instead, scholars of race and ethnicity have shown how diverse factors impact relations between Korean entrepreneurs and black customers. Others have questioned the very existence of black-Korean conflict, emphasizing the mundane and prosaic forms of interactions that predominate in Korean-owned businesses in black neighborhoods and the role of media in exaggerating tensions.[4]

In assessing the real and publicized tensions between these groups, these studies provide insightful analyses of commercial establishments such as grocery and retail stores but largely ignore service-based enterprises such as nail salons. In addition, by focusing mainly on race, and to some extent on class, they give marginal attention to the role that gender plays in intergroup relations, particularly in immigrant-owned small businesses. Sites such as Korean-owned nail salons, where large-scale conflicts have neither erupted nor drawn media attention, highlight how gendered practices of service provision can mediate race and class-based tensions. Specifically, by prioritizing gendered identities and practices as a source of commonality, the expressive form of body labor reframes black-Korean relations in nail salons.

My purpose here is not to summarize or critique the entire body of literature on black-Korean relations but rather to make a specific intervention, which is to analyze the impact of gendered work processes, specifically, the performance of body labor, on black-Korean relations. With a few notable exceptions this gender analysis has been largely absent in this literature, as well as in the study of race relations and immigrant incorporation more broadly.[5] Studies of black-Korean relations in ethnic small businesses often assume that these interactions occur mostly between men, as reflected in the male-centered terms that they use. For example, the term *middleman minority*, which has served as an influential theoretical concept in the literature, prioritizes class and neglects gender.[6] While it would be a positive step to expand this concept to include "middlewomen minorities," it is also necessary to develop new theoretical constructs that speak to unique processes operating among women. We cannot merely assume that parallel phenomena operate identically across gender lines but rather must modify and expand these concepts to account for the specific dynamics that occur between racially diverse women in ethnic small businesses.

The concept of body labor, and, specifically, the expressive form of body labor that can emerge in nail art salons, is one such analytical tool for bringing gender into the study of black-Korean relations. While creating space for certain possibilities, expressive body labor practices, in and of themselves, do not determine when gender commonalities are realized or quashed by other forms of difference. Korean nail salon owners and black customers can disrupt prevailing racial discourses through gendered practices, but the structures of racial difference and inequality persist as the subtext of their interactions and are easily rekindled into racialized tensions that override gender solidarity. Thus in this chapter I argue that the gendered practices of body labor create possibilities but do not offer a simple formula for easing tensions and generating solidarity between racially distinct women. Expressive body labor can disrupt one-dimensional framings of unbridgeable racial divisions, but these interactions do not play themselves out in identical and predictable ways, even across similar sites.

MANICURING BLACK-KOREAN RELATIONS

I went to a black-owned salon once but it took them an hour to do what the Koreans do in twenty minutes. The price was about the same. But I'm not going to waste forty minutes just because people tell me I should be into my own culture. . . . They all look Korean, but I don't know that for a fact. . . . I figure as long as they don't have no conflicts with me, I'm cool. I've never had a problem. How can I put this?—I never had nothing against them.

How do nail salon interactions influence relations between Koreans and blacks?
I guess it makes it better. They learn to like people of my race. It gets
them to understand Afro-Americans—or at least get used to us. I see the
regulars laugh and talk with them, but I don't. They be busy—when I
go, they just do my nails. I don't need talk or a massage—I'm not into
that. I get what I want and I leave.

Vicki, the twenty-one-year-old African American college student whose
opinion I solicited about black-Korean relations in nail salons, paid only
fleeting attention to her nail technician's race and ethnicity, prioritizing
Korean women's ability to create elaborate, durable, and artistic nails
over allegiance to black-owned businesses. Disrupting portrayals of
endemic racial tensions, she expressed appreciation to Korean women
for providing African American working-class women like her with
greater access to nail services. In all, she was satisfied with the cordial,
albeit perfunctory, body labor exchanges.

Black women, who would not necessarily view Korean small businesses
positively in all contexts, do have positive regard for nail salons as a result
of interactions and framings that are specific to these sites. The gendered
nature of the businesses deracializes the nail salons as less intrusive and
less exploitative of the black community. Unlike the clear ethnic designation of the "Korean delis" or green grocers, the ethnicity of the owners of
the salon that they frequent is unknown to many black customers, and
many do not know that the nail salons are mostly operated by Koreans.
Most customers instead lump the owners into a generic racial category of
"Asians" or "Orientals," or they extend the ethnic category of "Chinese"
to include all Asians (or at least East Asians). Zena, an elderly patron of
Downtown Nails, told me, "No other nationality is out here doing nails—I
don't see anyone from Pakistan, India in this neighborhood. It's not something that's learnt overnight. As far back as you can go, back to Marco
Polo days, Oriental people have been doing nails. Only got to read the history books and it's there." Referring to "Orientals" as possessing innate,
or at least, historically based expertise in the care and design of nails, Zena
frames the women who do nails as belonging to the same "nationality."
Thus she demonstrates the perception of Asia as a single Oriental nation,
rather than as a region with many countries and hundreds of ethnic groups.

I have found this to be a framework that is common in mainstream U.S. society as well as one expressed by black working-class customers in this study. By excluding Pakistan and India from this imagined nation, Zena reveals her view that South Asians are a separate racial category from East and Southeast Asians. Finally, she appeals to these racial constructions of Asian as an explanation for their domination of the nail salon niche.

Zena's comments, rather than erroneous or ignorant, are indicative of the social contexts that foster them. First, despite scientific arguments that no biological justification exists for systems of racial differentiation, let alone the superiority of one racial group over another, everyday constructions of race continually appeal to phenotypical differences to justify racial categories and inequalities.[7] To Zena, Koreans, Chinese, Vietnamese all look the same, whereas she regards Pakistanis and Indians as looking different. However, it is not only their similar physical appearance but their common clustering in the same occupational niche that forms the basis for her grouping East and Southeast Asians together. Indeed, based on ethnic concentration in the nail salon industry, Zena is arguably correct in her system of racial classification—Koreans, Chinese, and Vietnamese are all heavily represented in manicuring services, while Pakistanis and Indians are not. Thus Zena's racial categorization of Asians makes sense, given her everyday experience—"Orientals" refers to a single "nationality" of Asians who look similar, and all do nails.

Like Zena, Gail, an African American customer at Artistic Nails, applied a racially generalized view of Asian women as not only highly skilled at nails but also as contributing positively to the community through these skills:

> I figure this is like the arts, it looks like the Asian women arts. From the little that I see with the sculptures and stuff, I see that some of the designs are from their origins, so you know their paintings and so forth. You see a lot of that stuff in the nails, intricate designs. So I would figure that's why. Why is it on a nail? I don't know. That would be interesting, why Asian women do it on nails. I don't know that part. . . . The stereotype? They are in the community to just make their money and come to do their businesses here, but they live far away, blah blah blah. . . . There's plenty like that maybe, there is. . . . Then, again, you can argue, "Well, they are giving back the service. You pay your money."

Gail sees Asian women as desirable nail service providers who apply their cultural aesthetics to serving black women. Thus she regards Asian nail art salons as giving something back to the community by providing desirable and accessible nail services, as opposed to taking away resources, a criticism that has been leveled against other Korean-owned small businesses.

In addition, it is noteworthy that the black women in this study who do identify nail salon proprietors as specifically Korean, as opposed to generically Asian, frame the owners' "Koreanness" not in pejorative terms but as a plus. Latoya, an African American customer at Downtown Nails, explained: "A lot of African American women like to get their nails done. In the mid-eighties I think it really started happening. Before that, I don't remember seeing them so much. But now everybody—like Mary J. Blige—has long nails with designs. . . . Not me personally, but I heard stories from people that they think the Koreans are just better at it."

This positive appraisal of Koreans as the nail providers of choice refers both to their technical expertise and to the sense of higher status that black women derive from having Asian women (whether they categorize them according to specific Korean ethnicity or not) do their nails. An African American beauty salon owner in the neighborhood near Downtown Nails stated that she stopped offering nail services because "I just couldn't compete. All the girls know the Koreans are the best at nails. They want them doing it instead of us." Thus, in performing this work, Koreans have revamped nail services to make them not only more available but also more appealing to black women.

In the exchange of these services Korean nail artists and black customers invert dominant racial hierarchies through the dynamics of feminized service provision. Stephie, an African American customer at Artistic Nails, asserted that she, and most black women, regard nail salon work as low status, just one step above working in a restaurant:

> I'd say it's the same as, like, food. But I'm not a psychiatrist, I'm not trying to be, but I would think that maybe in terms of Chinese food and nails, they would put this up. . . . They think they are better or something, but, come on, they're doing nails instead of frying chicken or chicken wings in the back of a Chinese restaurant. It's a nail salon so they are up [compared to that], but most black people wouldn't do this kind of work. I don't know for sure, but I would think that. That's what I would think.

Thus rather than applying the framework of Asians' coming into black communities and displacing African Americans from business opportunities, Stephie sees Asians as filling a niche that most black women regard as low status and not desirable employment. Furthermore, she sees Asian women as somewhat deluded in assessing this work as higher status than it really is.

Even in cases where black customers regard Koreans as looking down on blacks, they are able to counter these perceptions by appealing to notions of Asians as slavishly subservient as opposed to admirably industrious. Doris, an African American nurse, was having a manicure at Downtown Nails, when I asked what she believes Asians think of blacks, and vice versa. She asserted:

> That they look down on American blacks. They say things like, "Why don't you have a house? I have a house and I just got here." It's true, we like to dress and look good—and eat good! But we're not willing to pile up nine hundred people in a one-room apartment to send our kids to a good college. They have a thing about status. . . . I have a BS in health administration, but I've never got a promotion. Thirteen years in the same hospital, and I've never got a promotion. I've been doing gunshot wounds in the ICU while the white nurses I started with have moved on to someone's private practice or retired. That's how it is here. They [Koreans] don't see that part, though. They just see that we like to party.

This framing, unlike the model minority stereotype referenced by white middle- and upper-class women, casts a different light on the work ethic of Asians. Rather than seeing Koreans' willingness to work hard as a positive attribute, African American women like Doris see Koreans as making unnecessary sacrifices that force them to live in substandard conditions, such as "nine hundred people" crammed into a small apartment. While she sees them as making these sacrifices for the good of their children, she also regards them as naive in their pursuit of higher status and their lack of understanding of racial discrimination in the United States.

Expressive body labor both reshapes the attitudes of black women toward Koreans and shifts Korean women's perceptions of blacks, albeit in mixed ways. How do Korean women's views of blacks change through their work in nail salons? Some, like Anne Kwan, reformulate derogatory stereotypes and fears regarding blacks through the process of engaging in intimate embodied interactions. "Before I came to this country, I could have never imagined touching another person's feet besides my husband. Let alone a black person. I remember the first time I saw how the inside of their hands are light, and I was so surprised. But now I don't think that they are so different." Others, like Jade, a nail technician at Downtown Nails, come to prefer black customers over whites, saying, "I had seen television broadcasts of the L.A. riots so I was afraid to go to black areas like Brooklyn or the Bronx. But after working there, I found that they were very friendly, and I'm not afraid of them anymore. I've learned that whites are more picky and demanding—in fact, I'm more afraid of whites now than blacks." Likewise, Young Kang, who worked at Downtown Nails, commented: "When I was in Korea, I thought blacks were poor and lazy. Now I understand that there is discrimination in this country so even people who want to work hard can't find a good job. I think blacks get angry when people don't understand them, but if you make an effort to understand them, they are very warm and friendly. . . . Because I am young like them, I think of them like friends. I like their style." Young developed positive feelings toward blacks through sustained contact with them in service interactions and in appreciation of their style of bodily display.

These experiences of greater identification with blacks through the body labor exchanges, however, is by no means universal. Performing nail services for black customers can reinforce Korean women's negative stereotypes of black women, ranging from disparaging of their bodies to fearing them as criminals. One worker at another salon serving predominantly black customers revealed her racial prejudices, saying, "Their hands are much dirtier, and their nails are harder to cut." Similarly, Joanne Shin, who had worked in both black and white neighborhoods, discussed differences between these locales, focusing on tipping practices but framing her comments in racialized constructions of black women's bodies: "There is only one difference between a black and white neighborhood; it takes more energy to do blacks than whites but there is no tip. I would be able to get $100 in tips for the same work that I do elsewhere, but I only get $10 in a black neighborhood. It's also harder to do blacks because blacks are generally larger than whites, and their muscles are harder." Another nail technician, Gloria Kim, explained how she suppresses rather than transforms negative feelings that manifest in servicing black customers:

> You have to be the most careful with black people because they think Koreans look down on them. White people can be racist toward us, but we just have to put up with it, we don't have to worry so much how we respond. I switched from the Long Island salon because I wanted a change. I don't know Brooklyn well, but I know this isn't a bad neighborhood, even though there are lots of blacks. I only saw whites in Long Island, and it made it less stressful; you know how to act with them; even though they may look down on us, it's still easier.

Thus close physical contact in no way guarantees more favorable individual or group-level relations. Instead, the physical and emotional dimensions of the work can reinforce derogatory stereotypes and strained relations. For these Korean manicurists the provision of services for black women, whom they view as both hypersensitive to race and as racially beneath Koreans, requires intense emotional management.

The experiences of manicurists who work for a short period in a black neighborhood and then move on to a higher-income white neighborhood tend to retrench rather than rework negative stereotypes of blacks. In many cases Korean women move out of black working-class neighborhoods as quickly as possible once they gain manicuring and language skills. Indeed, the very reason they are in these neighborhoods in the first place is that they cannot gain employment or establish a salon in a white middle-class area until they improve both their technical and business skills and language ability.

Even in cases where Korean manicurists stay long term in black low-income areas, they do not necessarily develop a rapport with and respect for their customers. As Jinny, the manager at Artistic Nails, revealed, negative stereotypes can become further ingrained through sustained work in black neighborhoods, especially when tensions are high. She told me, "About ten days after I started working here, I remember saying to myself, 'The people here are like talking animals.' I know I'm wrong. I'm bad, but I still [feel that way]. . . . I knew what kind of people were in here. But I didn't know that they were this much different." In short, a more favorable view of blacks as a consequence of performing body labor in nail salons in black working-class neighborhoods is far from a given, as many Korean workers and owners quickly move out of these salons, and even those who stay for longer stints can end up further inscribing derogatory stereotypes.

At the same time working with black customers necessitates suppression of blatantly racist attitudes and behavior, or at least their outward expression, and can pave the way for the development of more genuinely positive feelings. Whether as an adaptation based on their experiences in nail art salons, a reflection of a lower status position in American society, or an indication of different nail aesthetics and service priorities, customers' demands for pampering in the low-income black neighborhoods are significantly lower than in nail spas. In some cases this can allow Korean manicurists to develop genuine affinity with black customers and less of a sense of burnout from manufacturing affection or suppressing negative feelings, as they often do in serving white middle- and upper-class women.

In conclusion, black-Korean relations are rewritten through the performance of body labor in nail salons in multiple and unpredictable ways. In contrast to assumptions of animosity and hostility toward Korean-owned businesses, many black women regard the presence of nail salons in their communities favorably. They value these establishments as providing them with desired services and do not necessarily see them as taking away resources and opportunities. Korean women do not universally disdain black customers, but some reformulate prejudicial views of blacks and forge meaningful ties through providing body labor based on individual respect and community outreach. However, just as often, work in nail art salons reinforces negative racial ideologies. Thus the reworking of stereotypical forms of interaction in the salons is not to be expected but depends on the ways that the gendered processes of service work, enacted as expressive body labor, unfold in different sites. The following comparisons of Downtown and Artistic Nails demonstrate how particular body labor practices challenge or reproduce dominant racial representations and their impact on face-to-face interactions in different nail salons serving mostly black working-class customers.

DOWNTOWN NAILS

Squeezed between a Caribbean bakery and a discount clothing store, the worn-out signboard displays the single word *NAILS* and a painting of a graceful, well-manicured hand holding a long-stemmed rose. The sign points to a staircase that leads to the second-story entrance of Downtown Nails. Upon being buzzed in through the locked door, the customer is greeted with a display of hundreds of brightly colored nail designs that lines an entire wall. Sharina, an African American student at the nearby high school, sauntered into the salon at 11 o'clock on a Tuesday morning, plopped her backpack down on a chair, and said to the owner, Mrs. Lee, "I want a fill-in." Covering up new growth to match the existing color, a fill-in is to nails what dying the roots is to hair.

"Why you not in school?" Mrs. Lee asked, raising an eyebrow as she looked up from her task of removing caked-on nail polish from around the rims of the many small glass bottles littering her table, a chore that she reserved for these off-peak hours. "Don't get on my case," Sharina fired back. "I just want a fill-in, no advice, no Bible stuff, okay?" Mrs. Lee sighed, "Bible not stuff, Bible is God's word, lessons for good life." Sharina grabbed her backpack and lurched toward the front door. Mrs. Lee called out, "You come on, sit here." Sharina hesitated, still not sure whether she would stay or go. "Come on, come on," Mrs. Lee coaxed, motioning to the clean table next to her. Sharina reluctantly sat down, letting Mrs. Lee push back her cuticles and fill in her nails with a bright aqua polish.

As she finished, Mrs. Lee straightened up and looked Sharina in the eye. "OK, I make you deal. You no more skip school, I give you free service today." Sharina immediately protested, "I'm not skip—" but Mrs. Lee gave her a stern look and said, "Then ten dollar, please." Sharina looked torn but gave in, "OK, deal." Mrs. Lee smiled, and there was a moment of tenderness between them, as the teenage customer accepted this awkwardly negotiated gift, even with strings attached. "But for real, no more talking about Jesus," Sharina jabbed, determined to have the last word. Later, when I asked Mrs. Lee about her relationship with this endearing but difficult young customer, she said, "She's very smart, but gets in lots of trouble, family is no good." Mrs. Lee said she had known

Sharina since she was a child, when she would come into the salon with her mother, but they now appeared to be estranged and Sharina was living with her grandmother.

Service interactions between Mrs. Lee and Sharina demonstrate a different kind of body labor than that exhibited in upscale nail spas serving mostly white middle-class and upper-class women. Rather than focusing on pampering and attentiveness, nail art salons like Downtown Nails focus more on creating distinctive nail designs and expressing respect and caring, not only for individual customers but for the communities in which they operate. Both Mrs. Lee and her husband and co-owner, Mr. Lee, expressed respect and appreciation, albeit tinged with missionary zeal, toward their black customers, and their customers responded in kind. In its overwhelmingly positive customer relations, Downtown Nails was admittedly an outlier among Asian-owned salons located in black working-class neighborhoods. Nonetheless, it illuminated processes that lead to both smoother customer interactions and disruptions of negative racial stereotypes.

Downtown Nails enjoyed a steady customer volume with many purchases of expensive and intricate sets of services. Much of the salon's business did not come from regular manicures and pedicures but from extensions, tips, fillings, and both airbrushed and hand-painted designs. Indeed, several nail technicians, who were more likely to be referred to as "nail artists" than as manicurists, had acquired a strong base of regular customers. On a Saturday afternoon Downtown Nails was filled to capacity, and the wait for a preferred nail artist could be more than an hour. The customers engaged in animated conversations while sharing coco bread and bulla cakes from the downstairs bakery. The banter ranged from vivid accounts of a recent mugging near the salon to news about a pay freeze at the nearby hospital where some of the women were employed. The noise level in the salon was usually high, as various electronic nail sculpting tools created a constant buzz to match the flow of lively conversations among the mostly black customers, who included native-born African American women and Caribbean and African immigrants.

In addition to ethnic diversity, the customers at Downtown Nails spanned a range in socioeconomic status, but most were working- to

lower-middle class. The term *working-class,* however, deserves some qualification. Many of these customers were employed or underemployed
in low-wage unstable jobs, but at the same time they occupied a higher
class position relative to other residents in the neighborhood. In addition,
they may or may not have identified themselves as working class, as they
often aspired to middle-class status.[8] Workers in these salons differed
from those in more upscale locales as they tended to be recently arrived
immigrants from more working-class backgrounds with less English-
language fluency. They also were more likely to be working without legal
immigration status or licenses, although, as I discussed in Chapter 2, the
actual number that fall into this category is difficult to ascertain. The salon
also employed several Latina and African immigrant women.

The case of Downtown Nails is instructive because one of the co-
owners was a man. Even so, the setting remained a feminized space, as
men in the salon adjusted to and maintained a woman-centered establishment. The owners, Mr. and Mrs. Lee, a married couple, emigrated in the
1980s to pursue better educational opportunities for their children. They
came from a rural province in South Korea, where they both worked as
schoolteachers. Two years after they arrived in the United States, they
opened Downtown Nails in this location because the rent was affordable,
the customer base was strong, and they lived in a nearby neighborhood.
In 1992 they decided to open another salon on Long Island that Mrs. Lee
operated while Mr. Lee continued to manage the Brooklyn salon. Mr. Lee,
who was an artist and art teacher in South Korea, attracted many customers who traveled out of their way, a few from as far away as New Jersey,
to receive his special hand-painted floral, animal, and geometric designs.

After maintaining both salons for several years, the couple decided to
sell the Long Island salon, and Mrs. Lee returned to work at their original salon in Brooklyn. Unlike many Korean women, who want to leave
black neighborhoods as quickly as possible for employment in more suburban settings, Mrs. Lee had reversed this process, explaining that she
preferred the clientele at Downtown Nails:

> Working in the white neighborhood didn't match my personality. I don't deal
> well with picky customers. . . . In the black neighborhood, it's more relaxed.
> They don't leave tips but they don't expect so much service, either. . . . [On

Long Island] they want you to go slow and spend time with them. Here I just concentrate on doing a good job and working quickly. . . . It's a kind of art, and I get to use my talents. At first, I couldn't understand why they would want to wear such things on their nails. But now I understand it's their taste so I like doing designs that they like. . . . Most other people want to leave this neighborhood and move out to Long Island or New Jersey. But we are proud that we understand blacks and are able to get along with them. They are good people and they support us. . . . Having come here as immigrants, we know that Americans look down on minorities.

In explaining why she prefers working at Downtown Nails, Mrs. Lee demonstrates a complex service ethic toward her predominantly black customers. She both enjoyed her ability to please her customers and gained a sense of fulfillment from creating artistic nails. Furthermore, she identified with her customers as racial minorities and prided herself on positive intergroup relations. Compared with her experience in serving mostly white middle-class women at the Long Island salon, here Mrs. Lee invested less energy in being deferential, allowing for a more genuine affinity with her customers and less burnout.

The owners of Downtown Nails demonstrated an investment in this neighborhood, as they had chosen not to leave the area even though their economic circumstances had given them the choice. They expressed pride in their ability to create nail art, their understanding of the people in this Brooklyn neighborhood, and their ability to maintain positive customer relations. This salon was not necessarily representative of other salons in black neighborhoods nor was it simply an anomaly arising from the actions of extraordinary individuals. Instead, this case demonstrates how certain kinds of interactions emerge as the result of the interplay between social conditions and the ways that individuals respond to them. The mostly positive interactions at Downtown Nails do not signify a simplistic or universal valuing of gender commonalities over racial differences. Instead, relations at this salon demonstrate a situational emphasis on gendered service provision. In particular, the performance of expressive body labor, which prioritizes nails as a form of artistic expression while also expressing respect for the community, fosters more amiable, less racially charged relations between black customers and Korean service providers at this site.

DIMENSIONS OF EXPRESSIVE BODY LABOR

Jade Kim, a Korean nail artist at Downtown Nails, wore a thick cotton mask and plastic gloves as she wielded an electric filer and airbrush gun to create the long thick sculptured nails and elaborate designs that had won her a loyal following. Customers entering the salon were greeted with the acrid aroma of acrylic glue, but most seemed accustomed and resigned to the fumes and nail dust. Mrs. Lee, the owner, waved at customers she recognized and motioned them to sit and wait or to peruse the display of nail tips with airbrushed designs.

Regular customers made their way over to a shelf to find the plastic bags with their names scribbled in black marker that held disposable utensils that they could purchase for $4 and reuse on each visit. Absent were the elaborate sanitizing machines and solutions, let alone the soft pampering touches of nail spas. Instead, customers bore much of the responsibility for maintaining sanitation and avoiding infections, as well as for managing their own feelings with regard to the service or lack thereof.

A far cry from the spalike pampering experience of Uptown or Exclusive Nails, a nail job at Downtown Nails was closer to a stint on a factory assembly line—highly mechanized and potentially toxic. Workers often donned cotton masks and latex gloves as they wielded electric filers or applied acrylics. Despite these appearances, expressive body labor at Downtown Nails involved a complex mix of physical and emotional labor that accommodated customers' desires to express a unique sense of self through their nail designs and their expectations that service providers demonstrate respect toward both individuals and the community they served. The conversation, massages, and other services that nail spa customers value highly were regarded as extraneous by nail art customers. What mattered most here were the appearance and durability of the nails themselves. Alia, a twenty-two-year-old African American cashier, underscored the importance of original designs as the main factor drawing her to this salon: "They do it with their own hand—it comes from their own mind, their own creativity. So yeah, sure. I'll pay an extra ten bucks for that instead of having some that would look like anyone's nails. I like to have silver a lot, and I do fire lines—fire, like I'm hot [laughs]. I've gotten checkerboards, flowers, butterflies, characters

. . . like Mickey Mouse. I've gotten my name a lot. And rhinestones, yeah, I've done rhinestones, too." To meet the expectations of customers like Alia, body labor at Downtown Nails called for developing expertise in sculpting and painting original nail designs rather than in the soothing, pampering services offered at Uptown and Exclusive Nails. Thus the physical demands of body labor were not less but simply of a different type.

Similarly, the emotional dimensions of body labor at Downtown Nails were not different in degree so much as in kind. Black customers' expectations of emotional attentiveness are much lower than those of the white middle-class women at nail spas. Despite the lack of pampering, Serena, an African American grocery store cashier, assessed the emotional labor at Downtown Nails positively. "It's very good, I'm satisfied with it. They really just do the nails, no massages. That's fine with me," she told me. "I just go in with my Walkman and listen to some good music and maybe just have a little basic conversation." Customers at Downtown Nails were rarely on a first-name basis with the service providers, except perhaps the owners, and their preference for a particular nail artist depended more on her technical skills than her emotional attentiveness. Serena elaborated: "There are a few people I like, and I go to whoever's open, but I'll stay away from certain people. I know they're not good 'cause I hear other people complain—I see someone come back and say that their nail cracked the next day, or I see someone get nicked with a filer. . . . No, it's not because they're rude or anything, it's because I know they don't do a good job. . . . Just like some people just can't do hair, some people just can't do nails." Of her relations with her current manicurist, she said, "I feel comfortable with her, but it's more that she does an excellent job. If a wrap cracks or looks funny or I lose a nail, I'm not going back to her, no matter how nice she is." Other black customers at different salons expressed similar sentiments and reasoning, as an African American customer at a salon in Harlem said:

> This is Harlem, it's mostly minorities living here, and people don't really think about massages. I don't really care for it—I'm like, "Yeah, I'll take it if they do it." I don't feel bad about it because they charge for it, and I don't want to pay extra for a massage. I guess if I really thought about it, I would say it isn't right, they shouldn't do that [provide less service than

at other salons]. But that's what the customers here want. Women up here pay $45 for a full set with artwork, so all they care about is how it looks.

These customers associated emotional pampering in the form of conversation and physical touches such as massage as "extras" rather than intrinsic parts of the service, and they would rather forgo than pay for them. Furthermore, the kinds of nails they purchased—long and sculptured with elaborate designs—required artistic skills rather than emotional labor.

Customers at Downtown Nails focused more on demonstrations of respect and fairness that recognize the complex dynamics of Korean businesses operating in black neighborhoods. Mr. and Mrs. Lee responded to these expectations by thanking customers for their patronage, participating in community events, displaying Afrocentric designs, and playing R&B and rap music on the sound system. They allowed regular customers to run an informal tab when they were short of money. The Lees also maintained a change jar that customers dipped into for bus fare or other incidentals. It was not uncommon for customers to drop by, even when they were not getting their nails done, to use the bathroom or leave shopping bags behind the front desk while they ran errands.

These efforts at "giving back to the community" entail a distinct form of body labor that conforms to black working-class women's concerns with respect and fairness, in contrast to white middle-class women's feeling rules of privilege and pampering. Through these practices black customers reframe the Lees and their business, not as sucking resources out of the black community but as making a former luxury service both more accessible and more attuned to the needs of black women. One particular practice, a Christmas Eve party that the Lees sponsored annually at the salon, illuminates the expressive body labor practices that foster positive customer relations.

GIVING BACK TO THE COMMUNITY

Doing a heavily accented Santa Claus impersonation, Vera, a sixty-nine-year-old Trinidadian grandmother with shopping bags and two children in tow, blustered into the salon. "M-e-e-e-r-r-r-ry Christmas, Mr. Lee. I brought my grandchildren again to the party. I told my boys—no McDonald's today—today's on Mr. Lee. We been giving him our money all year long—now today's on Mr. Lee." She placed her hands on her hips and glanced around the salon, "Now, I asked for a car this year, Mr. Lee—where is it?"

Mr. Lee held up his hands, empty except for the airbrush gun that he was using to create an elaborate design on an adolescent client. "Sorry, no money, no honey," he muttered through his cotton mask. Vera, one of the oldest and most regular customers at the salon, scowled in mock anger, "You just lucky I didn't bring my five others, we'd eat you out of house and home!" The women seated at the manicure tables looked up and smiled. "Mommy, quit fussing and come over and feed your children," one customer chided. Mrs. Lee seemed mildly amused but did not break her concentration as she performed an elaborate full set. She pointed with her chin toward a folding table, "Lots of food over there." The modest spread for the eighth annual Christmas Eve party consisted of fried chicken, macaroni salad, and French fries, supplemented by West Indian pastries from the downstairs bakery.

This party loomed large in the minds of Downtown Nails' customers, who cited it as evidence that this salon was not merely making money but was giving something back to the community. Yvonne, a forty-two-year-old Jamaican customer and county government employee, said, "The only problem I have is that they [Koreans in this neighborhood] don't contribute to charity. Sometimes I've seen people canvassing for the homeless or some community project, and they outright refuse to pay any attention. If you are in a community, you should feel a part of it, and giving back a little is not too much to ask. Even this is showing appreciation [lifting up plate of fried chicken and potato salad]: it's a little gesture that makes the customer feel good." Other customers, both West Indian and African Americans, shared Yvonne's appreciation for the Christmas Eve party as a "little gesture" to the community.

How the salon came to host this party highlights several interacting forces—the owners' economic interests, the agency of customers, and the influence of events in the community, particularly a well-publicized boycott of a Korean-owned grocery store in a nearby neighborhood. Vera boasted only half-jokingly that she saved the nail salon by giving Mr. Lee the idea of holding the Christmas Eve party. "I taught him everything he knows—this place would be a mess without me, isn't that right, Mr. Lee?" Indeed, Mr. Lee conceded that at first he was not in favor of holding a party, but he was eventually swayed through repeated interactions with Vera and other customers, who convinced him that it would be an appropriate show of appreciation as well as a wise business decision.

> One day some of the customers just said to me, "Mr. Lee, we want you to have a party for us." I just laughed and thought they were joking, but they kept saying, "Let's do it, let's do it." It was three or four of the regular customers, and they started getting a little angry when I said no. So I thought about it and decided it would be a nice thing. There is a tradition in Korean businesses [in Korea] to give out calendars or some other small gift, but we never did that here in America. In the beginning we did a lot of work—we cooked Korean food ourselves, and some of the workers and customers brought in some side dishes. We tried to make it like a Korean-style party. . . . [The customers] didn't really like our food so much, so I asked them and they said they would rather have their own American-style food. So we started just ordering fried chicken, potato salad, chips, that kind of food—it made it much easier. But then some customers from the islands didn't seem so happy so we brought some of the cakes up from the Jamaican bakery.

> *Were you influenced to hold the party by the boycott of Korean grocery stores?*
> I was never affected by the boycott; business didn't slow down at all during that time. . . . At first, I just didn't pay much attention to customer relations because I was the only salon in this neighborhood. Then a lot more started opening up, other Koreans and then Vietnamese. Now many Koreans have moved out of the neighborhood, but the competition with Vietnamese is really fierce—because they are poorer, they work harder and charge less.

Mr. Lee's initial decision to host the party was thus largely driven by economic concerns, especially the threat of increasing competition in the neighborhood. However, close relations between him and his customers, built around the processes of intimate body labor, gave him the insight and incentive to adopt the kind of conciliatory business practices that other Korean establishments have been less successful in implementing.

Furthermore, despite Mr. Lee's insistence that he was not swayed by boycotts of other Korean-owned businesses, customers and Mrs. Lee attested otherwise. Interestingly, and not coincidentally, the Lees started hosting the party in 1990, the year of the boycott of the Korean-owned Red Apple market in Brooklyn. While Mr. Lee said that he was not affected by the boycott, Mrs. Lee disagreed: "We used to drive by that way, but once someone threw something at our windshield when they saw that we were Korean, so we started driving around a different way to get to the salon. It did feel tense for a long time, but we really didn't have any problems inside the salon." Mrs. Lee saw the boycott of other Korean-owned businesses as creating an atmosphere of tension, although outside rather than inside the salon.

Even in the midst of one of the most pivotal and highly publicized conflicts between blacks and Koreans, relations within the Lees' salons remained mostly cordial. Why was that the case? The holding of the Christmas Eve party suggests a certain openness to communicate and work out differences, an attitude that may have been fostered by the kind of services offered in the salon. Instead of framing instances of unsatisfactory service as examples of "black-Korean conflict," the customers focused on specific practices at this salon, such as "Mr. Lee was always rushing through the job." Any complaints referred to Mr. Lee's gender rather than his Korean ethnicity. Despite his presence, Downtown Nails remained a feminized space, as he mostly conformed to the norms of a woman-centered establishment in his demeanor and actions. In contrast, Korean men in other small businesses such as grocery stores often enact hypermasculine gender performances, donning army fatigues, baseball caps, and sweatshirts with sports team logos while barking out orders to employees and surveying the activities of customers. Mr. Lee, on the other hand, adjusted to a role of providing women-centered beauty services. As Yvonne noted, "Even though Mr. Lee is the boss, he doesn't act like he can get away with doing whatever he wants."

Mr. Lee now meets these expectations for gendered service most of the time but only after a difficult period of adjustment to his role as a beauty service provider. Many customers used to complain about his excessive roughness. Rather than attributing this roughness to his ethnicity and

Figure 14. Even when the owner is a man, salons remain women-dominated spaces, as this crowded waiting room shows. A woman gets an eyebrow waxing while the Korean owner helps a customer with her shoes and customers wait and visit with each other.

generalizing his behavior to all Koreans, the anomalous position of Mr. Lee as a man in a profession dominated by women served as an alternative explanation. Gender thus disrupted racial explanations of unsatisfactory service.

Customers' comments suggest that the nature of service relations in the salon enabled both customers and the proprietor to frame their differences in gender terms rather than adopting more antagonistic positions based on collective racial identities. The practices of expressive body labor at Downtown Nails thus ameliorated tensions that arose in the salon, instead of escalating them into protests against not only the offending Korean store but also all Korean-owned businesses in black communities. Their history of generally positive interactions at Downtown Nails motivated customers to try to smooth over relations, and the setting of the salon allowed these negotiations to take place. The frequency and intensity of interactions enable the customers to articulate specific complaints regarding the quality of service. Customers also did not generalize from their experience of impolite treatment by one Korean-owned nail salon to include all such establishments. In contrast with the distinct ethnic identification of the grocery stores that were often generically referred to as "Korean markets," the nail salons were not automatically characterized according to a racialized marker. While nearly all customers were aware that many grocery stores are owned by Koreans, most did not know or seem to care about the ethnicity of the owners and staff of the nail salons. As I noted earlier, the customers tend to lump salon personnel in one generic racial category of "Asian" or "Oriental" or they extend the ethnic category of "Chinese" to include all Asians. For most black patrons of nail salons, receiving respectful, skillful service that fulfills their standards of feminine beauty is more important than the race or ethnicity of the proprietors.

Why would the customers and store owner be able to negotiate and implement a conciliatory practice such as the Christmas Eve party in a nail salon but not in other businesses, such as grocery stores? The greater physical and emotional intimacy expressed through body labor enables the owner and the customer to respond to complaints with concrete measures to improve customer service and appreciation. Other specific practices that highlight contingent expressions of gender commonalities over racial differences emerge in regard to the regular policing of customers in some retail establishments. Jolene, a young African American customer at Downtown Nails, commented, "As a purchaser, I would rather go to a black-owned store—partly because I believe in supporting black-owned stores, but I think mainly because I'm treated better, none of that staring thing. In the salons you don't have that going on—I can't steal a manicure [laughter]." By joking that she can't steal a manicure, Jolene identified a crucial difference in nail salons versus other Korean-owned businesses. Simply put, nail salons sell services, not material goods, and the practices that stem from these distinct business operations highlight gender ties as opposed to racial differences.

Whereas interactions between proprietors and customers in retail businesses are often brusque and fleeting, expressive body labor spawns prolonged and often intimate exchanges. Furthermore, customers in establishments such as grocery stores are purchasing essentials rather than luxury items such as manicures, a difference that heightens the stakes of these negotiations. As Mrs. Cho, who operated a Korean-owned grocery store in the vicinity of Downtown Nails, said, "In the nail salons, if you have trouble, you can just fix it—you just paint it again. In the grocery store there is no proof if they are stealing or cheating you. . . . There are so many people coming and going, you never get to know the customers." That this Korean grocery store owner was a woman yet still experienced tensions with her black customers dispels the notion that women are naturally better at customer service and again highlights the specific gendered services offered in nail salons as enabling more amiable relations between women. In addition to the suspicion created by the need to guard against theft, the lack of opportunities for more sustained intimate contact with the customers in the grocery stores contributes to the potential outbreak of hostilities. Instead, in nail salons expressive body labor paves the way for more cordial and meaningful exchanges that have the potential to counter racial prejudices with gender affinities.

Rather than simply reflecting the values or personalities of Mr. and Mrs. Lee, measures such as the Christmas party evolve out of the culture of expressive body labor and the kind of relations forged within it. Several factors shape this more amiable context, including creation of a feminized space that excludes most men and downplays the masculinity of those who are present, and absence of items to steal, which reduces objectionable policing practices.

BLOW-UPS: WHEN RACE TRUMPS GENDER

While the expressive style of body labor and the larger social conditions that shape its performance can foster congenial relations, disagreements do arise, at times resulting in heated exchanges. For example, an interaction turned unpleasant when a customer protested to Mrs. Lee that she had acrylic tips attached just two days earlier and they had already fallen off. Mrs. Lee asked in Korean, "Who did this woman's nails?" and a nail technician responded, also in Korean, "I did them, but it was over a week ago. She must have broken them herself." The customer eyed them suspiciously, sensing that she was the subject of their conversation. Mrs. Lee then turned to the customer and said, "Not two days, one week. You pay again," and refused to redo the nails for free. The customer erupted, "You gonna rip me off. Why don't you all go back to Chinatown!" She then verbalized a string of nonsensical sounds imitating a Korean accent and stormed out of the salon.

Thus even Mrs. Lee, who sustained overwhelmingly cordial relations with her customers, could become embroiled in conflicts that quickly were framed in racial terms on both sides. Despite numerous positive interactions between Mrs. Lee and her customers, in the heat of the moment this history disappeared as customers invoked racial epithets to express anger at everything from getting cut to not getting a favored nail artist or not receiving desired services to perceiving themselves as the object of unflattering conversations in Korean. Whatever Mrs. Lee's attempts at trying to smooth over these blow-ups, the result was often the reinforcement of a polarized racial discourse. Nonetheless, these conflicts arose not because of fixed racial animosities but because of the fluid ways that service interactions become imbued with racial meanings.

While in the last example Mrs. Lee did not reciprocate with similarly charged racial language, in other instances I observed owners or nail techs shouting back in kind and escalating the conflict. Jamilla described such a scene.

It's kind of a Catch-22. Some customers feel like they're getting disrespected if you don't refer back to them or if you're having a side conversation. Then the Koreans get upset and think African Americans have an attitude, which then makes them talk more about us. You see, in the African American community, you can't outright say anything you want to say because we always have our guard up. We get it all the time, from the cops or whoever. I've seen it in the Hispanic community too—this thing about honor and respect—"Don't disrespect me just because I'm black or Hispanic. What I say does count."

Similarly, Serena described a scene that illustrates how failed exchanges of expressive body labor can quickly erupt into shouting matches that take on not only racial but also anti-immigrant overtones: "I've seen some customers really go off on them, 'You're not in your country, speak English!'" Thus botched service interactions between blacks and Koreans can feed racial animosity and fuel generalized antipathy toward immigrants.

Gender solidarity is highly situational and easily disrupted, not just between service providers and customers but among black customers. Furthermore, the tensions among customers can rebound onto Korean service providers and threaten the tentative ties of gender solidarity. Tensions between African American and Jamaican immigrant women at Downtown Nails show how allegiances based on race and gender or even socioeconomic status cannot be taken for granted but instead converge or diverge based on the contexts of these interactions.

For many years an African American enclave, the Brooklyn neighborhood surrounding Downtown Nails has seen its demographics shift dramatically with large numbers of new immigrants from the Caribbean, whom the salon customers perceived and referred to as "Jamaican." Relations within the salon reflected these changes in the neighborhood, as long-term African American residents complained about newer black immigrants, whom the long-time residents viewed, correctly or not, as complicit in neighborhood drug trafficking. Della, a middle-aged African American customer, described her perception of the Caribbean women who frequented Downtown Nails: "I can't stand when the girlfriends of those Jamaican drug lords come in here full of attitude. . . . What drives me crazy is when they come in, no matter how long you've been waiting, the Koreans take them first. They'll even fight over them because they give big tips. They'll just ignore other customers who've been waiting." Consistent with Della's comments, I observed several young women with strong West Indian accents come into the salon together and watched as Mrs. Lee, the owner of the salon, quickly attended to them. However, while Della attributed Mrs. Lee's motivation to a desire to earn more tips, Mrs. Lee offered a different perspective. "I don't want no trouble," she explained. "If they come, I take care of them first so they not anger, cause trouble." Thus she actually shared the African American

customers' perceptions of the Jamaican women as potential troublemak-
ers. Contrary to Della's perception, she attended to them first to move
them quickly out of the salon, not to earn more tips. However, customers
saw her preferential treatment of the Jamaican women not as an effort to
create a safer and more comfortable salon space but as motivated simply by profit. Despite the mostly positive relations between Mrs. Lee
and her customers, even a loyal and long-term customer like Della was
quick to frame perceived unfair salon practices through the discourse
of exploitation of black customers by Korean businesses. Whether Mrs.
Lee's actions were justifiable or not, any dissatisfaction with her business
practices quickly referenced this framework of exploitation.

Throughout this book I have critiqued the ideology that nail salons,
and beauty salons more broadly, function as women's community centers.
Here I have shown how this ideology falsely presumes a shared culture
even among customers of a single racial group. Instead, relations among
black customers often reflect differences based on class, occupational status, ethnicity, nativity, and age. These tensions challenge the totalizing
conclusion that gender trumps race in these establishments and once again
underscores the fluid and unpredictable forging of intersectional ties.

Overall, such blowups, while unpleasant, were infrequent at Downtown Nails, but they occurred on a daily basis at Artistic Nails. What
accounts for the differences in relations at these two nail art salons, as
they provided comparable services to a similar customer base?

ARTISTIC NAILS: THE FAILURES OF EXPRESSIVE BODY LABOR

Goldie Chun, the owner of Artistic Nails, leaned against the front door-
way, drinking a Snapple and fanning herself with a dog-eared copy of
Essence magazine. Business was slow, as the summer heat made her
unair-conditioned salon uncomfortably close. The door of the salon was
propped open, and a group of teenage girls in belly-baring tops and low-
rise jeans had congregated in front, talking and laughing, some smoking, others talking on cell phones. Goldie called out to them—"You want

manicure?" The girls consulted with each other, then shook their heads at her. Goldie responded, "Then you move away my store, too much smoking and loud!" One girl imitated Goldie with a heavy accent—"You too much smoking and loud!" They all looked at each other and laughed; one flicked a cigarette butt in her direction. Goldie shouted, "You get away or I call security!" They bristled and moved away. When I asked Goldie how often she experienced such interactions with her customers, she said, "Everyday! Ten times a day!"

Unlike Mrs. Lee, who chose to leave Long Island and preferred to work with black customers, Goldie disparaged the salon, the kind of services it offered, and the clientele it served. Goldie believed that she was pushed out of her previous location on Long Island by competition and had to move to a different locale and type of nail salon for economic survival. Now in her second year of ownership at Artistic Nails, Goldie relayed a vivid, humorous, and at times ugly account of her hard adjustment to this low-income black neighborhood:

> I could not handle everything. This is a big shop. There are over a hundred people in and out everyday. This is my second year at this shop. First year was so busy. Sixteen people worked nonstop. I opened at 9 A.M., and closed at 7:30 P.M. I took over this place at the end of May. Black people in summer time, from twelve-year-old kid to seventy-year-old lady, wanted to get a pedicure. Now, because of bad economy and 9/11, it got worse but, still, it is better than the other place in Long Island. . . . The white people do different style. For example, they never use the acrylics, but in this store about 90 percent is acrylic. Another different thing is workers. They are all Spanish. If the white people don't like the job and they don't like the shop, they don't come. They never say anything. They don't complain too much. But black people, no. They try not to pay. They try to steal it. They steal not only polish, even tools from the girls. . . . I put the sign "No Eating, No Pets," but it does not matter. They eat. The Long Island white people whenever they need manicure, they only come by themselves. These people, if mommy want to get a manicure, all the family come. Totally different. Eating and in and out, I cannot close the door. . . . The most difficult thing is that the black people do not want to pay. They want to pay less money. They are picky. It's not for the job. They try to pay less money. That's hard. . . . Black people, after fighting, the next time they walk in [as if] nothing happened before. That's the problem. Now, I guess,

so much [I] got used to it [and I am] so close to them now. At the beginning time, [I thought], "Oh, my god. These people are not human." Inside
myself, I talked to myself: "Now I understand why the white people dis-
criminate these people. They are not human." . . . I had such a hard time.
Now I know how to handle that.

Goldie was apologetic and poked fun at her prejudices toward blacks.
She had made a great effort to overcome these prejudices and improve
relations in the salon but to limited avail. While her efforts may have
been genuine, they were also idiosyncratic—small gestures such as giving candy to children—rather than integrating ongoing practices into the
everyday running of the salon or even once-a-year efforts such as the
Lees' Christmas Eve party at Downtown Nails. While Artistic Nails did
meet the demands of customers for creative designs and skillful sculpting of acrylic nails, on the emotional side it did not conform to expectations for respectfulness and community engagement.

Despite the many altercations in her salon, Goldie prided herself on
her relations with her customers and her ability to handle conflicts, and
even to assist other salon owners with theirs, and her self-congratulations
were not completely deluded. I witnessed numerous playful exchanges
between her and her customers. One day a customer came in and showed
off her new handbag to Goldie, who grabbed it and pretended it was
hers—"You like my new bag?" Goldie asked, striking a pose. Another
customer let out a low whistle, "You show it off, girl!" Goldie then sauntered down the aisle, as if it were a catwalk, swinging her hips and the
bag to the hoots and hollers of her customers. While these intermittent
exchanges may have helped to create momentary good feelings, they
did not add up to consistent measures that conveyed appreciation to
individual customers, let alone to the community that the salon served.
Instead, Goldie's approach to customer relations was often combative
and legalistic, as she explained:

Most of my clients say that I am different from other Korean nail salon
owners and I seem to be a more Americanized person because I can talk to
them. For example, the guy who owns the other salon, he does not speak
English at all. He got the salon five days after he got here [from Korea].

He just stays there and his aunt works there. I heard that there are a lot of problems, a lot of lawsuits. At first he did not know how to deal with them [black customers], so he just gave money to them and did whatever they asked. So I told him not to do that and to call me whenever he had a problem. Once, one lady sued him for breaking her pinky toe. Because she is too fat, she somehow broke her toe when she stepped down. I went and told her that the chair was inspected a few days ago and asked her for legal evidence. Then she did not come back.

While Goldie clearly demonstrated disdainful approaches to dealing with her clientele, at the same time her conflicts with her customers at Artistic Nails were not attributable solely to her personality or prejudices. Her interpersonal skills and cultural awareness left much to be desired, but other social factors beyond her control contributed to the tensions in her salon and her inability to smooth them over through practices of expressive body labor.

Although Downtown Nails and Artistic Nails served similar clienteles, these salons occupied different kinds of structural positions in the settings in which they were located. Downtown Nails had become a fixture in a neighborhood that maintained many other long-standing ethnic small businesses and thus a strong sense of community. Furthermore, its semiprivate second-story location allowed for more personal interactions and the development of sustained relationships involving many regular customers and a fairly stable employee pool. In contrast, Artistic Nails was one of many transient businesses that rented space in an anonymous outdoor strip mall. Its doors opened onto a plaza with heavy foot traffic that was controlled by both city police officers and private security guards hired by a largely absentee landlord. With nearly triple the number of manicure and pedicure stations, it was a much larger operation than the Lees' salon, and Goldie was hard pressed to stay on top of the high turnover in both customers and workers. In addition, because the salon sold nail polish and other products, the owner reproduced distasteful surveillance practices that other salons did not impose. Thus Goldie skipped many of the niceties of service provision and community outreach that Mrs. Lee, supported by her husband, extended to her customers at Downtown Nails.

The scenes that follow further demonstrate how structural conditions beyond the salons, in this case the mismanagement of the facilities by an absentee landlord, can result in misunderstandings that enforce mutually disparaging racial stereotypes between blacks and Koreans.

Three black women sat at pedicure stations, soaking their feet. As they exchanged small talk, the pedicurist, a petite Ecuadoran woman, jumped back and screamed, overturning her tray of instruments. The customers looked puzzled, then they too screamed and jumped up, their long skirts dipping into the soapy water and splattering it across the floor as they rushed to escape a large gray rat that was scurrying along the basin. The rat careened around the salon as Goldie chased it with a broom, shouting obscenities in Korean. Finally, it found the open front door and disappeared into the street.

The three customers, who had been huddling in a corner, burst out in laughter, hugging and reenacting the scene with impersonations of each other's frenzy. Jinny, the manager, walked over and barked orders to the pedicurist in Spanish to clean up the mess. She then told the customers they could sit back down and finish their pedicures. Her attempts to smooth things over, however, had the opposite effect, as the customers' joviality immediately morphed into irritation. "You need to keep this place cleaner. We could catch some disease from them rats," one customer complained. "Yeah, yeah, no problem, we disinfect," Jinny replied and walked away. Several hours later, after the salon had quieted down, Jinny brought the incident up with me as she started the end-of-day cleanup. "They think the rats come because we are cheap and don't want to keep the salon clean. It's not because of us, but the landlord doesn't pick up the trash often enough. He's a Jewish man, lives in Long Island, and never listens to us. I told him many times that the trash is stinking in summer and bringing bugs and rats, but he never listens." However, Jinny did not explain this problem with the landlord to the customers and appeared to dismiss their concerns, when in fact she shared them.

As Jinny was fluent in English and Spanish, the problem was not so much a lack of language ability but a lack of opportunity, and perhaps willingness to communicate, shaped by the lack of emphasis on attentive communication in the salon. Artistic Nails contrasted sharply with

Downtown Nails, where the proprietors consciously enacted expressive body labor practices that fostered close relations with customers. In contrast, the owner and manager at Artistic Nails neither engaged in a style of service provision that prioritized community building nor did the social context of the salon support such practices.

In short, Goldie's salon inadequately fulfilled the service ethos of expressive body labor, as evidenced in the skimping on hygienic and pampering procedures, the gruffness of emotional exchanges, the lack of shows of appreciation for customer patronage, and the suspicious treatment of customers as potential thieves. While Goldie was an easy target to blame for the difficult relations in her salon, and her abrasive personality and racial prejudices cannot be overlooked, other factors beyond her control contributed to the tensions with her customers. Structurally, the salon's location in a large strip mall did not encourage a more intimate women-only space and the accompanying intimacy that can foster strong gender ties. Furthermore, the individuals involved in these interactions were also less inclined or equipped to act upon the limited possibilities that did exist. Thus, in contrast to Downtown Nails, gender solidarity did not emerge at Artistic Nails and did not in turn act as a counterbalance to racial tensions in this salon.

The contrasting cases of Downtown and Artistic Nails reveal that gender can disrupt the dominant racial framework of black-Korean conflict but only in contingent spaces in which social actors concertedly undertake the work of rewriting this framework in meaningful ways. In other words, certain structural factors create possibilities for new kinds of relations between Koreans and blacks in nail salons, but it is up to individuals to capitalize on these opportunities to "manicure" new social ties. Gender—but not simply at the level of individual bodies or identities— makes a difference in how customer relations between Koreans and blacks are negotiated in the nail salons. Instead, gender mediates less racially charged relations between black customers and Korean entrepreneurs in nail salons through specific workplace practices and conditions associated with expressive body labor.

This analysis in no way suggests that black customers and Korean service providers in nail salons have more in common as women than they have differences as blacks and Koreans. The much-publicized case of Latasha Harlins, an African American teenage honor student who was fatally shot by Soon Ja Du, a Korean woman in a grocery store in Los Angeles, tragically disrupts essentialized notions of women as more nurturing and less volatile than men.[9] The case also eliminates a facile understanding that Korean women are innately better than Korean men at getting along with black women customers. Instead, it underscores the need to examine customer relations within the context of the kind of business, its practices, and the meanings given to those practices. Only within particular kinds of nail art salons, where priority is given to expressive body labor, are black and Korean women able to negotiate less hostile interracial relations.

CONCLUSION

Anticipating that some readers may oversimplify my arguments, a colleague who reviewed an early draft of this chapter asked, "So are you arguing that if more people got their nails done, we wouldn't have race riots?" I hope it is clear that my answer to this is no. No matter how positive the relations between Koreans and blacks within any given nail salon, these interactions can produce only literally cosmetic improvements with little or no impact on the structural conditions of urban poverty under which interracial tensions erupt into large-scale social unrest.

Nonetheless, if we take the manicure metaphorically as a process of layering and smoothing over face-to-face interactions, there may be something to be said for more people getting their nails done. While interracial conflicts result from systemic social problems, they erupt at the level of direct contact between individual members of different groups. The lens of body labor focuses us on what can go right or wrong in these moments of direct contact, not only within the circumscribed spaces of nail salons but in more generalized service encounters. The potential for misunderstandings and dissatisfaction remains high in service exchanges involving emotional and embodied dimensions across various social divisions. The same women who may temporarily reach across these boundaries and ally with each other when engaged in feminine beauty practices or when confronted with common threats, such as fear of crime, quickly drop this fragile sense of solidarity when service interactions go awry or once they leave these sites.

The specific practices that foster gender solidarity in nail art salons include efforts to "give back" to the communities in which they are located by demonstrating respect and appreciation for customers as well as abstaining from objectionable practices such as the policing of customers. While individual owners and managers decide how much to prioritize these efforts, they are also constrained by factors outside their salons. These factors include the racial and class configurations of the neighborhood, physical location of the salon, and degree to which the salon can be maintained as a women-centered space. Thus for women to sustain these fragile ties outside the salons, the larger social conditions that shape their lives outside the salons must also change.

Relations between women in nail art salons reveal that gender solidarity is not based solely on gender. Instead, black customers and Korean nail salon owners and technicians identify with each other as women and ignore differences based on race, ethnicity, class, and citizenship, *only* to the degree that their gender solidarity is supported by and makes sense in the context of a particular site. "Black-Korean conflict" may have largely disappeared from front-page headlines. However, the reality of racially distinct immigrant entrepreneurs who operate small businesses in poor underserved minority neighborhoods, persists as a formula for conflict that can disrupt women's tentative ties across their many differences.

Six

"You Could Get a Fungus"

ASIAN DISCOUNT NAIL SALONS
AS THE NEW YELLOW PERIL

Are the horror stories true? Holly Bonello, a nail technician . . . says of Asian salons: "I know of cases of families living in their salons. Many times they use each other's licenses. Their sanitation practices leave much to be desired, using the same drill bits and files without sanitizing them. . . . I have many clients who come to me to 'fix' problems caused by unsafe practices at these shops."

Suzette Hill, "The Asian Influence"

For the average consumer, opening a bottle of nail polish once every so often is a negligible risk. But for professionals exposed to them consistently, it can be a bigger problem.

Jeremy Caplan and Laura Fitzpatrick, "The Worst Jobs in America"

When they are the one waiting, they want everything to go fast, but as soon as they are the one getting a manicure, they want everyone to go slow.

Alice Nam, manicurist, Convenient Nails

Holly Bonello, the nail technician quoted by Suzette Hill in *Nails* magazine, articulates perceptions of Asian discount nail salons as cutting corners on hygiene and spreading infections and other diseases. Although the *Nails* article itself presents a balanced look at public health concerns, this particular technician frames these concerns in terms of negative stereotypes of Asian immigrants. In addition to describing Asians as living in squalor and neglecting sanitation practices in the workplace, her comments reveal denigrating characterizations of Asians as unclean, unskilled, and untrustworthy.

Rather than recognizing the multiple forces that collude in creating health risks, not just for customers but also for manicurists, certain customers transfer their anxieties and dissatisfaction with nail services to their individual manicurists and the racial groups to which they belong. In doing so these customers both overlook and contribute to the conditions that led *Time* magazine to name "nail salon worker" as one of the "worst jobs in America" in 2007.[1] As Grant Nakayama, an assistant enforcement administrator at the Environmental Protection Agency, said of Asian nail salon workers, "This is an unusual working population. . . . They work long hours. They might be women of childbearing age. They might bring children to the workplace. They may have less access to information about proper use because they might not be as fluent as the general population. These are all factors that go into a situation of creating needless exposure to chemicals."[2] Instead of focusing on these complex factors, which affect the health of both customers and workers, complaints about nail salons are framed in veiled racial terms that obscure the real sources of unsafe conditions. These include manufacturers' use of toxic chemicals, unfair labor practices, and pressures from owners and customers to keep prices low and to work quickly.

The term *chop shop* has emerged as derogatory shorthand for Asian discount nail salons. According to *Nailpro* magazine, the use of the term on Internet sites has "provoked racial insults and eventually sidetracked any meaningful conversation on the topic" of health and safety.[3] This term, along with comments like the nail technician's quoted earlier, resuscitate much older framings of Asian immigrants as the "yellow peril" who threaten to undermine U.S. society through physical contamination, inferior cultural practices, and economic competition. Interactions in discount nail salons reveal that such disparaging views of Asians persist, both despite and because of the ostensibly more favorable discourse of the Asian model minority. Contemporary debates about Asian nail salons as hotbeds of disease and violators of U.S. labor and living standards propagate "new yellow peril" stereotypes that are evocative of the anti-Asian sentiments that predominated more than a century ago. This chapter demonstrates both the resilience of the old yellow peril framework and the ways that it is rewritten in new sites such as nail salons.

As I explain in more detail later in this chapter, the "yellow peril" is a collection of racial stereotypes of Asians and Asian Americans as dirty, alien, evil, and bent on invading or undermining Western civilization. It began to flourish in the United States in the mid-1800s as white workers in California increasingly saw Chinese immigrants as economic threats. Eventually, such anti-Chinese and anti-Asian sentiment led to restrictive legislation, most notably the Chinese Exclusion Act of 1882, aimed at containing the perceived economic and cultural menace represented by Asians. Such depictions were applied to subsequent Asian immigrant groups such as the Japanese, Koreans, Filipinos, and Indians, and culminated after the Pearl Harbor attack with the internment of Japanese Americans. Contemporary examples of this yellow peril image of Asians and Asian Americans include continuing stereotypical portrayals in the mainstream media, the renewed linking of economic competition with racial hostility concerning China, and high-profile cases accusing Asian Americans of dangerous links with China, as in the spying allegations against the Los Alamos scientist Wen Ho Lee.[4]

This chapter explores how the discourse of the yellow peril emerges in new forms in Asian-owned nail salons through fears of physical contagion, cultural inferiority, and economic competition. Current discourses surrounding health risks in nail salons have deep historical roots in fears of Asian women as disease carriers. Although concerns have been voiced about nail salons in general, this chapter focuses on the particular ways that discussions of Asian-owned nail salons carry racial overtones and consequences for Asian Americans.

As I have throughout this book, I use the perspective of gendered work and body labor to illuminate the shifting racializations of Asian women within the U.S. service sector and the global service economy. Thus far I have argued that pampering body labor in upscale nail spas enforces the racial privilege of white middle- and upper-class women vis-à-vis their Asian manicurists. In contrast, at nail art salons serving black working-class women, the gendered processes of expressive body labor create an alternative form of identification that disrupts racial differences and inequalities, albeit temporarily. In this chapter I examine the dynamics of routinized body labor in discount nail salons serving a mixed racial and class clientele, arguing that the terms of generic gendered beauty exchanges divert attention from economic factors and onto the racial characteristics of Asians as the cause of unsatisfactory service. The consumer mentality that manicures should be fast and inexpensive drives down prices and services, creating undesirable conditions that then become associated with the Asian women who run the salons.

The McDonald's of the nail industry, discount nail salons, offer fast, inexpensive manicures and pedicures with no frills. However, no frills does not mean no work, as this form of service is not necessarily easier than that which prioritizes either pampering or artistic expression. Instead, it means that manicurists must work to counter negative stereotypes of Asians by providing adequate service under factory-like conditions for rock bottom prices. They have little time to pamper clients and instead concentrate on providing quick, safe manicures in contexts that are far from ideal.

These processes all hinge on service exchanges that target women's bodies and attend to their emotions in ways specific to race and class locations. This pattern of routinized body labor emerges in two salons—Crosstown Nails and Convenient Nails—that provide nondescript but reliable service aimed at a mass market. However, while nail technicians at discount nail salons strive to churn out standardized manicures and pedicures, they must attend to a range of customers who demand highly sensitive treatment of their bodies even when the price and conditions do not allow this. In other words, as the manicurist Alice Nam described at the beginning of this chapter, customers pay for routinized service but expect pampering. In this context even the most diligent manicurists' individual efforts cannot offset structural forces that make for fraught customer interactions.

Whereas in other chapters I have focused mainly on individual interactions and everyday acts of resistance in body labor exchanges, in this chapter I also address media representation and collective mobilization regarding occupational health, toxic products, and labor rights issues. Various community and labor rights organization are making headway in efforts to upgrade nail salon work, products, and health and safety protections, but the embodied and emotional dynamics of routinized body labor pose obstacles to raising workplace standards in nail salons.

GENDER, BODIES, AND THE NEW YELLOW PERIL

Why do successive waves of Asian immigrants continue to draw animosity from the U.S. mainstream based on fears of physical contamination, cultural pollution, and economic threat? What does the contemporaneous rhetoric of Asian Americans as both pollutant and model minority reveal about the tenuous position of this group in U.S. racial politics? How do gendered beliefs about Asian women fuel this rhetoric of invasion by a yellow menace? How can the perspective of body labor illuminate relations between women and their racial subtexts? This chapter demonstrates both the resilience of old yellow peril racial frameworks and the ways that they reemerge in new gendered worksites, such as nail salons.

The motif of Asians as the yellow peril stems from contradictory visions of the United States as an open democratic society but one firmly rooted in European culture and racial whiteness. Born of medieval European fears of Mongolian invasions, the concept of the yellow peril was transplanted and applied to the influx of Asian laborers to the United States in the late nineteenth century.[5] Anti-Asian sentiments culminated in a series of exclusion laws, most notably the Chinese Exclusion Act of 1882, and remained in place in some form until the Immigration Reform Act of 1965. Fueled by such popular images as the villainous Fu Manchu, the effete Charlie Chan, menacing propaganda posters targeting the Japanese during World War II, and virulently anti-Asian cartoons and editorials printed by the powerful Hearst publishing conglomerate, these depictions of Asian immigrants as dangerous pollutants stuck in the popular imagination, and Asian American communities have often suffered as a result.[6]

The doctrine of the yellow peril consistently invokes the alien body as the specter through which heathen invasions creep into and undermine more advanced civilizations. Nayan Shah, in his book *Contagious*

Divides: Epidemics and Race in San Francisco's Chinatown, documents historical depictions of Asian bodies as dangerous and impure. He writes, "For Chinese Americans, the journey from menace to model minority followed a deep undercurrent of ideas about citizenship, conduct and health. . . . At the turn of the century, 'health' and 'cleanliness' were embraced as integral aspects of American identity; and those who were perceived to be 'unhealthy,' such as Chinese men and women, were considered dangerous and inadmissible to the American nation.'"[7] While these representations focus on Chinese immigrants, they have repercussions for all Asian Americans. Similarly, contemporary yellow peril representations have emerged with a particularly pointed focus on physical contamination from China and Chinese immigrants, but this discourse spills over onto other Asian countries and Asian American groups.[8] Similar displacements in the past have targeted Asian Americans as a group when economic competition or military conflicts have arisen with North Korea, Vietnam, and Japan.[9] Thus the yellow peril motif may emerge around a particular Asian nation or ethnic group, but it is applied indiscriminately to all Asians.[10]

Rather than a linear progression from yellow peril to model minority, these two discourses have evolved as two sides of the same coin. On the one hand, Asian Americans earn praise for their hard work and entrepreneurship, as long as they are willing to assimilate into circumscribed economic and cultural roles. On the other hand, they draw condemnation when they are perceived as inadequately or unsafely fulfilling these roles, when they refuse to acquiesce to subordinated positions, or when they fulfill them too well and become an economic threat. Thus, as Gary Okihiro argues, "the concepts of the yellow peril and the model minority, although at apparent disjunction, form a seamless continuum."[11] These multiple forces coalesce as ambivalence toward Asia, Asian Americans, and Asian products, both material and cultural forms.

Bodily contamination discourses have emerged as a central element that drives the pendulum shifts from model minority to yellow peril. Allegations of Asian immigrants' threats to public health and decency have been invoked as political responses to economic competition. When the already uncertain welcome that has been extended to them is worn thin by economic competition, Asian immigrants become subject to a number of accusations related to physical and cultural pollution.[12]

How are both old and new yellow peril discourses shaped by gender? The body, and fears of contagion and contamination surrounding it, has served as the foundation of gendered recrimination of Asians as deviant and dangerous. Shah's research and other studies highlight how the racial journey from menace to model citizens involves conformity to mainstream standards of hygiene and sanitation as well as to the gender and sexual norms of white middle-class heterosexual marriage and domesticity. As a result of exclusionary laws, unstable employment premised on frequent migration and low wages, and virulent anti-Asian violence, few women and families in the nineteenth and early twentieth centuries were able or willing to migrate. The resulting preponderance of immigrant Chinese men spawned residential and familial forms, including bachelor boarding houses, relationships with concubines and prostitutes, and the infamous opium dens that violated the sensibilities of many social reformers and fed into already fierce anti-Chinese sentiments. While their sexual and reproductive capacities have resulted in hostilities directed at immigrant women broadly, these hostilities have taken particularly virulent forms against Asian women.[13]

The case for Asian exclusion was heavily shaped by fears of women's bodies as disease carriers as well as threats to sexual morality, as single Chinese women coming to the United States were labeled as prostitutes. As Sucheng Chan demonstrates, prominent court battles in California argued that "allowing the alleged Chinese prostitutes to enter would be akin to allowing persons with contagious diseases to enter."[14] Similarly, in 1875 the U.S. Congress passed the Page Law, one of the first in a series of Asian exclusion laws that barred felons and contract laborers from China and Japan and targeted Asian women, who were again assumed to be disease-carrying prostitutes. In *Entry Denied: Controlling Sexuality at the Border*, Eithne Luibhéid documents how medical advances of the late nineteenth century such as germ theory, which linked hygiene to disease, reflected and fueled racial fears of contamination through commercialized interracial sexual intercourse.[15] By singling out Chinese women for sexually amoral behavior (while ignoring the much larger problem of prostitution by white women), these laws laid the groundwork for the perceptions of Asian women as sexually available and lascivious that persist today.[16]

Thus a key link in the gendered construction of the yellow peril is the sexualization of Asian women as erotic and taboo objects of desire. Focusing on Hollywood depictions, the film studies scholar Gina Marchetti writes that "the yellow peril combines racist terror of alien countries, sexual anxieties, and the belief that the West will be overpowered and enveloped by the irresistible, dark, occult forces of the East. . . . This formulation necessarily rests on a fantasy that projects Euroamerican desires and dreads onto the alien other."[17] In this fantasy Asian women are rendered as the spoils of war, trophies that symbolize the triumph of white civilized men over a heathen, disease-ridden, and threatening Asia. This gendered construct of the yellow peril simultaneously fuels fears and desires of miscegenation in relationships between Asian women and white men.

But how do the gendered subtexts of the yellow peril play out in intimate but not necessarily sexualized service relationships between Asian and Western women? Manifesting in a very different kind of work, one that transpires mainly among women as opposed to between women and men, the gendered discourse of the yellow peril in nail salons takes on a new form, drawing less upon sexualized images but still resonating with racialized fears of bodily contagion through purchases of intimate services. Thus Asian-owned nail salons ground the gendered discourse of the yellow peril in contemporary sites of social interaction that illuminate much-less-studied aspects of relations between women in commercialized, embodied exchanges. Body labor provision in nail salons does not exist in a vacuum but reflects historical and contemporary perceptions of Asians propagated in the media and larger society.

RACIALIZED REPRESENTATIONS OF ASIAN NAIL SALONS

The character of Ms. Bunny Swan, a manicurist played by the comedian Alex Borstein on MAD TV, sports a black bowl hairdo, dark slanty eyeliner, and nonsensical English. She works at the Gorgeous Pretty Beauty Nail

Salon, which she pronounces "Gorga Pritty Booty Nay Salon." Although she is not explicitly identified as Asian on the show, her appearance, accent, and mannerisms strongly suggest this, and she is often described as Asian on unofficial sites.[18] This representation has prompted sharp criticism from Asian American groups. Guy Aoki, founding president of the Media Action Network for Asian Americans, criticized Borstein for "donning yellowface to play the gibberish-speaking nail-salon owner," adding that such derogatory portrayals become "the standards by which real-life Asian Americans are seen and treated."[19]

Whereas in other chapters I have focused mainly on ethnographic observations, here I also draw heavily upon media sources, including popular culture, news articles, and blogs. There are several reasons for this. As Aoki says, representations of Asians in the media shape perceptions of Asians in everyday life. Furthermore, much of the public debate about nail salon safety, and Asian-owned salons in particular, has emerged through media and policy discussion. Finally, customers were circumspect about criticizing salons and voicing blatant racial stereotypes directly to me in interviews, but such comments are widespread on the Internet. While they are not representative of interactions in Asian-owned discount salons, neither are they completely uncharacteristic. They are revealing for their own content as well as for the context that they provide for interactions in nail salons.

As a blog post entitled "'There Is a Humongous Fungus among Us'" from a twenty-year-old named Trish demonstrates, some dissatisfied customers frame an unsanitary manicure in blanket racial terms that condemn all Asian nail salons:

> Now, I love those Asians, especially their yummy food, but I'm telling you, I have not had good experiences at these nail salons. Twice in my life, I have gone and gotten to be, what I thought, pretty manicures . . . only to find, weeks later, that one of my nails started growing really weird. I have the nail fungus. It never fails. SOOOOO . . . I officially boycott the Asian nail salons. I know, I'm not being very P.C. about this, but you deal with the fungus and see how much you like it.[20]

In this post Trish first avows a love of Asians and Asian food, ostensibly as a way of averting accusations of generalized antipathy toward

Asians. However, she then freely launches into complaints not about the one or two offending salons that she has visited but about all Asian salons, which she plans to boycott en masse. In this case her complaints center on physical causes—the spread of nail fungus. In other cases the emotional aspects of service are more the source of discontent.

In a blog posting entitled "Asian Nail Salon Rudeness," the author, Jaime, who describes herself as a stay-at-home mom living in "Redneck-ville, United States," recounts having been treated with suspicion when purchasing nail polish from an Asian manicurist. She then fights the urge to retort with a racial slur: "'8 dolla,' she says and just stares at me. I refrain from asking, 'Me love you long time?' and instead reach into my pocket book and pull out the money and hand it to her. Even then she stands staring at me. . . . This isn't the first time this has happened. I don't know what it is about asian [sic] nail salons." After several readers criticized her comments, the author responded: "The 'Me Love you Long Time' thing was thought in my mind, as a JOKE [emphasis in original] . . . . In the end, this is my avenue to blog and to be honest, I don't think I've been hateful or rude in any of my reflections in regards to any race or nationality. Being ill treated as a consumer, irregardless of a person race or creed is just plain wrong in my opinion."[21]

Jaime's comments reveal several processes that shape nail salon interactions. Upon receiving service that she deemed rude, she quickly characterized the interaction in racial terms, although she denies doing so. Indeed, Jaime may not know that the line "me love you long time" references a well-known example of objectionable portrayals of Asian women in films, a Vietnamese prostitute in Stanley Kubrick's *Full Metal Jacket*. As the performance artist Allison Roh Park explains, "That phrase is so loaded. People don't understand the history behind that. . . . Asian women get exotified and hyper-sexualized to the point where it really affects our day-to-day life."[22] However, instead of acknowledging that she has used a racially charged phrase, intentionally or otherwise, Jaime appeals to her position as an "ill-treated" consumer to justify her reaction. Thus she invokes the service ideology of "the customer is always right" to sanction racist remarks.

These comments are much more extreme than those voiced by this study's participants. Nonetheless, they reveal strong reactions to the emotional and embodied exchanges in Asian discount nail salons that customers voiced in more subtle ways. At salons such as Crosstown Nails, similar themes of physical contamination and cultural otherness shape the performance of routinized body labor and the meanings that are given to these exchanges.

CROSSTOWN NAILS AND ROUTINIZED BODY LABOR

"For what it is, they do a great job. It's not the Red Door or Georgette Clinger, but it gets the job done. If you want an herbal wrap or a spalike experience, you would see the minute you walked in that you're not going to get it here. I come to this nail salon because it's in and out in twenty minutes." Kimberly, a customer at Crosstown Nails, captured the service ethos at this salon, which could be characterized as "beauty for everywoman." At this salon anyone can get a decent professional manicure, even those with little time or money. Unlike pampering body labor, the routinized form of body labor conferred at discount nail salons does not include excessive doting on the needs of customers. This does not mean that manicurists are not attentive to body labor but that they perform it in different ways, as they strive to instill a sense of "good enough" service under less than ideal conditions.

Located between a fashionable, high-rent, racially diverse residential district and a lower-income but also racially mixed neighborhood, Crosstown Nails captured the range of interactions that unfold in discount nail salons. The salon was clean but sparse and utilitarian. In addition to manicures and pedicures, it offered bikini, leg, and eyebrow waxing, all delivered in the same no-frills style. Susan Lee, forty-six, opened this salon in 1989 and was the sole owner. Divorced with one son, she emigrated in 1982 from Seoul with her husband, a graduate student. Before emigrating, she graduated college with a degree in tourism, worked as a travel agent in South Korea, and traveled often to Europe. In New York City she first worked in a retail store in Manhattan, then began to work in a nail salon in Brooklyn to support her husband's studies. After their marriage ended, she brought her mother from Korea and with her help opened a convenience store, which failed shortly thereafter. Susan opened Crosstown Nails a year later, and the business thrived, allowing her to open another nail salon several blocks away. However, she found it too stressful to operate both salons, and the income from the second salon was lower, so she closed it after two years. When I interviewed her, she was living in Queens with her mother and son.

All full-time employees at Crosstown Nails were Korean; two were relatives and one was a hometown friend, and several technicians, mostly Latinas and one Japanese international student, worked part time. The salon had a casual welcoming feel, as the workers knew each other well and had many regular customers. Because of its largely residential location, its busiest hours were on the weekend, during lunch hour, and after work on weekdays. I conducted fieldwork at Crosstown Nails for five months and interviewed the owner, workers, and customers, who held a range of occupations from high school teacher, hairdresser, student-bartender, homemaker, retired insurance bookkeeper, clinical researcher, and theater technician–musician to management consultant.

In stark contrast to the Uptown Nails and Exclusive Nails customers, who felt strong attachments to their manicurists, few customers at Crosstown Nails even knew their manicurist by name. One customer described the salon interactions as less intimate than those she experienced in Korean-owned groceries. "The nail salons are less personal in a weird way. I go to the grocery store, and they know me, and we pass along info about school or whatever. . . . In the nail salons, because of the volume, they're trying to get the maximum number of people in and out. I guess you still end up having more interaction with them, but the expectations are also higher." Thus she had significantly lowered her expectations in consideration of the minimal services offered at this salon. Another customer told me, "For the most part, I think they are distant with the customers. Some regulars are very friendly with them, they know all their names, but for the most part, it's distant." Communication tended toward practical instructions, and customers were more likely to converse with other customers than with their manicurists or, more often, simply "zone out" in front of the television or read a magazine. For all its lack of amenities Crosstown Nails often had customers waiting, but even when it was busy, the line moved quickly as each customer was whisked in and out of the manicuring seat with crisp efficiency. The manicurist may have offered to give a massage, but it was perfunctory and lasted barely a minute.

Describing a common calculus that many customers use to justify these no-frills manicures, Danielle, a regular Crosstown customer, explained:

> I like that it's inexpensive and clean. I don't like it when they are rushing you to get out. When it's busy, they can get careless. They can put on the polish too thick, which means it'll just peel off in a few days. Or they disregard specific things you want them to do. . . . When they get rushed, the most rigid hygiene standards are not followed. Like, I know I've soaked in the same dish that someone else has just used. At the more expensive salons they don't reuse anything. They have a sealed pouch, and they dramatically break it open for you to show you that it's new. . . . I'm not a nail veteran, but I know that there are much nicer places in Manhattan. I went to one that charged $60 for a manicure. It was also Korean owned but very fancy. They use really high-end products, everything smells fantastic. . . . There's not much conversation, and that doesn't really bother me. . . . [At this salon] it's quicker and more like an assembly line, but it costs less than half.

Although she praised the pampering services at other salons, in the end Danielle opted for a manicure that "costs less than half." She knew that she was forgoing pampering treatment as well as more elaborate sanitation procedures, yet she and many other customers continued to make this choice. While the market for discount salons depends on women like Danielle, these low-budget consumers also put pressure on these salons to keep costs low and work quickly, thereby inadvertently contributing to the risks involved in a manicure.

Customer expectations for fast, inexpensive service also impact the emotional delivery of services. In some cases service interactions are not simply scaled down but are decidedly short and tense, especially when the salons are very busy. One customer described an exchange that almost escalated into an altercation:

> The most positive experiences are when I'm greeted warmly. The most negative was I came last week with my friend and we were sitting next to

each other talking while we were having our manicures. She finished first, and they wanted her to move to the dryers, but we were in the middle of talking so she said, "I'd like to wait for my friend." And the Korean woman said, "You come now." My friend's the type who goes from zero to sixty like that [snaps fingers]. It didn't escalate, but they were both clearly annoyed.

Customers regard such rushing by manicurists as a measure of rudeness, rather than an extension of working conditions in the salons and their own demands for quick and inexpensive services.

Alice Nam, the manicurist at Convenient Nails, offered her perspective on how customers respond to these rushed exchanges. She said, "Sometimes they are sitting for half an hour under the dryer reading a magazine and others are waiting, but if we check them and say they are dry, they think we are rushing them." Thus manicurists must engage in emotional management that seeks to make customers happy with less. This means that they must make decisions about how to regulate their work priorities, which often means cutting out the niceties of conversation, massage, or any special accommodations.

This routinized style of service provision often conflicts with the expectations of customers. Even though they recognize that they are paying much less for these services, they still hold on to fairly high standards of physical and emotional attentiveness. At Crosstown Nails customers often make special requests and are miffed when they are ignored or refused. For example, one customer was trying to decide on a color and asked that two different polishes be mixed together. The manicurist looked at her blankly, then said curtly, "No mixing." Rather than pretending not to understand or otherwise finessing these requests, as manicurists at nail spas do, manicurists at discount salons simply say no. In another case a customer asked to use the bathroom before having her polish applied. She got up, and by the time she returned, another customer had taken her seat and she was asked to wait. Even though she was clearly annoyed, the staff made little or no attempt to mollify her.

Whatever efforts are made at pampering service are much more likely to come from the owner than the manicurists, particularly when the owner wants to keep waiting customers from leaving. Susan, the owner of Crosstown Nails, positioned herself at the reception area, eagerly engaging with customers who were beginning to fidget as they waited for the next available manicurist. "Jennifer, long time no see you!" With mock anger Susan said, "Let me see your hand—oh, terrible, terrible. How such beautiful girl lets her nails get so ugly?" The customer smiled halfheartedly. "It's because the wait here is always so long. I can go near my work, and I never have to wait more than five minutes." Making an exaggerated face reflecting hurt feelings, Susan countered, "We busy because we do best job! You wait just two more minutes, I get you coffee. You like cream and sugar?" She then turned to one of the manicurists and said curtly in Korean, "Finish up quickly. The customers will leave if it takes too long."

In this case the customer did not jump from miffed feelings to yellow peril stereotypes, but this slippage can occur easily in other instances. On another occasion Susan informed a waiting customer who was conversing with her friend that a manicuring station had opened. The customer looked up but kept talking and did not move. Susan repeated that the manicurist was ready for her, and the customer retorted, "OK, OK!" I then overheard her comment to her friend: "These little Asian ladies are so pushy!" Thus, in addition to attributing health risks to Asian-owned nail salons, certain customers also blame the rushed and impersonal aspect of discount nail salons on the "Asian-ness" of their service providers.

Such comments speak to another dimension of the yellow peril that attributes cultural traits such as rudeness to Asians. As I have argued throughout this book, such cultural attributions, whether of subservience, greed, or in this case rudeness, overlook the work conditions of body labor that foster certain behavior by Asian manicurists. The customer in this case frames the abruptness of the manicurist as a particularly Asian quality, rather than as a necessary adaptation to working in a routinized service setting. At the risk of triggering notions of Asian pushiness, manicurists and owners in these settings must walk a fine line between providing quick service while not rushing customers.

Whereas communication with customers at nail spas often focuses on complimenting and pampering and at nail art salons on demonstrating respect, at discount salons the focus is more on easing impatience and keeping customers from walking out the door. The mollifying is mostly done by the owner, as manicurists focus on simply keeping up with customer flows and not making mistakes. Susan's efforts to cajole and ingratiate herself with her patrons were often exhausting and embarrassing to observe. However, they were not simply a reflection of her personality or her desire to improve business, although the fruits of her work were evident in a booming salon with a large and loyal following. Instead, Susan's nearly hyperactive attempts to smooth over customer relations were an outgrowth of the clientele she served, the kind of services her salon offered, and the negative racial stereotypes that could be triggered in service interactions. These factors call forth body labor that attends to physical and emotional needs as well as to the racial and class contexts in which these services are performed.

BROKERING CLASS AND RACE

Discount nail salons such as Crosstown Nails, which serve a mixed clientele, become a laboratory of emergent multiracial and class relations. New immigrants negotiate and intercede in the construction of Asians as the yellow peril and in the dominant black-white paradigm that provides the backdrop for the racialization of other groups. Furthermore, immigrants, and Asians in particular, are incorporated not only into racial frameworks but also into those related to class, specifically, the stubborn belief in the United States as a classless society. This context of heightened racial discourses and invisible class divisions frames the hazards of routinized body labor through the controlling image of yellow peril threats.

This obfuscation of class and race calls forth particular negotiations of body labor. Customers in discount nail salons pay less, but they fail to acknowledge how the lower prices shape the terms of these exchanges. Rather than acknowledge their own limited means to purchase manicures as a significant reason for their dissatisfaction with these services, certain customers blame Asian manicurists, singling out their race as the source of any disappointments or difficulties. Thus they ignore how their own class position determines the kind of services that they are able to afford, and they fail to comprehend the economic forces that drive the trend toward standardized, mass-marketed beauty services. The myth of the classless society translates into racial explanations that obscure the class divisions and economic forces shaping gendered service delivery.

Because of the diversity of customers that patronize these salons, owners and manicurists often play the role of cultural brokers, both between themselves and customers and among the many different customers. Manicurists at routinized salons must communicate a sense of fairness, which often involves managing relations between customers of different racial and class backgrounds. Discount nail salons cater to women who have not purchased nail services in the past but are attracted by the price and convenience. Julia, a white bartender and regular customer at Crosstown Nails, commented, "I'm kind of a ragamuffin, so it kind of surprises me that I get them done as often as I do, which is still much less than most people in the city. It's just so easy to do here, and cheap." Julia's description of herself as a ragamuffin suggests that she did not adhere to strict codes of femininity in her dress or other beauty routines, as indicated by her casual peasant skirt and lack of makeup. Nonetheless, easy and cheap access drew her into purchasing regular manicures. Thus the secret of success for discount salons such as Crosstown Nails is their ability to appeal to customers who lack both excess disposable income and strong commitments to feminine beauty and normally would not indulge in a professional manicure.

Unlike nail spa or nail art customers, many customers at Crosstown Nails sought manicures neither as a pampering experience nor as creative expression but as a utilitarian measure to enhance a self-presentation suggesting class privilege, as I discussed in chapter 3. The purchase of professional nail services as a way of indicating class status cuts across racial lines. Furthermore, the greater importance of class over race in influencing nail styles and expectations of body labor is apparent in that the nail aesthetics of black and white middle-class customers are similar. Most routinized settings like Crosstown Nails do not offer nail art but specialize in basic and traditionally feminine manicures for all customers.

Merna, an Afro-Caribbean clinical researcher, commented, "I only get them done about every two months. I don't want to get attached to it. For some women it's such a ritual, it becomes a job—maintaining the tips and stuff. I'm presenting my hands all day long so it's worth it to me to spend some time and money to make sure they look good." Merna regards manicured nails as a professional asset, hence a class marker, more than an expression of her gender or racial identity. The style of her nails and the meaning she gives to having them done is more similar to the motivations of white middle-class customers at Uptown and Crosstown Nails than to those of the black working-class customers at Downtown Nails. Both Merna and Julia revealed a preference for hassle-free and inexpensive manicures. Thus both black and white women of modest means patronize Asian discount salons, suggesting that class is more significant than race in determining who opts for this routinized form of body labor. The style of nails and the meaning given to them are radically different from both the pampering of nail spas and the originality and self-expression in nail art salons.

While the importance of class in shaping the expectations of customers and the kinds of services they desire is often lost on the customers themselves, manicurists and owners in discount salons are acutely aware of the ways that class shapes who visits their salons and the kinds of services they expect. Speaking about the importance of nails as a class marker for her customers, Susan commented, "They care so much about their nails here because it shows what kind of person they are. In Korea rich people are all dressed up—shoes, bag, makeup, hair. But here even rich people just walk around in t-shirts, no makeup—casual style. But if they have their nails done, they can show off that they have money or are fashionable." Thus this owner recognizes customers' investment in their nails as an assertion of class privilege. Unfortunately, manicurists are hard pressed to deliver on this investment through the budget manicures that they offer. The mix of high expectations and low ability to pay for manicures breeds dissatisfaction by customers, but they displace their resentment away from their own limited class resources, and those of the salon, onto the race of the manicurists or salon proprietors.

Unacknowledged race and class divisions also shape relations among customers. Fears regarding Asian nail salons as pollutants draw not only upon negative views of the Asian service providers but also on suspicions of the other bodies encountered in these establishments. Crosstown Nails attracted a range of customers and placed them in physical proximity to each other. The mixed race and class composition of the clientele and neighborhood bred uncomfortable dynamics between customers that service providers had to broker in addition to their own interactions with customers. On several occasions I observed customers, especially when they were immediately following another customer, ask manicurists to change utensils or ensure that they had sanitized them. One woman sat down and said in hushed tones to the manicurist, trying not to let the previous customer hear her, "I think that woman was really sweaty—this seat is warm and wet. Can I move somewhere else?" In a forum post responding to a question about Asian nail salons, a customer wrote more overtly about the woman next to her: "She had this nasty cut on her big toe and still had the nerve to get a pedi. The main reason I got grossed out was knowing that after a pedi, the tubs are just wiped clean, not sterilized at all between customers."[23] The sense that the bodies of other customers are potentially dirty or dangerous increases the customers' concerns with sanitation practices and their resultant policing of manicurists. These concerns about other customers are heightened in racially and socioeconomically diverse settings.

In addition to regulating physical contact, customers in discount salons also attempt to limit their interaction with other customers in terms of conversational exchanges. At Crosstown Nails a young white woman was sitting next to a talkative older black woman, who attempted to engage in conversation despite clear signals of discomfort by the white woman. Susan noticed the interactions and directed a manicurist who was about to go on break to instead check on the young woman. Thus the potentially charged interactions between customers of different backgrounds also necessitate that the owner and manicurists step in and smooth things over.

Furthermore, the salons do not exist in isolation from the neighborhoods in which they are located, and community members venture inside the salon doors, at times drawing customers and service providers into tense interactions. On one afternoon a young black man laden with bags of toys, calculators, pens, and other tchotchkes came into Crosstown Nails hawking his wares. Susan, the owner, greeted him politely, looked over his merchandise, considered buying a small stuffed white dog for her son, then said regretfully, "No, thank you." Only when he approached an elderly white customer and pressured her to buy something did Susan ask him to leave. She avoided an incident with the vendor but at the same time tried not to offend the customers. After he left, Susan quickly went over to the white customer whom he had approached and commented on her nails, "French manicure looks good on you. Color matches your dress." She then immediately checked in with a black customer who was waiting, letting her know that she was next. Later, when I asked her about the vendor, she responded, "If I kick them out, blacks may get angry, but if I let them stay, whites don't like it." Whether the customers would actually respond in this way or not, Susan anticipated their reactions as such and took action to defuse them. Serving both black and white customers ranging from working to middle class, Susan had developed a second sense that put her on constant emotional alert in service to her diverse clientele. The wear and tear was evident as she rushed to the backroom during breaks to quickly inhale a cigarette or two.

Routinized body labor involves smoothing over tensions from both the provision of a budget manicure and management of the diverse bodies encountered in this setting. These factors add up to customers' heightened concern with the sanitary conditions of the salons, and owners' and manicurists' attempts to appease them. In this context the fears of customers for their own health far outweigh any concerns that they might have about the working conditions of salon employees. While customers have voiced concerns about their own health risks, more attention is needed to safeguard working conditions for manicurists and regulate cosmetics manufacturers.

Figure 15.   Nail salon work involves potentially toxic chemical exposures for workers, but customers most often focus on their own health protections, often overlooking labor rights issues and regulation of cosmetics manufacturers.

WHOSE HEALTH MATTERS?

Yellow peril discourses frame Asian manicurists as contaminators, ignoring the ways that the manicurists' health is compromised by the work they perform for others. Pressures to work quickly undermine manicurists' ability to follow safety and health procedures not only for their customers' protection but for their own. While routinized body labor fulfills both the emotional and physical needs of customers to access a former luxury service, albeit a dramatically scaled-down version, the performance of this work can translate into debilitating, long-term conditions for manicurists. Although customers express sensitivity to their own health risks, they are much less concerned about the health of their manicurists.

When I asked them to describe the worst thing about their jobs, almost all the workers I interviewed cited toxic exposures in the salons. One

manicurist summed up the problem in a succinct one-word response—
nemseh (the smell)—grimacing and holding her nose. Almost all the
women described experiencing, at the very least, runny noses and watery
eyes, and others had more serious illnesses, ranging from migraine head-
aches to chronic skin rashes to respiratory and digestive problems.

In addition to the fumes from the polishes, workers are exposed to
known toxins in nail polish remover and in the acrylics and glue used
for tips and extensions; these chemicals include dibutyl phthalate, formaldehyde, toluene, acetone, benzene, methylene chloride, glycol ethers,
and the banned but still used methylmethacrylates. Constant handling
of these solvents exposes workers to carcinogenic, allergenic, and/or
reproductively harmful substances. One study found that manicurists
had levels of dibutyl phthalates twice as high as those found in the general population.[24] A 2004 survey of salon employees in New York City
revealed that 37 percent suffered from skin problems, 37 percent from
eye irritations, 57 percent from allergies, 66 percent from neck or back
discomfort, and 18 percent from asthma.[25] In one year, Thu Pham, a health
worker in the Vietnamese community in Springfield, Massachusetts, saw
thirty-two women who work in nail salons with asthma, fungal infections,
and rashes and six women who miscarried.[26] Both owners and workers
described to me the occupational health issues related to nail salon work:

> I heard of someone who worked when she was pregnant, and the baby
> has some problems. People told her not to, but I guess she needed the
> money, and she thought it would be okay. This salon has good ventilation,
> and we keep it clean, but I still get rashes and sneezing. (Mary Lee)
> Of course [it affects my health]! My shoulder, I have a pinched nerve
> there. I have trouble with my right elbow. (Jenny Park)
> At our store we don't do acrylics, and it's well ventilated so it is better
> than other places, but nowadays my nose bleeds about two hours after
> finishing a big job like a tip set or wrap. I can't stand the smell of nail pol-
> ish anymore. (Jiwon Cho)
> Ah, my hands. I wake up unable to move my hands, they tighten.
> (Joanne Shin)

Julia Liou of Asian Health Services in the San Francisco Bay Area and
cofounder of the California Healthy Nail Salon Collaborative, described

risk factors in nail salon work. While she focused on Vietnamese workers in California, her comments are applicable to nail salon workers across ethnicities in different areas of the country. "It's been suspected that there is an increased incidence of breast cancer, and statistics show that cervical cancer is higher among Vietnamese women. Again, its hard to say what the cause is, but in California, 59 to 80 percent of the nail salons are Vietnamese. Most of these women are of reproductive age."[27] As the mission statement of the California Healthy Nail Salon Collaborative states, "Given their occupational exposures, history of immigration, cultural practices, lack of awareness about health risks, and limited access to health care, this worker population has a complex health profile."

This complex health profile is also a major factor in determining women's departure from the nail industry and fosters a circular employment path involving other forms of low-wage work, such as garment factories and grocery stores. Most women think that nail salon work is the best of these options in terms of status (even though the pay is actually comparable), but many cannot stay for more than a few years because they develop allergies and other occupation-related illnesses. Often they will leave and find other work until they have recovered enough to return, as this manicurist described:

> As I moved around from job to job, the *byong* [illness] would also move around in my body. When I worked in the [garment] factory, it was in my neck and shoulders. When I worked in the grocery store, it was in my back and legs. When I'm here [in the salon], it's right here [*she placed her hand over her mouth and nose*]. I worked for awhile vending outside in the hot sun, and it went here [*she touched the top of her head*] , and my hair started to fall out! But I worry most about my health here—because I don't know how bad it is, sometimes I just feel dizzy—there's nothing you can do.

Asked about chemical exposures in the salons, customers like Christine responded with concerns about their own health, not that of the workers: "The glue fumes are awful, but I've never had any kind of allergic reaction to them. They're just bothersome, one of the things you just have to put up with." Then I asked whether she was aware of any negative effects that the fumes were having on the women who worked there.

"You know, to tell you the truth, I never thought about it," she replied, laughing nervously. "This is probably one of those really un-PC things to do, huh? Like buying grapes or something." Thus Christine acknowledged both the "un-PC" dimensions of frequenting nail salons and that she had not considered these previously.

In some cases customers not only are unaware of health risks but also object to their service providers' attempts to protect themselves by using masks and gloves. Jackie Hong, a nail salon owner, commented: "I don't use gloves but use cotton masks when I do a tip set. There's too much dust when you're filing. Customers are okay with both the glove and cotton masks now, but when I first started using them, they asked many questions. They would ask if I was sick or would be insulted because they thought that I didn't want to touch them." Similarly, Jenny Park said, "When I first wore them [masks], they [customers] asked if I had a cold and suggested that if I did, I [should] go home and take a break."

Donna, a Crosstown customer, corroborated the unfavorable reaction of customers when manicurists adopt visible measures to protect their health: "They should put up a sign about what they do for sterilization. It would ease the worry. . . . I've never seen them wear masks or gloves—I guess if I did, I would worry more about what I'm breathing in because I'm not wearing a mask." Her comments suggest that efforts by manicurists to protect their health can create a backlash wherein customers become even more wary about their own health risks. Research has shown that gloves protect manicurists against skin irritations.[28] However, manicurists refrain from visible measures to protect their health because they recognize that customers are sensitive to their use. This sensitivity may be slowly changing, as dental and medical professionals now commonly use masks and gloves. However, the norms of beauty services are slower to shift as the ethos of pampering service persists even in discount establishments.

State regulations also prioritize customer protections over the occupational safety and health of manicurists. As Alexandra Gorman Scranton, coauthor of the report, "Glossed Over: Health Hazards Associated with Toxic Exposure in Nail Salons," and director of science and research for Women's Voices for the Earth, one of several groups that founded the Campaign for Safe Cosmetics, explained: "There is a definite lack of regulation which could protect nail salon workers from chemical exposure. This means that inspections of nail salons (which are often few and far between anyway) rarely if ever, touch on the issues of chemical exposure. The focus tends to be more on infection control, which while certainly important is not the only health hazard in a salon." Thus Gorman Scranton noted that any increase in regulation is more likely to target practices that protect customers from infection rather than manicurists from toxic exposures.[29]

In short, nail salon workers' health takes a backseat to that of their customers. Furthermore, fears of drawing attention to their salons and triggering negative stereotypes can divide workers and owners, as individual manicurists' efforts to practice safe manicuring procedures can be undermined by owners' desires to downplay health risks and increase customer flow and profits. Fortunately, various groups are organizing and advocating to address working conditions and toxic exposures in nail salons. However, these efforts to upgrade nail salon work must walk a fine line, to address problems without fueling negative stereotypes of Asian discount nail salons.

ADVOCATING FOR MANICURISTS' OCCUPATIONAL HEALTH

"It's like a modern-day DDT story—it's analogous to the exposure that farmworkers have experienced," said Julia Liou, who cofounded the California Healthy Nail Salon Collaborative, a coalition of twenty-five organizations that focuses on policy, research, outreach, and education in the nail salon industry. While the coalition takes a multipronged approach, its emphasis is on "holding the manufacturers accountable." While the coalition recognizes and addresses the problems caused by unsafe sanitary practices, it also emphasizes toxic chemical use by manufacturers and lack of regulation, at both the state and federal level, that contribute to hazardous conditions in the salons for both customers and workers.[30]

Recently, progress has been made in the regulation of phthalates and other chemicals in cosmetics products in the United States, but the problem of lack of comprehensive regulation and enforcement remains.[31] Richard Rabin, an environmental engineer with the Massachusetts Occupational Safety and Health Association, said, "OSHA [the U.S. Occupational Safety and Health Administration] doesn't cover many of the hazards largely because they're under their radar gun. . . . There are also concerns over chemicals that OSHA doesn't even have a rule for."[32] Concerns have also been voiced about the influence of the industry's own Cosmetics Ingredient Review on setting standards.[33] In this context of lax regulation, the collaborative has worked to draw attention to workers as the most vulnerable population with regard to toxic exposure in the salons. At the same time it uses a strategy of building alliances among workers, owners, and customers to address health threats that affect them all. Liou said, "We don't want to scare people. There has been a lot of negative publicity around the salons, and they don't want to scare customers away. This is their livelihood, so we approach it as, 'Safe practices are better for your business. It's good for everyone.'" Liou acknowledged that efforts to upgrade nail salon work operate in a sensitive climate in which underlying negative representations of Asian nail salons can easily be triggered.[34]

The perspective of body labor illuminates how the work itself, especially the processes of intimate physical and emotional contact, taps into anxieties about these services, a dynamic that further complicates organizing strategies in the nail salon industry. Various organizations, led mostly by Asian American community groups, have begun campaigns to link public health of customers with occupational safety and health of workers while acknowledging the potential backlash against Asian nail salons. Efforts have included outreach and participatory research with salon owners and workers and partnerships between federal, state, and local government, community organizations, and the local business community. In 2007 many of these groups joined together to form the National Healthy Nail Salon Alliance, which has been effective in pressuring cosmetic companies to remove from their products the "toxic trio" of toluene, formaldehyde, and dibutyl phthalate and in building a movement for "green salons." These efforts have identified and publicized best practices in nail salons for the protection of both workers and consumers, and they have significantly raised awareness in communities across the country.[35]

However, even when clearly understood by nail technicians, best practices are sometimes difficult to follow when they could upset customers or owners. There is often a wide gap between what manicurists know they should do and what they actually are able to do. For example, the Asian Law Caucus and the University of California, San Francisco's Community Occupational Health Project have publicized guidelines for nail salon workers to protect themselves and customers against infection. These include wearing gloves, frequent hand washing, and disinfecting of tools. In addition, they recommend precise steps to take if a client bleeds: "Hand the client a cotton ball to stop the bleeding; use liquid styptic on a cotton applicator; ask the client to throw out the cotton ball; if you get blood on your skin, wash your hands immediately with soap and water."[36]

While these procedures seem straightforward, one experienced nail salon worker in Manhattan, thirty-seven-year-old Julie Suh, shed light on the difficulties of implementing these protocols in the workplace:

> When you use gloves, customers feel bad so I don't use them. . . . Most [manicurists] don't use gloves. They only use them when they are using a lot of chemicals. I don't wear a mask, but some do because the filing makes dust go into the air. . . . The owner doesn't like it when you wear a mask with regular customers . . . because she wants you to talk to them. . . . In black and Hispanic neighborhoods people wear more masks because they do a lot of tips, but where I work it's mainly manicures. It would be strange if no one is wearing a mask or gloves and you're the only one wearing them.

I asked her to identify the hardest part of her job. "I'm afraid I'm going to make the people bleed," she replied. "People who've done it for five years still make people bleed and it scares me. . . . If you make them bleed, the customer gets really upset. You just have to apologize a lot and take care of them. . . . You can't put on gloves for that little amount of blood. To save time you have to touch it, then just throw it away. I never heard of anyone contracting a disease, but I worry about it. I have a family so that's what I worry most about." Rather than being able to institute measures to protect their own health, manicurists like Julie must respond to customers' needs, both physical and emotional, even if this means subordinating proper hygienic protocols as well as their own health protection.

Workers' ability to institute practices to protect their own and their customers' health confronts the ethos of beauty service, which strives to create an oasis without problems, rather than drawing attention to them. Therefore, organizing campaigns face customer resistance to acknowledging the dangers of toxic products, let alone being willing to participate in collective action to address these issues. Joy Onasch, community program manager at the Toxics Use Reduction Institute at the University of Massachusetts Lowell, described how efforts to raise public awareness about chemical exposures in nail salons bump up against a general lack of understanding regarding regulation of toxic consumer products: "I don't want to generalize about the American public, but it may be that that they are less aware about toxins, not just in personal care products but in pesticides, cleaning products, lead fishing weights, etc. There are a variety of products that cause exposure. There may also be a false sense of security—people believe the government is making sure that their products are safe, and that is not necessarily the case."[37] In sum, a general ignorance or even denial prevails regarding the lack of oversight of the cosmetics industry in the United States. The success of the beauty service industry relies on creating a relaxing, care-free experience for customers, thus making it difficult for owners, workers, and customers to identify and act on potential health threats. Furthermore, the latent discourse of the yellow peril becomes an easy default explanation for any problems encountered in these salons—the blame is put on Asians for being unclean, as opposed to blaming products and manufacturers for being unsafe.

LABOR ORGANIZING IN NAIL SALONS

Customers, manufacturers, and regulators are not the only ones guilty of overlooking attention to workers' health, as certain owners also give little priority to healthy and safe working conditions. Because owners often pressure manicurists to work quickly, workers are hard pressed to follow time-consuming disinfecting and cleaning protocols. Thus occupational safety and health issues are closely connected to working conditions and labor rights in the salons. How do the dynamics of body labor and routinized service provision influence labor organizing and advocacy efforts?

Labor rights organizers have successfully mobilized and represented nail salon workers against owners. Several organizations have represented nail salon workers in back-wage cases. The Asian American Legal Defense and Education Fund (AALDEF) and YKASEC–Empowering the Korean American Community collaborated in support of former nail salon workers from Flushing, New York, and won a back-wage settlement of $17,500 in January 2006. In July 2006 the U.S. Department of Labor won $222,036 in back wages and interest for 152 workers at six New York City salons for violations of the federal Fair Labor Standards Act.[38]

According to a 2007 report from the Brennan Center for Justice, "The nail salon segment has been growing rapidly in recent years, and is also where we most consistently found minimum wage and overtime violations."[39] Nail salons for the most part also follow lax protocols regarding legally mandated breaks.[40] One manicurist in Queens told me, "I don't know any salons that give you an hour break at a set time every day. Sometimes we have to eat in ten minutes depending on whether it's busy or slow. Sometimes its so busy, the boss won't even tell you can take a break so you just have to keep working." Many workers complain of irregular meal and break times, unhealthy working conditions, including exposure to toxic chemicals, low wages, and lack of overtime pay.

Ethnic business associations that could advocate on behalf of manicurists have tended instead to downplay labor rights and toxic exposure issues. When I asked Esther, a long-term Korean manicurist in Manhattan, whether she participates in any nail industry or ethnic community organizations, or if they have helped her in any way, she guffawed, "They do not care about people like me—they are just trying to help the owners make more money. . . . They have known for years that this is not good for our health, but they don't want to make it an issue because the owners don't want to make it known." Esther pointed out that owners and industry representatives, fearing negative publicity, may in fact be more invested in keeping toxic exposure issues quiet than in improving working conditions. Michelle Wong, copresident of the Yale Chapter of the National Asian Pacific American Women's Forum, told me that some nail salon owners hesitated to participate in her organization's advocacy work in New Haven. Her group spearheaded outreach efforts to nail salons by sponsoring workshops on toxic exposure and ways to minimize hazards. Although she regards the outreach as a success, she noted some barriers and limitations that her organization encountered with regard to employer participation:

> Both employers and workers are trying to maximize the number of customers daily, and in some cases this might mean using acetone nail polish remover, which works much more quickly than acetone-free products. . . . We found that the owners were slightly hesitant [about conducting a workshop in their salon] and thus we did not get the chance to work with them. . . . We also don't know if they have made an effort to change to other less toxic products. These products are currently not as readily available and are more costly alternatives.[41]

As Wong pointed out, it is costly to use safer products and practices, and owners alone should not be saddled with these costs. In order to lessen toxic exposures, manufacturers must also shoulder the responsibility for developing and marketing products that are safe and affordable, and customers must be willing to pay for them.

Alexandra Gorman Scranton further elaborated on the delicacy of framing health issues in the salons so as not to place blame solely on individual owners, workers, and salons, saying, "In order to engage nail salon workers and owners, we found it is best not to use language which appears to put the blame on them [for using products containing toxic chemicals]. We also found a resistance to language which implied that visiting a nail salon was dangerous for a consumer. We found that successful language focused on the chemicals themselves and the manufacturers' responsibility for ensuring their products were safe to use."[42] In stressing the importance of not placing blame on nail salon owners and workers, Gorman Scranton acknowledged that such blame can

dissuade customers from visiting these establishments. Increasing consumer awareness can simply lead to boycotting these salons, as opposed
to pushing for better products, conditions, and oversight.

The tendency to blame Asian manicurists not only for customers'
health problems but for their own is seen in what industry representative
Debbie Doerlamm, who runs beautytech.com, told the *Nation:* "The technicians that are going to get sick are those girls who are normally of Oriental background. They are not well trained, they don't get the education
and they have very poor work habits."[43] Thus debates about salon health
and safety reveal a yellow peril undercurrent that can backlash against
Asian-owned nail salons, diverting attention from the manufacturing of
toxic products and the violations of occupational safety and labor rights
in these sites, and instead criticizing manicurists for these problems.

NAIL SALONS AS ECONOMIC THREAT

While framed as public health and safety concerns, criticisms of Asian
discount salons often conceal an underlying fear of economic competition with regard to attracting customers and protecting jobs. Manicurist,
and cosmetologist more broadly, is a job that has traditionally been dominated by both native-born black and white women.[44] More and more of
these jobs are now being filled by Asian immigrants, but does this mean
that immigrants are taking jobs from native-born Americans?

The impact of immigrants on the job prospects of native-born Americans is one of the most contentious questions in current immigration policy debates, and it reverberates in the yellow peril discourse surrounding
discount nail salons. The economists Maya Federman, David Harrington,
and Kathy Krynski applied this question to the nail industry, reframing it
as, "Are immigrants displacing natives or finding new nails to polish?"
In their case study of Vietnamese manicurists in California between 1987
and 2002, Federman and colleagues found that displacement does occur,
but mostly because fewer natives are entering the field, not because they
are being pushed out of existing jobs. Furthermore, this shift is offset by
significant job creation. Some non-Vietnamese have left the nail industry,

but it is unclear how much of a shift would have occurred anyway, as natives are more likely to see the work of manicurist as temporary employment. Federman, Harrington, and Krynski show that "Vietnamese immigrants and natives do not compete for a fixed number of jobs" and that "most of the displacement stemmed from a reduction in the number of non-Vietnamese choosing to enter the occupation rather than a quickened exit of those already working as manicurists."[45] While Federman and colleagues focus on Vietnamese-owned salons, their findings suggest that the perception of Asians as stealing jobs from native-born Americans is often erroneous. Their study speaks to a general gap between public opinion, which excoriates immigrants for stealing jobs, and academic scholarship, which has consistently refuted any sizable negative impact of immigrants on the job prospects of natives.[46]

Such concerns about competition have also been a factor in debates regarding the regulation of nail salons and Korean-owned salons in particular. In chapter 1, I discussed how the lack of regulation provided opportunities for Korean immigrant women to enter this niche in the early days of its emergence. Since 1994, however, such open access has been curtailed by new and strict laws that mandate 250 hours of accredited training to receive a "nail specialty" license. Strict regulations supposedly were implemented because of concerns about health and sanitation, but as Pyong Gap Min argues, "Many of the manicurists were nurses and teachers back home. . . . Sanitation is not new to them and it is not the real issue in the reaction to Korean businesses."[47] An article in *Crain's New York Business* captured two different views of the drive toward regulation, one held by Cynthia Ahn, who served as a representative on New York State's Appearance Enhancement Advisory Committee, and the other by James N. Baldwin, executive deputy secretary of state.

"My feeling," [Ahn] says, is that the American beauty salons "felt they were losing business" to the Koreans, and they felt "they needed some protection, to make things really difficult (for the Koreans)." But [Baldwin] says the state had been studying the whole area of cosmetology for the last eight to 10 years—long before the Korean nail salons were a factor—with an eye toward updating requirements that had become outdated. "We're willing to work with them (the Korean salon owners) and the sponsors of the legislation to develop amendments that would be sensitive to their situation," he says.[48]

It is difficult to prove that competition from Korean-owned nail salons was a primary motivating force in the regulation of nail salons in New York. However, as Baldwin noted, the state had been considering regulations for nearly a decade but did not implement them until Korean-owned salons proliferated. Whatever the actual reasons driving regulation, the perception that these efforts were fueled by fears of competition from their salons was strong among some Korean salon owners and representatives.

A report titled "Is New York City Killing Entrepreneurship?" sees this strict licensing of manicurists as misguided, saying it would be comparable to requiring licenses for individual servers in restaurants rather than prioritizing inspections of the establishments themselves. In addition, it notes the discrepancies in requirements for ethnic-dominated niches, such as 250 hours to become a nail technician and nine hundred hours to become a licensed hair braider, as opposed to the mere 116 hours necessary to work as an emergency medical technician or the forty-seven hours to qualify as a security guard allowed to wield deadly force. The report concludes that the high level of regulation of nail technicians and other immigrant-dominated service niches discourages employment, fosters unfair competitive advantages for those already well established in comparable service niches (such as beauty salons), and often is not justified to protect the public interest.[49] While I do not share this report's libertarian position that state intervention in principle should be limited, I agree that regulation often reflects interests other than public health and safety. Licensing and inspections can be important avenues for protecting both consumers and workers, but they can also restrict and intimidate immigrants in small business.

Similar concerns that state regulators have targeted their salons have emerged among Vietnamese in California, in this case with regard to salon inspections. Trang Nguyen, community outreach organizer with Asian Communities for Reproductive Justice in Oakland, noted that inspectors often seemed excessively punitive toward Vietnamese nail salon workers, rather than working with salons to upgrade health condi-tions. She said, "It is unreasonable to penalize the worker for a violation committed by the owner. . . . Many workers are working hard to earn as little as $300 a month and were fined $1,000 to $2,000 per violation, not knowing why they were being fined." Nguyen further pointed out the lack of Vietnamese inspectors and written materials as another obstacle for Vietnamese salons in conforming with state regulations.[50]

During a public comment session of the California Board of Barber-ing and Cosmetology, meeting in Los Angeles in November 2008, sev-eral members of the Vietnamese community voiced their sense that the inspection process is harsh and even discriminatory toward Vietnamese salons. The minutes of this meeting report: "Phi Long Mai stated he was treated rudely and like a criminal during an inspection. He noted his chair renters were very scared. He feels discriminated against with the inspectors. . . . Kevin Nguyen, member of the audience, agreed the rules and regulations needed to be followed. . . . He believed inspectors were not polite and discriminated against them because English was not their first language. He believed inspectors should teach along with giving fines." A committee member responded that "they take these concerns very seriously" and urged those who felt they had been treated unfairly to file a complaint.[51] These discussions do not necessarily prove a pat-tern of discrimination, but they do reveal tensions and misunderstand-ings between state officials and Asian—in this case Vietnamese—salons regarding regulation.

Some customers in my study also believed that economic concerns underlie much of the criticism of Asian-owned nail salons. Toni, a cus-tomer at Crosstown Nails, shared her experiences regarding one beauty salon owner's negative portrayal:

> I used to go to this beauty salon to get my nails done, but they just didn't do as good of a job and it was usually a wait. The owner must have noticed that I stopped getting my nails done there, and when I came in to get my hair done, she called me to task for it. She was actually pretty rude about it, telling me that the Korean salons weren't sanitary and that I would get a fungus. . . . It was pretty clear to me that she had a chip on her shoulder about losing customers to the nail salons.

While Toni herself was wary of hygiene practices in these salons, she perceived that beauty salon owners criticize the sanitary practices of Asian nail salons less out of health concerns and more out of fears of business competition. Several other customers voiced similar perceptions, with one saying, "It's obvious that the beauty salons don't like these nail salons."

In addition to concerns about competition, another economic dimension of the yellow peril stereotype that customers reference focuses on objectionable business practices and stereotypes of Asians as driven by greed. Jane, a customer at Convenient Nails, said:

> I don't want to play into those awful Asian stereotypes. It's hard to talk about these things, but there is the stereotype that they are ruthless in business and that can sometimes get enforced when they're trying to rush you through. The stereotype that they're too bookish applies mostly to kids, but the ruthless stereotype is what I think about with regard to businesses. Then, again, if people have that way of looking at the world, they will find evidence of it anywhere. I try not to attribute things to a person's heritage—if a person is unpleasant, they're just an unpleasant person. But it's easier to fall into that way of thinking than I'd like to admit. They probably think that we're ridiculous and lazy, that we can't even do our own nails.

According to Jane, the stereotype she regards as most prevalent of Asians is not that of the industrious model minority or the high-achieving student but that of being "ruthless in business." Her comments resonate with perceptions of Asians as "money-grubbing foreigners" and reveal another dimension of yellow peril fears that focuses less on contamination and more on cutthroat competitiveness. While the substance of the stereotype may be different, the end result is the same, as themes of both contamination and competition solidify unsavory views of Asians.

CONCLUSION

Asian immigrants are not in fact "stealing" the jobs of native-born manicurists but are replacing those who leave, in addition to expanding the number of jobs in this niche. Nonetheless, like many debates involving contemporary immigration, the actual economic contributions of immigrants receive much less attention than their perceived negative impact, not just economically but culturally. Yellow peril discourses become easily ignited in a climate of anti-immigrant and anti-Asian sentiment. These circumstances demand that nail technicians not only provide fast, inexpensive manicures but also mitigate negative racial stereotypes. However, the conditions of their work make it difficult to rewrite this persistent subtext of Asians as contaminants.

The tendency for customers to universalize from an unsatisfactory interaction with a single Asian manicurist to condemnations of Asian-owned nail salons as a whole would seem preposterous in service enterprises dominated by other racial and ethnic groups. Would a bad experience with an Italian server lead a customer to boycott all Italian restaurants? Or would a disappointing session with a Swedish massage therapist result in wholesale dismissal of any such establishment? As I have discussed, the designation "Asian" when attached to nail salons is different from the ethnic basis of Italian food or the equating of "Swedish" with specific massage techniques. In contrast, little, if anything, about a manicure is essentially Asian, even though customers and manicurists may swear otherwise. Nonetheless, the tendency to attribute racial meanings to certain kinds of business enterprises and practices is much more prevalent with regard to Asians or other minorities than white ethnic groups.[52]

While some individual manicurists and salons are guilty of failing to follow proper protocols, health risks in nail salons are magnified by larger forces, including manufacturers' use of toxic chemicals in the products, regulators' focus on penalizing rather than educating manicurists, pressure from owners to cut corners, and customer expectations that a manicure be both quick and low cost. Furthermore, the yellow peril discourse heightens distrust of individual Asian manicurists and Asian-owned nail salons as a whole, leading to accusations that they have downgraded the manicure and made it an unsanitary exchange. Drawing again on the parallel example of the food service industry, this would be comparable to placing sole blame for a contaminated meal on the server who delivered it, without taking into consideration the management of the restaurant or the production and processing of the food itself. Likewise, routinized manicuring services at discount nails salons reflect larger factors that are related to the industry as a whole and are beyond the exclusive control of individual manicurists or owners, although owners have greater accountability, particularly with regard to labor rights violations.

In recent years a number of community organizations have mobilized efforts to improve health and safety standards in Asian-owned nail salons. These efforts are important and encouraging, especially when they take a multipronged approach of addressing labor rights, regulation of toxic cosmetic products, and public education targeting both service providers and customers. Unfortunately, the dynamics of emotional and embodied intimacy in routinized body labor often undermine rather than encourage public campaigns that address common interests of women on both sides of the manicuring table. Rather than scapegoating an already vulnerable population of immigrant women workers, customers could serve as a voice both for protecting themselves and for upholding health and labor standards in the nail industry. Instead, customers are more likely to single out the practices of individual owners and workers and Asian nail salons as a whole, invoking racial stereotypes and blaming them for conditions that they have not created—and suffer from, often far more than their customers.

Conclusion

WHAT IS A MANICURE WORTH?

A half-dozen protesters stood in front of a Manhattan nail salon carrying crumpled cardboard signs emblazoned: "Hey Nail Plaza! Women workers should have the right to breaks"; "Sweatshops are not glamorous"; "No gloves, no masks, no pedicure!"

They represented several different organizations and had gathered in support of a dismissed worker, Do Yea (Susan) Kim, who had filed a lawsuit accusing the salon of not giving breaks or paying overtime.[1] Despite the protesters' efforts, many customers crossed the picket line and entered the salon. Two well-dressed elderly white women left the salon, huddling together with nervous smiles. One protester yelled, "Don't support this salon—they don't respect workers' rights." One of the customers yelled, "That's not true. She takes good care of us. She's very nice." The protester retorted, "She's nice to you, not to her workers!

All you care about are your nails, you don't know what's going on in there!" The customer called back—"Yes, we do!"—and then hustled away. Later another woman, a former customer at this salon, stopped by and commented, "I'm actually really surprised to see so many people still going in there. This is the Upper West Side, we have a reputation of being very liberal, big Hillary supporters. We're known for supporting the underdog—unions, teachers. . . . I guess people are attached to their manicurist so they're willing to break the picket."

Here the physical and emotional intimacy involved in the exchange of a manicure translates into customers' loyalty to a particular owner and salon, and overrides concerns with labor rights. Women who arguably would not cross a picket line in other circumstances are willing to do so in order to be cared for by a favorite manicurist in a familiar and comfortable setting. As in this example, the exchange of body labor often blurs, conceals, and justifies inequalities in the workplace and poses a barrier to organizing. At the same time by making it difficult to replace the service provider, these same attachments can increase the value of this work and provide an impetus for positive change in the nail industry.

What calculus do we use to determine the worth of a manicure? Do we rely simply upon its exchange value in the mass market and the laws of supply and demand to justify its low price? If not, what other factors should determine the value of this service exchange? Once we make a determination of its value, what actions can we take to ensure that it is appropriately compensated under proper working conditions? How can relations among nail salon customers, manicurists, and nail salon owners inhibit or support upgrading the conditions of this work? I hope these questions give reason for pause. In this book I have sought to make the case that manicuring work, like much service work performed by immigrants and women, constitutes a package of often unacknowledged and uncompensated services that, when broken down into their constituent parts, possess far greater value and importance than is currently recognized.

Throughout this book I have given examples of manicurists who, in the course of caring for their customers' nails, provide everything from massage, elder care, counseling for teens, community outreach to therapy for stressed-out clients. If we added even a fraction of the estimated costs of these services, they would ramp up manicure prices well beyond those charged for even the most luxurious manicures. Instead of being an insignificant cosmetic indulgence, a manicure is a complex social exchange. In chapter 1, I demonstrated how this service emerges from local and global forces that bring strangers together in intimate physical and emotional contact. In chapters 2 and 3, I focused on the redefinition of identities, or the "manicuring" of both customers and nail service providers through the exchange of body labor. In subsequent chapters I delved into the nature of the work itself, focusing on its embodied and emotional dimensions and their consequences for racial discourses and relations. In this conclusion I aim to pull together these findings to map out directions for improving relations and upgrading work in this service niche.

The procurement of the manicure enmeshes women in complex relations that are situated in larger systems of gendered employment, racial hierarchy, class inequality, and global migration flows. For customers the weekly or biweekly visit to the nail salon can serve as a salve for an array of frustrations and pressures that they face in their lives, ranging from unattainable standards of beauty and challenges of balancing career and motherhood to obstacles in their educational and professional advancement. Women attest to receiving various personal boosts from their manicures, from improved appearance and higher self-esteem to status enhancement at work, in their communities, and in their personal relationships. However, this interlude, while mostly enjoyable in and of itself, rarely translates into understanding or appreciation of the women who provide their manicures.

Variations in the gendered performance of body labor demonstrate that women inhabit different bodies and different social worlds and that they bring these with them into the manicuring chair, thereby shaping the terms of the manicure and its social meanings, particularly, but not exclusively, with regard to gender. For manicurists, both owners and workers, nail salon work offers opportunities for employment and economic mobility that are largely lacking for them in the primary labor market. This work also affords collegiality with coworkers, a sense of community, and a vehicle for economic and cultural assimilation. At the same time the body labor that they perform extracts a high emotional and physical toll that affects their identities, families, and terms of incorporation into their new country. In order to provide these services manicurists engage in physically demanding work that carries various occupational health–related risks. Furthermore, they perform high levels of emotional labor that are heightened in particular by negotiations of body contact and cultural and language differences. As owners they invest all their savings in these increasingly risky and low-return enterprises while sacrificing time and care for their families. As workers they labor long hours, often without breaks and adequate pay.

In return, how do we, both individually and as a nation, treat those who provide these services? The disparity between the services that manicurists render and the sense of appreciation and respect that they receive is yet another example of the large gap between the contributions of immigrants and their level of acceptance in this country. While they increase the affordability and availability of an array of services and material goods, newcomers to the United States encounter an increasingly virulent anti-immigrant backlash. Often referred to as the "New Nativism," according to Lynn Fujiwara, "the past decade [the 1990s] of anti-immigrant sentiment and discourse resonates racialized hostility and insists on saving America for 'Americans.'"[2] This anti-immigrant discourse has resulted in a number of legislative actions. In 1994 California voters approved Proposition 187, also known as the "Save Our State" initiative, which prohibited the provision of public services, including education, welfare, and health benefits, to undocumented immigrants and their children. Although later declared unconstitutional, it was the first in a wave of anti-immigrant legislation that continues apace. The 1996 Personal Responsibility and Work Opportunity Act echoed aspects of Proposition 187 at the federal level by making citizenship a condition for receipt of any public benefits, except for emergency services (even so, cases abound of undocumented immigrants' being turned away even from this most essential care). The Illegal Immigrant Reform and Immigrant Responsibility Act, enacted the same year, made it more difficult to gain political asylum in the United States and penalized those who would support or hire undocumented immigrants. Following the events of September 11, 2001, anti-immigrant fervor escalated dangerously as immigrant status became increasingly conflated with terrorism. The USA PATRIOT Act of 2001 extended government powers of surveillance and detention without due process, applicable not only to noncitizens but also citizens, and allowed for widespread and arbitrary exclusion and deportation.[3] In New Bedford, Massachusetts, on March 6, 2007, three hundred federal agents stormed a factory that made military vests under a U.S. government defense contract and detained more than 350 undocumented workers, mainly from El Salvador and Guatemala. As many of those detained and eventually deported were women with young children, these actions resulted in the separation of numerous children, including infants, from their parents.[4]

How have Asian immigrants fared in this latest round of anti-immigrant backlash? Their reception by the U.S. government and society has been decidedly mixed. On the one hand, Asians have been touted as the model minority and commended for their industriousness and family values. At the same time this welcome mat, even for arguably the most desirable members of this immigrant group, can be pulled up at a moment's notice and replaced with the yellow peril fears of physical and cultural contamination that have fueled decades of systematic exclusion.

Characterizations of Asian women in particular flip back and forth between the sinister and highly sexualized dragon lady motif and the bumbling yet docile servant, and the manicurist easily slips into this pantheon. Negative views of Asian manicurists, and immigrants more broadly, are disseminated by a popular culture that often fuels one-dimensional racial representations, as in the Bunny Swan character discussed in chapter 6. Unfortunately, such depictions continue to provide an unspoken backdrop for everyday interactions in nail salons.

ASIAN NAIL SALONS AS SOCIAL BAROMETERS

Upon receiving a bad manicure or encountering a surly manicurist, few customers think to blame the working conditions in a given salon, let alone to consider the dynamics of the global service economy that contribute to an unsatisfactory manicuring experience. Instead, they frame these experiences at the level of individual personality or responsibility—"I'm never going back to her again"—or to generalized group condemnation—"Asian manicurists are rude"—or unclean, unskilled, untrustworthy. Conflicting expectations regarding the appropriate practices and demeanor of service delivery do not simply result in miffed feelings between individuals. Because these exchanges so often involve women of different racial, socioeconomic, and citizenship status, they become fodder for group-level stereotypes and animosities.

Stereotypes of Asian women are not monolithic but instead are malleable according to the multiple social contexts and relations in which they emerge. As I discuss in chapters 4 to 6, different racial, class, and gender representations of Asian immigrant women frame their work at different kinds of salons and with different kinds of customers. The three types of salons (nail spas, nail art salons, and discount salons) and styles of service (pampering, expressive, and routinized) reflect distinct characterizations of Asian women and represent different forms of gendered work. Furthermore, these styles of body labor are simultaneously distinct and interdependent—each caters to certain clientele by excluding or at least distancing from others. Pampering body labor earns its cachet by distinguishing upscale nail spas and their mostly white middle- and upper-class clientele from the inexpensive generic services offered in discount nail salons and the marginalized forms of feminine body display in expressive nail art salons. Likewise, nail art salons appeal to working-class black women because they enable and validate articulations of femininity that depart from narrow normative definitions of women and beauty. Finally, discount nail salons serve the myth of a classless society by creating the semblance of equal access to a once-restricted luxury service. Rather than superficial cosmetic processes, these different styles of body labor reflect and reproduce gendered forms of racial and class privilege.

Customers' beliefs that body labor, in all its different forms, is something that comes naturally to Asian women disguise structural forces that shape Asian immigrant women's work in this niche and reproduce gendered versions of racial stereotypes. The discourses of the model minority, black-Korean conflict, and the yellow peril are not simply racial constructions but invoke notions of class, citizenship, and immigration status as well as gender. In establishing and operating these businesses, Asian women both respond to existing social divisions and play a role in maintaining them. At times, they can also subvert them.

THE POWER AND LIMITATIONS OF BEAUTY

What lessons can scholars, activists, policy makers, and customers learn from the complex negotiation of embodied intimacy, gendered work, and racial discourses in nail salons? In the last twenty years a significant body of literature has debated the power of beauty in women's lives, sparking public debate and personal outrage. While these studies have focused predominantly on beauty ideals propagated through corporate advertising and media, these are not the main influences articulated by the women I interviewed. Instead, the women in this study situated their manicures within their identities in multiple sites—their workplaces, families, significant relationships, and racial and ethnic communities. Furthermore, women themselves become participants in reinforcing the rules of beauty in various institutional contexts, as well as in redefining and resisting them.

While nails can serve as a vehicle for women to claim and celebrate their own bodies, the power of beauty often derives from and reinforces powerlessness in other areas of women's lives. Women absorb an onslaught of messages telling them that their own personal failings, particularly the failures of their bodies, are responsible for the difficulties they confront. Thus it is not surprising that they seek solutions to their problems by manicuring their own bodies. It is also not surprising that these efforts end up enforcing norms of femininity, even alternative forms, rather than mobilizing women's resistance to social barriers and inequalities.

Maxine Leeds Craig explores similar issues related to hair. Interrogating the rise and fall of natural hairstyles among black women and men, particularly the Afro in the black power movement, she writes, "Black men, and I would argue, all women live in what might be considered 'marked' or stigmatized bodies. Only the unmarked can trivialize the fleeting, joyous cultural victory experienced when dominant meaning is subverted and what was formerly ridiculed is finally celebrated." At the same time, as Craig further asserts, "without a movement, any woman's body was just her own—not a symbol of unity, just her own."[5] Like hairstyles, manicuring practices must not be underestimated as a potential source of power in women's lives, especially when other sources of power are diminished or unattainable. At the same time the pursuit of power through individual beauty regimens fails to transform social structures that inhibit women's power. Lacking social programs and political movements that address their concerns, women turn to privatized solutions for what are in fact widespread social problems. While on the surface the most private of these solutions is the care, adornment, and alteration of their own bodies, these practices in fact immerse them in public contact in complex social contexts.

Throughout this book I have presented findings that illustrate the inequalities between women in manicuring interactions and how patterns of service provision shape racial meanings and hierarchies. I have critiqued the literature on beauty as focusing one-sidedly on the manipulation and victimization of women, and as ignoring how some women as beauty consumers can exploit less privileged women as beauty service workers. I have hit hard on this need to address the inequalities in nail salon work, as I do not think it is enough for certain women to free themselves from the shackles of oppressive beauty ideologies and practices if they continue to support or simply ignore the conditions under which other women labor in the beauty service industry. I hope this book will increase feminist commitments to creating more egalitarian relations, not only between women who provide beauty services and those who purchase them but also between women in other sites of the global economy who are shaped by both embodied and emotional intimacy and inequality.

BODIES AND EMOTIONS IN THE GLOBAL ECONOMY

Globalization means that our lives are more intricately connected with virtual strangers from across the world than most of us feel comfortable with or care to acknowledge. Rather than denying or skirting the tensions that arise when we find ourselves in an encounter with someone whom we barely know, yet whom we are paying to provide us with an intimate service, we need to recognize and then consciously respond to the various challenges that such interactions pose.

Commercialized interactions that mingle economics and emotional and embodied intimacy show no signs of abating and in fact are proliferating. In the United States we are no more likely to return to a world in which only a few women purchase manicures than we are to go back to a time when most women cooked every meal from scratch, cleaned their own homes, and took care of their children full time. The buying and selling of nail care services can be situated on a continuum with the buying and selling of other body-related services. While I do not claim to speak to these directly, the processes involved in manicuring exchanges can illuminate related dynamics in other settings in which bodies and body work are commodified, including not only facials, massages, plastic surgery, and other beauty services but also, arguably, sex work, surrogacy, and the marketing of organs. Clearly, there are major differences in the nature and degree of bodily commodification in these various services, but all share a common and disquieting position at a historical juncture where the body meets the market.

By focusing on body labor in nail salons, I expand Hochschild's pathbreaking work on emotional labor by adding an embodied perspective. Hochschild's concept of emotional labor, as well as her more recent work on "the commercialization of intimate life," unsettles us for several reasons.[6] We all want to believe that the network of service providers upon which we depend is comprised of people who genuinely care, not only about doing a good job but about us as people. It would be very difficult to subject ourselves to a procedure such as a manicure, let alone to a full body massage or plastic surgery if we could not muster up faith in the manicurist, massage therapist, or cosmetic surgeon as both a skilled professional and someone invested in our feelings, appearance, and overall personal welfare. In other words, as consumers we collude in this fiction of personal caring in order to ease our anxieties regarding the vulnerabilities of our own bodies and emotions and the awkwardness of entrusting these into the hands of strangers.

Certainly, the caring that we receive from body-service providers is not a complete fiction, as many of these providers are compassionate individuals who are drawn into these professions out of a genuine desire to help others. But by not allowing these service exchanges to reflect the natural ebb and flow of human relations and emotions, as well as failing to acknowledge the unequal social hierarchies in which they are performed, consumers of manicuring services—and of intimate body and emotional labor more broadly—impose a high degree of artificiality upon them.

What is gained and lost in the nonnegotiable service culture of the "customer is always right" and its ceaseless demands for smiles and soft touches? What would it take for the participants in these exchanges to engage in honest service encounters as equal human beings and, in doing so, to weather the inevitable bumps and fluctuations in attention and affection? And if we are not up to this task, what are the options? Do we then continue to insist on commercialized arrangements in which we pay, and most often underpay, people for their services and to demand that they are obligated not simply to complete their contracted work but also to make us feel good about ourselves in the process? These are not simply rhetorical questions but inquiries into the very nature of human relations within global capitalism. I acknowledge that it may seem a stretch to go from examining the provision of manicures to reflecting upon the fundamental nature of embodied and emotional ties in twenty-first-century social life. At the same time the evidence from my research demonstrates that service interactions in nail salons, and the beauty industry in general, often obscure both undesirable working conditions and labor relations and new forms of service relations in the global service economy. Under the veneer of caring for customers' physical and emotional needs, these relations are normalized, personalized, and abstracted from the social structures that undergird them. Thus closer attention to body labor in nail salons can offer lessons about envisioning and working toward more equal and humanizing relations inside these establishments as well as in the larger societies in which they operate.

MANICURING CHANGE

The months of protesting at Nail Plaza on behalf of Do Yea Kim ended with an important victory. Represented by the Asian American Legal

Defense and Education Fund and the law firm of Paul, Weiss, Rifkind, Wharton and Garrison, Kim filed a lawsuit charging lack of overtime pay and wrongful termination. In October 2007 a federal jury awarded her $182,000 in back pay, overtime, and damages.[7] The victory galvanized efforts to draw attention to and improve working conditions in nail salons. In chapter 6, I discussed a number of these, including occupational safety and public health approaches concentrating on community outreach and education, labor rights organizing focusing on owner-worker relations and enforcing labor laws in salons, and coalitional work targeted at legislation and regulation of manufacturers' use of toxic chemicals in nail products.

In formulating strategies for change in the nail industry, it is helpful to examine approaches in other industries that involve similar dimensions of intimate body and emotional labor. As numerous scholars have demonstrated, much labor that falls under the rubric of "care work," which encompasses child care, elder care, and care of sick and disabled people— and, I would add, care of bodies and their appearance—is grossly unregulated and undercompensated. In these burgeoning care industries various organizations are seeking to address issues confronting both employers and employees. On the one hand, these include efforts to protect the consumer, ranging from clearer standards to enforcement of violations. This, however, is only half the story. The other half that needs to be addressed are the wages, working conditions, and rights of the employees and the policies and institutional supports necessary to guarantee them.

Mary Romero provides lessons from domestic work in her book *Maid in the U.S.A.* She describes professional women who, uncomfortable with the dynamics of hiring immigrant women of color as domestics, become "dodgers and duckers" and hire college students to do their cleaning, usually for much higher wages. Others adopt a "common victim" stance that posits them as "just as exploited as the women they employ" and "denies that the burden of sexism has been shifted to another woman."[8] Both strategies end up denying that certain women's privileges allow them to hire other women to care for their homes or their loved ones, often for substandard wages and in poor working conditions. Similarly, these dodging and ducking strategies are inadequate for dealing with the contradictions of paying another woman to care for one's body. It does little to address the inequalities of beauty services simply to avoid patronizing Asian-owned salons in favor of purchasing manicures from a native-born cosmetologist at a full-service beauty salon, usually for a higher price. Nor is it particularly useful for a customer of race and class privilege to claim commonality with low-wage immigrant women of color as equal victims of gender discrimination. These strategies either skirt the issues or grasp too readily at easy but inadequate solutions. Instead, customers can choose the harder but more effective road of supporting their manicurists by paying them adequately for their services, treating them with respect, demanding that salons follow proper safety and health standards protecting both customers and workers, and joining with them in efforts to improve cosmetic products and regulations.

In order to succeed, efforts to upgrade the work of manicurists must confront differences and divisions between women. Just as raising wages for domestic labor performed mostly by women of color threatens the ability of relatively privileged women to afford the services of nannies and maids, so can raising the price of manicuring services performed by Asian immigrant women undermine the ability of certain customers to purchase them. In addition, the work necessary to improve the conditions of nail salon work can also cut into the profits that Asian immigrant small business owners generate, at times at their workers' expense. Even when relations between women in nail salons—whether owners, workers, or customers—foster some sense of mutual assistance or understanding, they are often predicated on unequal power and conflicting interests.

How does the embodied and emotional intimacy of this work shape prospects for collaborative efforts between owners, workers, and customers to upgrade nail salon work? Other scholars have argued that close physical and emotional ties between workers and employers, as well as between workers and customers, largely mask and help to perpetuate unequal power relations and exploitative conditions in various industries, ranging from sex work to nursing to domestic service.[9] For better or worse, I find these patterns replicated in the nail industry, as even customers who profess that their manicurists are their friends are unwilling to support them in improving the conditions of their work.

It cannot be assumed that the intimacy involved in nail salon work, or any work, translates into mutual investment by all parties—owners, workers, and customers—in improving the various conditions involved in this work. In fact, the opposite is more often true. As Paula England and Nancy Folbre assert, "the principle that money cannot buy love may have the unintended and perverse consequence of perpetuating low pay for face-to-face service work."[10] In other words, the belief that intimate relations and the processes through which they are enacted should not be commercialized ends up devaluing work that involves care, or as emphasized in this study, emotional and body labor. The case of nail salon work lends further support to this argument, as different forms of body labor raise the stakes of customer interaction but not the compensation for or valuing of this work. Despite these tensions, points of common interest between women in salons exist and can be nurtured.

In mapping out the complexities of body labor, I have highlighted small opportunities for social change that lie in negotiating more equitable service interactions between women of different classes, racial and ethnic backgrounds, and immigrant status. While these interactions often mimic structures of power and privilege, they also create openings to contest these structures. Asian manicurists at nail spas undermine the privilege of their white middle-class customers by talking about them or refusing to perform certain work. The Korean owners of Downtown Nails learned to respect and show appreciation for their black working-class patrons. Routinized service at discount nail salons roughly equalizes the treatment of women across race and class. From the customer's side a weekly trip to the local nail salon can become a lesson in relating to a woman of a radically different social position whom she would rarely encounter in her own social milieu. The dynamics of body labor can increase the value of the work by emphasizing that the worker is not simply a machine on an assembly line but a person with specific skills for attending to the unique bodies and feelings of the customer.

Evelyn Nakano Glenn writes that "contesting race and gender hierarchies may involve challenging everyday assumptions and practices, take forms that do not involve direct confrontation, and occur in locations not considered political."[11] Exchanges involving body labor in

Asian-owned nail salons are one such location where these everyday assumptions and practices of privilege and inequality can be recognized and perhaps renegotiated. Because these emotional and embodied interactions reflect larger systems of status and power, by rewriting the unspoken feeling and embodied rules of these interactions, women can take small but important steps in the creation of more equal relations with other women.

MANICURING UTOPIAS

What are the possibilities of the manicure as a meaningful social, physical, and emotional exchange? Arguably, group grooming exercises are the foundation of sociability in many species, from cheetahs to chimps. Why should our own be any different? Indeed, social scientists have long observed the importance of ritualistic acts of adorning and tending the body in "uncivilized" societies, but these same ritualistic behaviors in modern, Western societies often escape this anthropological gaze. Thus it may be useful to look at manicuring practices outside our own familiar environs and then return to look anew at the nail salon around the corner.

For his National Book Award–winning work, *The Noonday Demon: An Atlas of Depression,* Andrew Solomon went to Cambodia to interview survivors of Pol Pot's killing fields and explored the emotional makeup of people who survive such atrocities. In Phnom Penh he learned of an extraordinary woman, Phaly Nuon, who survived witnessing the murder of her daughter and the starvation of her infant child.[12] After many years of struggling to come to terms with these tragedies, she now devotes her life to helping other women reclaim their lives. According to Solomon, Nuon has developed her own three-step healing process of learning first to forget, then to work, and finally to love. She grounds this process in traditional Khmer herbal medicine, Western antidepressants, and, yes, the giving and receiving of manicures. She explains her use of manicures in a way that makes this unconventional approach to overcoming trauma seem not only unremarkable but perfectly sensible:

I teach them how to give one another manicures and pedicures and how to take care of their fingernails, because doing that makes them feel beautiful, and they want so much to feel beautiful. It also puts them in contact with the bodies of other people and makes them give up their bodies to the care of others. . . . While they are together washing and putting on nail polish, they begin to talk together, and bit by bit they learn to trust one another, and by the end of it all, they have learned how to make friends, so that they will never have to be so lonely and so alone again.[13]

Nuon thus engages women in the exchange of manicures as a way of bringing them back into their bodies, then back into caring and trusting contact with other human bodies, and finally back into their own lives and social worlds.

What can Nuon teach us about the possibilities of the manicure as a vehicle for forging authentic connections to self and others in societies that are increasingly based on inauthentic and commercialized relations? Is her use of the manicure as a therapeutic practice specific to the history and culture of a Southeast Asian country ravaged by war and terror? Or are there lessons that can be transported to midtown Manhattan, Brooklyn, and Queens or even to downtowns, small towns, and suburbs throughout the United States and other countries? I hesitate to jump between such disparate contexts to make naive comparisons between sites that are in fact worlds apart. Nonetheless, I cannot help but wonder, is Nuon really on to something, and are we remiss to ignore her wisdom in using the manicure as a healing and humanizing exchange?

I wish I could hear from the women themselves who participated in Nuon's program—what was it about giving and receiving manicures that enabled them to connect with each other in meaningful and supportive ways? While I cannot speak directly to or for their experiences, I can garner some insights from my own research on women working in New York City nail salons. When I asked these women what they would change to improve this work, their responses were simple. Many pointed to the working conditions of the salons—"Have better ventilation and less strong smell"—or labor and wage issues—"More breaks and better pay"—but a surprising number also spoke to more intangible aspects of salon relations. Gloria Kim, a veteran manicurist with more than fifteen years of experience, told me: "Though on busy days I'm unable even to go to the bathroom or eat, I do this work because I like it. I feel that relationships are closer in a nail salon than grocery stores. I am facing the person as I am working with her. I have many regular customers. I have been here for quite a long time, and we've become close through conversations. For example, if I share with a customer that I have a toothache, the next time she comes around, she will ask me about it."

In a similar vein, Nancy at Uptown Nails explained her feelings about her customers and her hopes for mutual respect and concern:

> We have to get very close to the customers, like this [holding her hands together] so we try best to get along with them. If you don't like someone and you have to do this—hold their hand and talk to them face to face—it can be very difficult. This is service work—so you know you have to act a certain way. Of course I don't like doing the pedicures, having to kneel down, and the foot smell. But I just think of it as part of giving the service . . . I try very hard to ask them about their families and how they feel. It would be nice if once in a while they asked me, too.

These simple things—responding with concern when a manicurist says she has a toothache, asking in return about her family and health—are what make or break a manicurist's day. They can give her the sense that her work is not merely tolerable but has purpose and dignity.

These simple things do not seem too much to ask. However, until a manicure is seen as more than a personal indulgence or a ritual of bonding between women, the intensive embodied and emotional work that it entails and the conditions under which it is performed will remain largely invisible and unequal—and these small requests to upgrade the work will most likely go unanswered. Unless women become active agents in recognizing and changing the social relations that shape a manicure, they will continue to be nailed by the divisions and hierarchies that place them, often at odds, on opposite sides of the manicuring table.

Notes

The epigraphs are from Hochschild (2003: 8); Lorber and Moore (2007: 240); and Glenn (1992: 37).

1. Frank 1990.
2. Fonow and Cook 2005: 2216.
3. Hochschild 1983: 5.
4. Industry figures estimate that while 45 percent of U.S. nail technicians are Asian women, the figures are much higher in particular cities. In New York City an estimated 80 percent of the manicurists are Korean, and in California 75 percent are Vietnamese (Nails 2008: 62).

5. For discussion of media depictions of beauty salons, see Scanlon (2007). The history of beauty salons serving and operated by African American women reveals that they have in fact played the role of community center, where black women socialize and network, although not across racial lines. See Willett (2002) and Harvey (2005).

6. Lowe 1996: 158.

7. On intersections of race, gender, immigration, and work in the constructions of Asian and Asian American women, see Espiritu (2003, 2008), Vo and Sciachitano (2000), Chin (2005), E. Lee (2005), Chan (1991b), Parreñas (2001), Grace Chang (2000), Choy (2003), Foo (2007), and Yamanaka and McClelland (1994).

8. While Collins's "controlling images" is related to the terms *representations* and *stereotypes*, she asserts that "controlling images are most closely tied to power relations of race, class, gender and sexuality" (2005: 350). Thus I apply the concept of controlling images to Asian immigrant women while also using more familiar terms such as *representations* and *stereotypes* when appropriate.

9. I saw Cho's performance on October 5, 2003, at the Calvin Theater in Northampton, Massachusetts.

10. I use the term *white* to refer to a racial category that designates those of European ancestry and the term *black* to refer to a racial category that includes African Americans, Afro-Caribbeans, and Africans. At the same time I recognize these terms carry meaning beyond ancestry. Consistent with literature on the social construction of race, I use these terms to highlight the common racial categories that are used to group together diverse populations. At the same time I acknowledge them as problematic terms that often subsume differences in culture and historical experiences, particularly by rendering "whiteness" as both a dominant and an invisible category (Bonilla-Silva and Doane 2003; Brattain 2001; Frankenberg 1993). Where individual respondents designate their racial and ethnic identities otherwise, I use their self-descriptions. I also designate ethnicity and nationality when these distinctions relate to analytical points.

11. In this book I use the term *manicurist* as a general and inclusive term to include various techniques of providing nail services, as well as various jobs within the nail industry. Where greater specificity is useful, I use other terms, such as *nail technician, nail artist,* and *pedicurist.* I also recognize that differences between salon owners, managers, and workers are significant, and I distinguish between these varying positions where the differences are salient. This discussion is informed by scholarship that analyzes the class and status differences between coethnic employers and employees in the ethnic economy (Light and Bonacich 1988; Model 1988; Sanders and Nee 1987; Zhou and Logan 1989).

12. I have used the extended case method, which, according to Michael Burawoy, "tells us about society as a whole rather than about the population of

similar cases" (1991: 281). Thus I have examined cases of specific kinds of nail salons, not to formulate generalizations about all similar nail salons but instead to explore the larger social structures and processes in which they are embedded.

13. I concentrate on women, recognizing that this focus is only one angle of a much more complicated gender perspective. Whether men actually frequent these establishments or not, a feminized niche like the nail salon also heavily implicates men, including their expectations regarding women's appearance and their influence on gendered labor markets and the gendered organization of households.

14. Gilroy 1993: 85.

15. Baumgardner, in collaboration with Amy Richards (2000, 2005), has published influential works on feminist politics.

16 Jennifer Baumgardner, "Nails," 2000, www.spoonbenders.com/nails .htm. This link is no longer active.

17. Hochschild and Machung 1997; Wolf 1991: 24–27.

18. Hochschild and Ehrenreich 2004. On immigrant women in domestic service, see Hondagneu-Sotelo (2001), Parreñas (2001), and Romero (2002). For domestic work outside the United States, see Lan (2006).

19. Critiques of women's search for beauty include Banner (1983), Bordo (1993), Chapkis (1986), and Wolf (1991).

20. These terms—intersectional, transnational, and postcolonial feminisms— refer to related but distinct frameworks that challenge false universals regarding women's shared experiences and the primacy of gender. They situate gender within specific historical, cultural, economic, and political contexts but with different emphases. Intersectional perspectives focus on race, gender, and class as simultaneous and interconnected social processes that shape social relations and identities (Andersen and Collins 2006; McCall 2005; Weber 2004; Brown and Misra 2003; Chow, Wilkinson, and Zinn 1996; Zinn and Dill 1996; West and Fenstermaker 1995; Glenn 1992; Crenshaw 1991; Amott and Matthaei 1991; Collins 1991; hooks 1981; Hurtado 1989; and King 1988). Transnational feminists examine constructions of nation, race, gender, sexuality, and class within a framework of imperialism and global capitalism, highlighting resistance, including—but not confined to—challenges to the state and nationalist ideologies (Grewal and Kaplan 2004; Kaplan, Alarcon, and Moallem 1999; Mohanty 2003; Shohat 1999). Postcolonial feminists emphasize the impact of processes associated with colonialism and decolonization and the ongoing ways that colonial legacies continue to shape culture, power, and inequality, particularly with regard to the imposition and contestation of Western gender norms (Minh-ha 1989; Mohanty 1991; Narayan 1997; Spivak 1988). These feminist frameworks draw from and share affinities with black, multicultural, and Third World feminisms (Anzaldúa 1990; Lorde 1984; and Moraga and Anzaldúa 1981).

21. Pascale (2006) discusses how understandings of race, gender, and class depend on commonsense, or seemingly obvious, assumptions that often preclude conscious examination.

22. The dichotomous framings of race and gender were evidenced in the 2008 Democratic presidential primaries when Hillary Clinton was characterized as the "woman" candidate and Barack Obama as the "black" candidate, as opposed to recognizing both race and gender in Clinton's identity as a white woman and Obama's as a black man.

23. Hochschild's original case study of flight attendants and subsequent applications to other female-dominated occupations have emphasized the gendered employment experiences of native-born white women—as paralegals (Pierce 1995), nannies and au pairs (Macdonald and Sirianni 1996), fast food and insurance sales people (Leidner 1993), and police officers (S. Martin 1999).

24. As Davis argues, "Recent feminist theory on the body has displayed a marked ambivalence towards the material body and a tendency to privilege the body as metaphor. Priority is given to the deconstructive project—that is, to dismantling the mind/body split in Western philosophy or debunking gendered symbols and dichotomies rather than attending to individuals' actual material bodies or their everyday interactions with their bodies and through their bodies with the world around them" (1995: 1). Theoretical and empirical studies of women's bodies have focused on the social construction of ideas about the female body and how these constructions control and are resisted by women, particularly in debates about sexuality, appearance, and bodily behavior. See Bordo (1989), Janet Lee (1994), E. Martin (1987), Morgan (1991), and Weitz (1998).

25. Studies that address the embodied and emotional dimensions of work in various occupations and contexts include Bernstein (2007), Wolkowitz (2006), Bolton (2005), Oerton (2004), Gimlin (1996), Oerton and Phoenix (2001), Jervis (2001), Twigg (2000), and E. Martin (1996). Pei-Chia Lan (2000, 2003) has developed the related term "bodily labor" to analyze cosmetic sales in Taiwan.

26. Kraut 2006: 115.

27. Hochschild defines these terms as follows: "I use the term *emotional labor* to mean the management of feeling to create a publicly observable facial and bodily display; emotional labor is sold for a wage and therefore has *exchange value*. I use the synonymous terms *emotion work* or *emotion management* to refer to these same acts done in a private context where they have use value" (Hochschild 1983: 7n). Hochschild distinguishes emotion work as the control of feelings performed in a private context and emotional labor as the management of feelings in exchange for a wage. However, these terms have been subsequently adopted in various ways, with *emotion work* often used as an umbrella term for both paid and unpaid emotion management and *emotional labor* to specify the commercialized control of feeling display. Thus, while I build on her distinctions, I have adapted

them to correspond with the prevalent use of *body work* in scholarly literature to designate both paid and unpaid work on the body and I use *body labor* to refer specifically to the commercialization of bodies and feelings in work on the body that involves a fee. See Wolkowitz (2006) for further discussion of these terms.

28.   Hochschild 1983: 7. This definition builds upon her case study of flight attendants and the specific feeling rules that govern this job as it was performed by white middle-class women largely for the benefit of white middle-class and upper-class men. While Hochschild emphasizes variation in forms of emotional labor, including a case study of bill collectors and the aggressive style of emotional labor they perform, much less attention has been directed at the multiple forms, contexts, and consequences of emotional labor.

29.   The Committee Against Anti-Asian Violence (CAAAV) provided important contacts and insights, but did not sponsor this research and is not responsible for it. Its Women Workers Project continues to mobilize support for Asian immigrant women employed in such service sectors as domestic work, nail salons, and laundries. I served as a board member of CAAAV from 1992 to 1994.

30.   Feminist methodology has problematized the role of the ethnographer toward her subjects and issued a call for greater "reflexivity" regarding how the social background of the researcher affects the data and their presentation and how the research subjects view the work. See hooks (1990), Fonow and Cook (1991 and 2005), Haney (1996), Reinharz (1992), DeVault (1999), Naples (2003), Richardson (1997), D. Smith (1998), and Visweswaran (1994).

31.   I have attempted to account for the influence on the research subjects, data collection, findings, and interpretation of my own background as a middle-class second-generation Korean woman. See Kang (2000).

32.   Potential avenues for ongoing research include examinations of specific labor recruitment mechanisms that result in certain Asian groups' clustering in this niche; comparative analysis of the experiences of different racial and ethnic groups in the nail industry; comparisons of coethnic and interracial relations between immigrant employers and workers in this industry; men as manicurists and customers; and policy and advocacy to upgrade work in this industry. For research on other dimensions of Asian-owned nail salons, see Roelofs et al. (2008), oh (2007), and Federman, Harrington, and Krynski (2006).

1. "THERE'S NO BUSINESS LIKE THE NAIL BUSINESS"

The epigraphs are from Haughney (2003) and Townsend (1989).

1.   Sassen 2001.
2.   Hochschild 2003.

3. In addition to Hochschild, several scholars have explored the processes through which capitalism expands into private life. See Braverman (1974) and Glenn (1992).

4. See Putnam (2000).

5. On the growth in hair-cutting chains, see Gallagher (2003).

6. Zelizer 2005: 34.

7. Standley 2007.

8. See Blair-Loy (2003), Cohen (1996), and Padavic and Reskin (2002). The U.S. Bureau of Labor Statistics reported in February 2000, "In 1950 about one in three women participated in the labor force. By 1998, nearly three of every five women of working age were in the labor force."

9. Dickson 2005.

10. Nails 2008: 62.

11. U.S. Bureau of Labor Statistics 2007.

12. Postrel (2004) points out the huge discrepancy between the Bureau of Labor Statistics estimates and industry estimates, arguing that "the bureau has missed more than 300,000 manicurists. It puts the total at around 30,000, compared with the count of 372,000—up from 189,000 a decade ago—by Nails magazine, using private survey and state licensing data. Even if not all licensed manicurists are practicing, the bureau number is off by an order of magnitude. There are 53,000 nail salons in the country, most of them with more than one manicurist. The industry supports two major trade magazines, each with about 60,000 subscribers."

13. Nails 2005: 27. This survey reported a significant shift in nail salon services, with traditional manicures accounting for only 18.5 percent, while acrylics, nail art, and other artificial enhancements made up 44.7 percent.

14. A dentist, Dr. Stuart Nordstrom, is widely credited with creating the chemical substance used in acrylics. Nordstrom experimented with dental liquid and powders and went on to start a successful nail products company and create numerous substances widely used in the nail industry. See Postrel (1997).

15. Sachs 2001.

16. Willett 2000; Candelario 2000.

17. Craig 2002; Banks 2000.

18. Nails 2002: 38, and 2005: 42.

19. U.S. Census Bureau 2004.

20. Sassen 2001.

21. Saskia Sassen-Koob, "Labor Migration and the New Industrial Division of Labor," in Nash and Fernandez-Kelly 1983: 195.

22. For studies of the socioeconomic restructuring of New York City, see Bean and Stevens (2003), Foner (1987), Logan and Alba (1999), Mollenkopf and Castells (1991), Sassen (1989), and Waldinger (1987).

23. Hill 1997a: 100.

24. Sassen 1998: 154.

25. The U.S. Bureau of Labor Statistics reports in its 2008–2009 *Occupational Outlook Handbook,* "All States require barbers, cosmetologists, and other personal appearance workers to be licensed, with the exceptions of shampooers and makeup artists. Qualifications for a license vary by State, but generally a person must have a high school diploma or GED, be at least 16 years old, and have graduated from a State-licensed barber or cosmetology school. After graduating from a State approved training program, students take a State licensing examination. . . . Most States require separate licensing examinations for manicurists, pedicurists, and skin care specialists" (see "Service Occupations: Cleaning, Food, and Persona," p. 6, http://stats.bls.gov/oco/reprints/ocoro10.pdf). According to Willett (2005), many states have required manicurists to be licensed since the 1930s and 1940s.

26. Wurdinger 1992.

27. Hill 1997a: 102.

28. D. Lee 1999.

29. K. Park 1991: 8.

30. On factors influencing Korean women's migration to the United States, see K. Park (1991), B. Kim (1977), N. Kim (2008), E. Lee (2005), Kim and Yu (1996), Bonacich, Hossain, and Park (1987).

31. See Bello and Rosenfeld (1990), Garran (1998), Goldstein (1998), and E. Kim (1999).

32. For further discussion of South Korea's rapid industrial development, authoritarian state regimes, and resistance movements, see N. Lee (2007), Rhee (1994), and Shin (1999).

33. S. Moon 2005.

34. Danico 2004, Le 2007a, and L. Park 2005.

35. Chan 1991a, Takaki 1995, and Zolberg 2006.

36. U.S. Office of Immigration Statistics 2007.

37. United Nations 1999.

38. Kye Song Lee, interview by author, May 30, 2000, St. Louis, Missouri. The *Korean American Nail and Beauty Journal* has been renamed *Beauty Times.*

The U.S. Bureau of Labor Statistics reports a median hourly wage for manicurists and pedicurists of $9.46 and annual median earnings of $19,670 in May 2008 (www.bls.gov/oes/current/oes395092.htm).

39. Min 1997: 14.

40. The census figures are from "Fact Sheet: New York City: Census 2000 Demographic Profile Highlights: Selected Population Group: Korean Alone," 2000, http://factfinder.census.gov. To access these statistics, click on Fact Sheet/Fact Sheet for a Race, Ethnic, or Ancestry Group. Under "Asian Alone," select "Korean Alone" and on the new screen fill in "New York" for the location. Census tabulations for 2006 may be found in "New York City, New York:

ACS Demographic and Housing Estimates: 2005–2007," http://factfinder. census.gov/servlet/ADPTable?_bm=y&-geo_id=16000US3651000&-qr_ name=ACS_2007_3YR_G00_DP3YR5&-ds_name=ACS_2007_3YR_G00_&-_ lang=en&-redoLog=false&-_sse=on.

41. Espiritu 2008: 87.

42. *Sae Gae Times,* January 29, 1991, cited in Min 1996.

43. An Sik Nam, interview by author, August 31, 2000.

44. Ibid.

2. "WHAT OTHER WORK IS THERE?"

The first two epigraphs are from interviews I conducted for this study; the third is from Pessar (2003: 31).

1. For critiques of the "model minority" stereotype, see Chan (1991b), Fong (2007), Kawai (2005), Sun and Starosta (2006), and T. Yu (2006).

2. Hondagneu-Sotelo 1994, 2003. The growing literature on gender and migration includes Ong (2003), Benhabib and Resnik (2009), George (2005), Pessar (2003), Espiritu (2008), Hondagneu-Sotelo and Avila (1997), Huisman and Hondagneu-Sotelo (2005), Kibria (1993), and Lamphere, Zavella, Gonzalez, and Evans (1993).

3. On the phenomenon of American fever in South Korea and its influence on postwar emigration, see "American Fever," chap. 2 in Yuh 2002: 42–83.

4. N. Kim 2008: 44.

5. As I noted in chapter 1 (see note 38, p. 261), estimates of earnings in nail salons vary significantly between U.S. Census and industry figures.

6. E. Lee 2005.

7. Rather than using the terms *Hispanic* or *Latina,* Korean immigrants instead often refer to Spanish-speaking immigrants simply as "Spanish."

8. Hochschild 1989.

9. Parreñas 2005.

10. L. Park 2005.

11. Gans 1979. Findings on the assimilation patterns of the "new second generation," post-1965 children of immigrants, reveal mixed patterns of mobility depending on education, neighborhood, parents' socioeconomic status, transnational ties, and racial and ethnic identity. See Portes, Fernandez-Kelly, and Haller (2009); Mollenkopf (2009), Kasinitz (2008), Farley and Alba (2002), Levitt and Waters (2002), Portes and Rumbaut (2001), Perlmann and Waldinger (1997), Neckerman, Carter, and Lee (1999); Portes and Zhou (1993).

12. Glass and Riley 1998.

13. Parreñas 2000; Moya 2007.

14. Menjivar 2003: 120.

15. Min 1990: 33.

16. K. Kim and Hurh 1988: 162.

17. Kibria 1993, 1994.

18. Espiritu 2003: 95.

19. Min 1990, 1996.

20. Hays 2003; Lareau 2002; Sidel 1998.

21. See C. Freeman (1999), Fujiwara (2005), Kibria (1993), and Parreñas (2005).

22. Sennett and Cobb 1993.

23 Hyun 2006. For other studies related to Asian Americans' blocked mobility in professional employment, see De Jong and Madamba (2001), P. Kim and Lewis (1994), Tang (1993), Woo (2002), Wu (1997), and Young and Fox (2002).

24. On the factors shaping Asian employment and self-employment in ethnic-owned small businesses, see Light and Bonacich (1988), Min (1990, 1996), Le (2007a), and Zhou and Bankston (1995).

25. Parreñas (2001: 150) develops this concept with regard to Filipina domestics, who move down in terms of occupational prestige but up in terms of earnings by migrating to the United States.

26. Grace Chang 2000; Glenn 1992; Hondagneu-Sotelo 2001; Romero 2002.

27. Ngai 2004: 2. On the complexity of determining the size, impact and responses to illegal immigration, see Passel and Cohn (2008), Durand and Massey (2004), Massey et al. (2005), Passel (1999), Congressional Budget Office (2007), and Nadadur (2009).

28. For example, in its brochure the Christian Nail School in Manhattan advertises a two-month full-time nail technician course for roughly $2,000 and offers support in filing for licenses and visas.

29. On the difficulties of undocumented immigrants seeking legal status, see Johnson (2007), Das Gupta (2006), Swarns and Drew (2003), Menjivar (2000), and Mahler (1996).

30. K. Park 1997: 26.

31. Perea 1997: 2.

32. McDonnell 1997, cited in Hamilton and Chinchilla 2001: 189.

33. Cho 1997: 165.

34. As I discussed in the introduction, these behaviors are not limited to men but can include women customers as well.

35. On the practices, environment, and impacts of sexual harassment in a range of workplaces, see Collinson and Collinson (1996), Cortina and Wasti (2005), Dansky and Kilpatrick (1997), and Huerta et al. (2006).

36. Kyeyoung Park (1997) discusses how many Korean immigrants see the establishment of a small business as a sign of having achieved status and security (anjong) in their new country.

3. HOOKED ON NAILS

The first two epigraphs come from interviews I conducted for this study; the third is from Atwood (1998: 29).

1. Bourdieu 1984 : 6–7.

2. Bourdieu 1990: 52–53.

3. Collins 2005: 193–94. Sexuality is also an important force that shapes gendered constructions of women's appearance. Regrettably, I was not able to address this dimension fully in my study, and this chapter focuses on heterosexual partnerships and identities. For analysis of appearance among lesbian, bisexual, and transgender women, see Atkins (1998), and Cogan (1999).

4. Bettie 2003: 15.

5. The idea of "cultural dupes" (Horkheimer and Adorno 1972) refers to the notion that the masses are manipulated into buying into popular culture, particularly through the media, as a central component of selling capitalism. Stuart Hall argues instead that culture is a site of continuous struggle involving both consent and opposition to dominant cultural forms. See Hall (1981, 1990).

6. For discussion of the influence of age on women's beauty practices see Furman's *Facing the Mirror* (1997).

7. Collins 2005: 193.

8. Chancer 1998: 146–48.

9. On different cultural constructions of motherhood, see Kaplan (1997); Crittenden (2001), and Hays (1996, 2003).

10. McCormack 2005: 661.

11. Roberts 1997: 152.

12. The social historian Julie A. Willett (2005) discusses the class distinction associated with manicured nails in an earlier era: "By the 1920s and 1930s, smooth, well-manicured hands revealed not simply a woman's attentiveness but her class background" (60). For more discussion of the class background of beauty service customers, see Peiss (1998).

13. The concept of elite educated women who "opt out" of the labor force to raise children was popularized by Belkin (2003). Subsequent scholarship has challenged whether women are in fact leaving the workforce or if other economic factors such as recession and unemployment account for the fluctuations in their participation (Boushey 2005). Others have focused on the pressures that make women feel pushed out as opposed to opting out of paid work (Stone 2007).

14. For a variety of perspectives on the mommy wars, see Peskowitz (2005), Steiner (2006), and Douglas and Michaels (2004).

15. Hays 1996.

16. For a classic study of social stigma, see Goffman (1974). For stigmatization of poor black single mothers, see Haight, Finet, Bamba, and Helton (2009), Hardaway and McLoyd (2009); Reutter et al. (2009).

17. McCormack 2005: 670.

18. While Kaplan's study focuses on black teen mothers, her analysis of the poverty of relationships is applicable to other mothers (Kaplan 1997).

19. Dellinger and Williams 1997: 174.

20. On discrimination against middle-class blacks see Feagin and Feagin (1999), Feagin and McKinney (2002), Feagin and Sikes (1994), and Waters (1990, 2001).

21. Rose Weitz (2001) writes about the centrality of women's hairstyles to their sense of attractiveness as well as how the significance of hair is shaped by multiple forms of power.

22. On the oppressive nature of beauty, see Wolf (1991) and Greer (1999). On women's potential agency and empowerment through beauty, see Friday (1996). On tensions between beauty as an oppressive versus subversive force, see Davis (1995) and Bordo (2004). Michel Foucault's work (1979, 1986) on the disciplinary technologies of creating "docile bodies," and feminist critiques of his work have been influential in these debates (Bordo 1989). Judith Butler (1999) shows that embodied performances of femininity, such as drag, can "trouble" dominant categories of sex and gender and create possibilities for resistance.

23. Scholars have addressed settings ranging from hair salons to cosmetic surgeons' offices to beauty pageants to organizations for fat acceptance to communities of resettled refugees to emphasize the shifting and complex meanings of beauty and the importance of social and historical constraints in shaping its practices (Banet-Weiser 1999; Chancer 1998; Gimlan 1996; Huisman and Hondagneu-Sotelo 2005; Peiss 1998; Gagne and McGaughey 2002).

24. Gimlin 2002: 9.

25. Huisman and Hondagneu-Sotelo 2005: 63.

26. For scholarship on hierarchical evaluations of women's appearance based on race, see hooks (1990), King-O'Riain (2006), and Hunter (2005).

27. Banet-Weiser 1999: 9.

4. "I JUST PUT KOREANS AND NAILS TOGETHER"

The Ishle Park epigraph is from *The Temperature of This Water* (2004: 94).

1. Tuan (1998) argues that representations of Asian Americans shift precariously from laudatory portrayals as "honorary whites" to derogatory designations as "forever foreigners."

2. According to the Internet Movie Database, the *Seinfeld* episode "The Understudy," written by Marjorie Gross and Carol Leifer, first aired on NBC on May 18, 1995; see www.imdb.com/title/tt0697802/combined.

3. According to Foucault, the body has come under increasing surveillance and control in modern societies through disciplinary institutions such as prisons, schools, factories, and the military. He argues, "A 'political anatomy,' which was also a 'mechanics of power,' was being born; it defined how one may have a hold over others' bodies, not only so that they may do what one wishes, but so that they may operate as one wishes, with the techniques, the speed and the efficiency that one determines. Thus, discipline produces subjected and practiced bodies, 'docile' bodies" (Foucault 1979: 138).

4. Bartky 1988: 64.

5. Fong 2007: 65.

6. Takagi 1992: 58–59. On dimensions of the Asian model minority discourse, see Chou and Feagin (2008), Inkelas (2006), Kawai (2005), Osajima (1988), Shim (1998), and Taylor, Landreth, and Bang (2005).

7. Palumbo-Liu 1999: 150.

8. On the diverse patterns of incorporation of Asian Americans, see Chou and Feagin (2008), Le (2007a), Sakamoto and Xie (2006), Woo (2000), and Xie and Goyette (2004).

9. Okihiro 1995.

10. Espiritu 2008: 124.

11. Edward Said (1979) defines Orientalism as "a style of thought based upon ontological and epistemological distinction made between 'the Orient' and (most of the time) 'the Occident' . . . despite or beyond any correspondence, or lack thereof, with a 'real' Orient" (5). While the women in this study do not necessarily reference this academic concept, their thinking nonetheless reflects exoticized, essentialist notions indicative of Orientalist ways of thinking.

12. Williams 2006: 19.

13. Wurdinger 1992: 38.

14. On the assimilation in the United States of Russian and other immigrants from the former Soviet Union, see Chiswick (1997), Gold (1995), and Kishinevsky (2004).

15. I have discussed the influence of my own Korean ethnicity on shaping interactions with respondents, particularly in moments such as this, when the customer addressed her comments directly to me in referring to "you Koreans." See Kang (2000).

16. While a variety of customers (ranging from a black female executive to a retired Jewish male financier to the fifteen-year-old daughter of the operator of the South Asian newsstand in front of the store) patronize this salon intermittently,

the majority are white native-born professional women. They included a lawyer, flight attendant, secretary, professor, personal trainer, accessories importer, pharmacist, homemaker, fashion designer, and real estate broker.

17. Goffman 1959: 119.

18. R. Lee 1999: 38.

19. Leidner (1993) uses this term to characterize work that requires direct contact with customers and clients, and she elaborates on the complex dimensions of conversation in this work.

20. Hagedorn's book focuses on such depictions as they relate to Filipinos. In a telling scene one character discusses the origin of the term *dogeaters:* "You know where the term 'dogeater' came from? The Americans, of course" (Hagedorn 1991: 40).

21. See Macedo, Gounari, and Dendrinos (2003), Boyle (2004), and Pennycook (1998).

22. See Shim, Kim, and Martin (2008).

23. Wolkowitz 2006: 98.

5. BLACK PEOPLE "HAVE NOT BEEN THE ONES WHO GET PAMPERED"

The first two epigraphs are from interviews I conducted for this study; the third is from Abelmann and Lie 1995: 159.

1. Tavernise (2005). Foxy Brown received probation in the 2004 nail salon incident but later was charged with assaulting a neighbor and a beauty supply store employee (Edidin 2007).

2. C. Kim 2000: 3.

3. Park (1996: 492) discusses the response of the Los Angeles Korean American community to "Black Korea." Ice Cube's controversial album, *Death Certificate,* on which the song appeared in 1991, "was the first rap CD to debut at number 1 on *Billboard's* pop chart," according to Ogbar (1999: 170).

4. Scholarship on race relations has challenged inflammatory media representations of tensions between Koreans and blacks and has provided understandings of the historical development, structural conditions, political mobilization, and contemporary discourse surrounding these conflicts. These investigations probe a range of factors, from individual prejudice and lack of language and cultural understanding to disparate forms of economic incorporation for immigrants versus native-born minorities to racial scapegoating to the mobilization of black communities seeking community autonomy to representations in media

and public discourse. Important contributions to the study of black-Korean rela-tions include Abelmann and Lie (1995); Cheng and Espiritu (1989); Cho (1993); Gooding-Williams (1993); Jo (1992); Kim (2000); C. Kim (1999); H. Lee (1993); Jen-nifer Lee (2002a, 2002b); Light, Har-Chvi, and Kan (1994); Min (1996); Ong, Park, and Tong (1994); Kyeyoung Park (1996, 1997); and Yoon (1997).

For this study the existence of some degree of hostility in other Korean-owned establishments—based on historical events and recent scholarship—is taken as a starting point, although not unproblematically. While I agree that media depic-tions of conflicts in grocery stores have been inflammatory and inaccurate, I argue that some degree of hostility is present in actual everyday interactions, allowing these stereotypical representations to take root regarding Korean businesses and the ethnic entrepreneurs who operate them. Jennifer Lee (1999, 2000b) focuses on everyday prosaic encounters to capture the wide variation in black-Korean merchant-customer relations but notes a propensity toward "racial coding" of economic exchanges. Similarly, I highlight variation according to neighborhood composition, characteristics of customers, and degree of familiarity but also note how conflicts quickly become framed in racial terms.

5. Scholars who have examined the intersections of race and gender in con-structions of Koreans and other Asians include Alumkal (1999), N. Kim (2006a), E. Lee (2005), Yuh (2002), K. Park (1997), and Pyke and Johnson (2003).

6. Middleman theory frames the tensions experienced by small busi-ness owners in minority neighborhoods as the result of the structural position of immigrant entrepreneurs as intermediaries for ruling elites and the masses (Blalock 1967; Bonacich 1973; John Butler 1991; Light and Bonacich 1991; Min 1990). Antagonism toward immigrant-owned small businesses is thus viewed not as a feature of racial or ethnic differences but of their class position's buffer-ing elite producers from poor customers. Min acknowledges the relatively less conflictual relations in Korean-owned service versus retail establishments but accounts for this by asserting that businesses such as the nail salons do not con-form to the middleman criteria (Min 1996: 198) rather than by examining distinct processes within the salons.

7. On ascriptions of race through skin tone and appearance, see Glenn (2009), Diggs-Brown and Steinhorn (2000), Herring (2003), and Hunter (2005).

8. Those interviewed include a student–package clerk, server, student-mother, cashier, therapist, ambulatory service staff, nurse, county government administra-tive assistant, laboratory technician, nanny, and elementary school principal.

9. This shooting was captured on videotape and, in the months leading up to the 1992 civil uprising, was aired repeatedly on local news. Harlin's death, and the light sentence given to the woman who shot her, fueled anger by African Americans toward Korean merchants. See Lee (2002a), Kim (1999), and Steven-son (2004).

6. "YOU COULD GET A FUNGUS"

The first epigraph is from Hill (1997b: 64); the second is from Caplan and Fitzpatrick (2007). The third is from an interview I conducted for this study.

1. Caplan and Fitzpatrick 2007. The *Time* article provides the following justification for including nail salon workers on this "worst jobs" list: "Forty-two percent of nail technicians are Asian immigrant women, according to industry estimates, and many have little recourse when exposed to dangerous health conditions. Cosmetics ingredients don't fall under the jurisdiction of either the EPA or the Food and Drug Administration, and many such products sold in the U.S. today contain known toxins."

2. Greenhouse 2007b.

3. Rost 2008: 75. Rost reports that industry representatives intervened on Web sites to encourage the use of the alternative term "nonstandard salon." However, references to "Asian chop shops" are still common. See Arnold (n.d.), who says: "Many [use the term to] refer to a nail salon that is primarily all Asian nail techs, a place where you do not need an appointment or do not have a personal nail tech and [that has] cheaper prices than a traditional salon[,] a 'Chop Shop.'" An example of the use of the term to link Asian nail salons with unsanitary practices appears in an online review of a salon in Austin, Texas. The unsigned review, dated January 25, 2008, warns, "BEWARE!! FRAUDULENT CHOP SHOP!! This place is a cheap Asian chop shop. Your nails will look awful and you'll spend hundreds getting your new staph and nail fungus infection treated at your local podiatrist" (http://local.yahoo.com/profile?id=19415748&review_id=3). For coverage of general concerns regarding salon safety, see Greenhouse (2007a, 2007b), Torres (2007), Ahrens (2000), and Blumenthal (1987).

4. On the history of anti-Chinese sentiments, see Kwong and Miscevic (2007), Chan (1991a), Okihiro (2001), and Takaki (1989). On the internment of Japanese Americans, see Daniels (1993) and Weglyn (1996). For discussion of media representations of Asian Americans, see R. Lee (1999), Hamamoto (1994), and Marchetti (1993). On current politics regarding suspicions of Asian Americans and their links to China, see Gordon Chang (2002), C. Lee (2000), and Le (2007b). After serving nine months in solitary confinement, Wen Ho Lee received a $1.6 million settlement for the inappropriate handling of his case by the government and media (Farhi 2006).

5. One prominent historical text that propagated the yellow peril discourse was G. G. Rupert's *The Yellow Peril; or, the Orient vs. the Occident as Viewed by Modern Statesmen and Ancient Prophets* (1911). For further analysis of the yellow peril see N. Kim (2008), Okihiro (1994), and Espiritu (2008).

6.   R. Lee 1999; Marchetti 1993; H. Yu 2000. See also New York University's Asian/Pacific/American Studies Program and Institute's 2005 exhibit "Archivist of the 'Yellow Peril,'" part of a collection of more than eight thousand popular culture representations of the yellow peril assembled by a New York film editor, Yoshio Kishi. For more information go to www.apa.nyu.edu/gallery/kishi/.

7.   Shah 2001: 3, 12.

8.   Regarding China's economic and political policies and how they affect Chinese Americans, see Lin (2008), Le (2007b), and Wang (1998).

9.   On ways that conflicts with Asian countries have affected Asian Americans, see Dower (1986), J. Freeman (1991), Nakanishi (1993), Harth (2003), and Morris (2005).

10.   One of the most infamous examples of anti-Asian violence is the brutal 1982 murder of Vincent Chin by unemployed Detroit autoworkers who blamed Japan for their economic woes. Although Chin was Chinese American, his murderers lumped him together with Japanese and blamed him for the troubles of the U.S. automobile industry. See Chou and Feagin (2008), P. Hall and Hwang (2001), Ma (2000), and Sethi (1994).

11.   Okihiro 1994: 141.

12.   On connections between model minority and yellow peril discourses, see Kawai (2005), Shim (1998), and Wong (1986).

13.   On anti-Asian sentiment and gendered discourses, see Shah (2001), Tchen (2001), Tyner (2006), Uchida (1998), Yanagisako (1995), and Yu (2000).

14.   Chan 1991b: 101.

15.   Luibhéid 2002.

16.   For discussion of the sexual politics surrounding Asian immigrant women, see Chan (1991b), Lowe (1996), Peffer (1999), and Yung (1995).

17.   Marchetti 1993: 2.

18.   One Web site, the Urban Dictionary, says of the character, "Ms. Swan is from somewhere in Asia" (www.urbandictionary.com/define.php?term=bunny+swan). A Web site called Yellowface Top 10, states, "It's difficult to view this character and not think that she's Asian. . . . Ms. Swan was a sobering reminder that Hollywood still regards Asians as fair game for race-based humor" (http://forums.yellowworld.org/showthread.php?t=10781).

19.   Aoki 2000: F3.

20.   Trish, "There Is a Humongous Fungus among Us," Trish's Dish, August 12, 2008, http://trisha-dish.blogspot.com/2008/07/there-is-humongous-fungus-among-us.html.

21.   For Jaime's blog entry, November 21, 2007, see http://momaroundthe clock.blogspot.com/2007/11/nail-salon-rudeness.html.

22.   Roh Park is quoted in an MTV article noting the diffusion of this line into a number of popular songs (Vineyard 2008).

23.   Response to City-Data Forum question "Does anyone get their pedicures/manicures done at Asian nail salons?" from HappySpring, October 28, 2008, www.city-data.com/forum/fashion-beauty/446665-does-anyone-get-their-pedicures-manicures-3.html.

24.   Kwapniewski et al. 2008.

25.   The survey of one hundred workers was conducted by the New York Committee for Occupational Safety and Health and a Korean workers' group, Empowering the Korean American Community (cited in Greenhouse 2007a).

26.   M. Chang 2005–2006: 50.

27.   Julia Liou, interview by author, August 8, 2007.

28.   Roelofs et al. 2008.

29.   Alexander Gorman Scranton, e-mail to author, August 8, 2007. The report "Glossed Over" was released in March 2007 by Women's Voices for the Earth and eleven other environmental and health groups. It focuses on efforts to stop the use of hazardous chemicals, such as toluene, formaldehyde, and dibutyl phthalate, by OPI, the leading supplier of products to U.S. nail salons. See Women's Voices for the Earth (2007).

30.   Julia Liou, interview by author, August 8, 2007. Participating in the collaborative are nail salon owners and workers from Los Angeles and the San Francisco Bay Area, as well as a range of other organizations, including prominent Asian American community organizations (Asian Health Services, the Asian Law Caucus, and the National Asian Pacific American Women's Forum), public health–related organizations (the Breast Cancer Fund, Physicians for Social Responsibility, L.A.), environmental action groups (Women's Voices of the Earth), labor rights groups and unions (United Food and Commercial Workers), and government agencies (U.S. Environmental Protection Agency Region 9 and California Department of Health Services Environmental and Occupational Health Branches).

31.   In response to organizing and publicity efforts, California has led the way in state regulation with the passage in 2005 of the California Safe Cosmetics Act (California Department of Public Health 2007). At the national level, the Environmental Working Group (2007–2009) writes, "In July 2008, as a result of pressure from EWG and other health groups, the U.S. Congress passed legislation banning six phthalates from children's toys and cosmetics."

32.   M. Chang 2005–2006: 50.

33.   See M. Chang (2005–2006) and Sole-Smith (2006).

34.   Liou interview.

35.   Organizations that have engaged in these efforts include the National Asian Pacific American Women's Forum (national office and Yale chapter), Women's Voices for the Earth, California-based POLISH (Participatory Research, Organizing and Leadership Initiative for Safety and Health), Boston Public

Health Commission's Safe Nail Salon Project, Nail Salon Project in Houston, Oregon Collaborative for Healthy Nail Salons, Toxic Use Reduction Institute at the University of Massachusetts at Lowell, Committee Against Anti-Asian Violence Women's Worker's Project in New York City, and the Environmental Coalition of South Seattle in partnership with King County, the Community Coalition for Environmental Justice, and region 10 of the U.S. Environmental Protection Agency. On efforts to eliminate dibutyl phthalate, formaldehyde, and toluene, see the National Healthy Nail Salon Allliance's report, "Phasing out the 'Toxic Trio,'" May 2009, www.womenandenvironment.org/campaignsandprograms/SafeCosmetics/campaignsandprograms/SafeCosmetics/nail_report.pdf.

36. Asian Law Caucus 2005: 8–9.

37. Joy Onasch, interview by author, August 16, 2007.

38. U.S. Department of Labor 2006.

39. Bernhardt, McGrath, and DeFilippis 2007.

40. According to sec. 162 of the New York State Labor Standards Act, employees who work more than six hours are entitled to one 30-minute meal break, and those who work past 7 P.M. (as many manicurists do) are entitled to another twenty-minute meal break. See New York State Department of Labor, www.labor.state.ny.us/workerprotection/laborstandards/employer/meals.shtm.

41. Michelle Wong, e-mail to author, July 29, 2007.

42. Gorman Scranton to author.

43. Sole-Smith 2007.

44. Willett 2000 and 2005; Harvey 2005; Peiss 1998.

45. Federman, Harrington, and Krynski (2006: 315). Their study finds that Vietnamese seemed to be "much more committed to the occupation" in that fewer Vietnamese left the industry after six years than did non-Vietnamese in only two years. My sample of Korean manicurists in New York is consistent with their findings in that the majority of my respondents had been employed in nail salon work for more than six years and expected to stay in this work at least five to ten years more.

46. Other studies regarding the impact of immigrants on the job prospects of native-born workers include Espenshade and Huber (1999); Fix and Passel (1994); Massey, Durand, and Malone (2002); Massey and Taylor (2004); Smith and Edmonson (1998).

47. Wurdinger 1992: 42.

48. Cited in Retkwa 1993.

49. Mellor 1996.

50. Trang Nguyen, e-mail to author, August 15, 2007, and interview by author, November 11, 2009.

51. Board of Barbering and Cosmetology 2008.

52.   On the differing ways that individuals and groups are racialized and the contrasts between whites and nonwhites, see Bonilla-Silva and Doane (2003), Chou and Feagin (2008), and Sullivan (2006).

7. CONCLUSION

1.   From participant observation fieldnotes at Nail Plaza protest on August 11, 2007, at Amsterdam and Sixty-seventh Street in Manhattan. This protest was a precursor to the fall 2007 kickoff of the Justice Will Be Served Nail Salon Workers Network, sponsored by the National Mobilization Against Sweatshops, Chinese Staff and Workers Association, and the 318 Restaurant Workers' Union. The campaign, according to a handbill, called for: "1) Justice for the Nail Plaza workers; 2) City-funding for a study and treatment program for nail salon workers; and 3) Government regulations to protect workers in the nail salon industry."

2.   Fujiwara 1998: 62.

3.   Jonas 2006.

4.   See Abraham and Ballou (2007).

5.   Craig 2002: 160.

6.   Hochschild 2003.

7.   The settlement was unexpectedly generous, as the court also awarded attorney fees and other costs, for a total of $330,000. Steven K. Choi, a lawyer for the plaintiffs, said, "I think it speaks to how strongly that our client was right and our employers were wrong" (Jennifer 8. Lee 2007). However, the defendants, Mou San Rim and Dong Rim Park, filed for bankruptcy after the ruling, and Do Yea Kim had not received any of the settlement as this book went to press. For coverage of Kim's case, see Gonnerman (2007) and Jennifer 8. Lee (2009).

8.   Romero 2002: 197–98.

9.   Choy 2003; Glenn 1986; Hochschild 2003; Hondagneu-Sotelo 2003; Kempadoo and Doezema 1998; Parreñas 2001.

10.   England and Folbre 1999: 46.

11.   Glenn 2002: 16–17.

12.   Nuon has received or been nominated for major humanitarian awards, including the 1998 Ramon Magsaysay Award for Community Leadership. Her organization, the Future Light Orphanage, "provides livelihood training and mental health counseling to over a hundred war widows in neighboring villages, as well as education and medical and clothing assistance to hundreds of needy children." See Ramon Magsaysay Award Foundation, www.rmaf.org.ph/Awardees/Citation/CitationNuonPhaly.htm.

13.   Solomon 2002: 36.

References

Abelmann, Nancy, and John Lie. 1995. *Blue Dreams: Korean Americans and the L.A. Riots*. Cambridge, Mass.: Harvard University Press.

Abraham, Yvonne, and Brian R. Ballou. 2007. "350 Are Held in Immigration Raid: New Bedford Factory Employed Illegals, U.S. Says." *Boston Globe*, March 7, www.boston.com/news/local/articles/2007/03/07/350_are_held_in_immigration_raid/.

Ahrens, Tracy. 2000. "Nail Enhancements Increasing, So Are Risks." *(Kankakee, Ill.) Daily Journal*, August 25, www.beautytech.com/articles/nailrisks.pdf.

Alumkal, Antony W. 1999. "Preserving Patriarchy: Assimilation, Gender Norms, and Second-Generation Korean American Evangelicals." *Qualitative Sociology* 22: 127–40.

Amott, Teresa, and Julie Matthaei. 1991. *Race, Gender and Work: A Multicultural Economic History of Women in the United States*. Boston: South End Press.

Andersen, Margaret, and Patricia Hill Collins, eds. 2006. *Race, Class, and Gender: An Anthology.* Belmont, Calif.: Wadsworth.

Anzaldúa, Gloria, ed. 1990. *Making Face, Making Soul/Haciendo Caras: Creative and Critical Perspectives by Feminists of Color.* San Francisco: Aunt Lute Books.

Aoki, Guy. 2000. "Asian Americans Living in a 'Bamboozled' World." *Los Angeles Times,* October 23, p. F3.

Arnold, Jennifer. n.d. "Assessing the Safety of 'Chop Shop' Nail Salons," Helium.com, www.helium.com/items/111794-assessing-the-safety-of-chop-shop-nail-salons.

Asian Law Caucus and University of California San Francisco Community Occupational Health Project. 2005. "Oakland Healthy Nail Salon Project: Infection Protection: Protect Yourself against Germs and Infections," January 4.

Atkins, Dawn. 1998. *Looking Queer: Body Image and Identity in Lesbian, Bisexual, Gay, and Transgender Communities.* New York: Haworth.

Atwood, Margaret. 1998. *The Handmaid's Tale: A Novel.* New York: Anchor.

Banet-Weiser, Sarah. 1999. *The Most Beautiful Girl in the World: Beauty Pageants and National Identity.* Berkeley: University of California Press.

Banks, Ingrid. 2000. *Hair Matters: Beauty, Power, and Black Women's Consciousness.* New York: New York University Press.

Banner, Lois. 1983. *American Beauty.* New York: Alfred A. Knopf.

Bartky, Sandra Lee. 1988. "Foucault, Femininity, and the Modernization of Patriarchal Power." In Irene Diamond and Lee Quimby, eds., *Feminism and Foucault: Reflections on Resistance.* Boston: Northeastern University Press.

Baumgardner, Jennifer, and Amy Richards. 2000. *Manifesta: Young Women, Feminism, and the Future.* New York: Farrar, Straus and Giroux.

———. 2005. *Grassroots: A Field Guide for Feminist Activism.* New York: Farrar, Straus and Giroux.

Bean, Frank D., and Gillian Stevens. 2003. *America's Newcomers and the Dynamics of Diversity.* New York: Russell Sage Foundation.

Belkin, Lisa. 2003. "The Opt-Out Revolution." *New York Times,* October 26, www.nytimes.com/2003/10/26/magazine/26WOMEN.html.

Bello, Walden F., and Stephanie Rosenfeld. 1990. *Dragons in Distress: Asia's Miracle Economies in Crisis.* San Francisco: Institute for Food and Development Policy.

Benhabib, Seyla, and Judith Resnik, eds. 2009. *Migrations and Mobilities: Citizenship, Borders and Gender.* New York: New York University Press.

Bernhardt, Annette, Siobhan McGrath, and James DeFilippis. 2007. "Unregulated Work in the Personal Services Industry in New York City." Chapter M in "Unregulated Work in the Global City," Brennan Center for Justice report, December 20, www.brennancenter.org/page/-/d/download_file_49382.pdf.

Bernstein, Elizabeth. 2007. *Temporarily Yours: Intimacy, Authenticity, and the Commerce of Sex.* Chicago: University of Chicago Press.

Bettie, Julie. 2003. *Women without Class: Girls, Race and Identity.* Berkeley: University of California Press.

Blair-Loy, M. 2003. *Competing Devotions: Career and Family among Women Executives.* Cambridge, Mass.: Harvard University Press.

Blalock, Herbert M. 1967. *Toward a Theory of Minority-Group Relations.* New York: John Wiley.

Blumenthal, Deborah. 1987. "Hygiene in Nail Salons Termed Risk." *New York Times,* November 21, www.nytimes.com/1987/11/21/style/consumers-world-hygiene-in-nail-salons-termed-risk.html?scp=1&sq=blumenthal%201987%20nail%20salon&st=cse.

Board of Barbering and Cosmetology. California Department of Consumer Affairs. 2008. "Advisory Committee Meeting of the Bureau of Barbering and Cosmetology, Minutes of November 18," Los Angeles, www.barbercosmo.ca.gov/about_us/meetings/minutes_20081118.pdf.

Bolton, Sharon. 2005. "Women's Work, Dirty Work: The Gynaecology Nurse as 'Other.'" *Gender, Work & Organization* 12: 169–86.

Bonacich, Edna. 1973. "A Theory of Middleman Minorities." *American Sociological Review* 38: 690–711.

Bonacich, Edna, M. Hossain, and J. Park. 1987. "Korean Immigrant Working-women in the Early 1980s." In E. Yu and E. H. Phillips, eds., *Korean Women in Transition: At Home and Abroad.* Los Angeles: Center for Korean-American and Korean Studies, California State University.

Bonilla-Silva, Eduardo, and Ashley Doane Jr. 2003. "New Racism, Color-Blind Racism, and the Future of Whiteness in America." In Eduardo Bonilla-Silva and Ashley Doane Jr. , eds., *Whiteout: The Continuing Significance of Racism and Whiteness.* New York: Routledge.

Bordo, Susan. 1989. "The Body and the Reproduction of Femininity: A Feminist Appropriation of Foucault." In Alison Jaggar and Susan Bordo, eds., *Gender/ Body/Knowledge: A Feminist Reconstruction of Being and Knowing.* New Brunswick, N.J.: Rutgers University Press.

———. 2004. *Unbearable Weight: Feminism, Western Culture and the Body (Tenth Anniversary Edition).* Berkeley: University of California Press.

Bourdieu, Pierre. 1984. *Distinction: A Social Critique of Judgements of Taste.* Cambridge, Mass.: Harvard University Press.

———. 1990. *The Logic of Practice.* Palo Alto, Calif.: Stanford University Press.

Boushey, Heather. 2005. "Are Women Opting Out? Debunking the Myth." Briefing paper, Center for Economic and Policy Research, Washington, D.C.

Boyle, Joseph. 2004. "Linguistic Imperialism and the History of English Language Teaching in Hong Kong." In Kwok-kan Tam and Timothy Weiss, eds., *English and Globalization: Perspectives from Hong Kong and China.* Hong Kong: Chinese University Press.

Brattain, Michelle. 2001. *The Politics of Whiteness: Race, Workers, and Culture in the Modern South*. Princeton, N.J.: Princeton University Press.

Braverman, Harry. 1974. *Labour and Monopoly Capital: The Degradation of Labor in the Twentieth Century*. New York: Monthly Review Press.

Browne, Irene, and Joya Misra. 2003. "The Intersection of Gender and Race in the Labor Market." *Annual Review of Sociology* 29: 487–513.

Burawoy, Michael, ed. 1991. *Ethnography Unbound*. Berkeley: University of California Press.

Butler, John. 1991. *Entrepreneurship and Self-Help among Black Americans: A Reconsideration of Race and Economics*. Albany: State University of New York Press.

Butler, Judith. 1999. *Gender Trouble: Feminism and the Subversion of Identity*. London: Routledge.

California Department of Public Health. 2007. "California Safe Cosmetics Program," www.cdph.ca.gov/programs/cosmetics/Pages/default.aspx.

Candelario, Ginetta. 2000. "Hair Race-ing: Dominican Beauty Culture and Identity Production." *Meridians Feminism, Race, and Transnationalism* 1: 128–56.

Caplan, Jeremy, and Laura Fitzpatrick. 2007. "The Worst Jobs in America." *Time*, July 30, www.time.com/time/business/article/0,8599,1648055,00.html.

Chan, Sucheng. 1991a. *Asian Americans: An Interpretive History*. Boston: Twayne.

———. 1991b. "The Exclusion of Chinese Women." In Sucheng Chan, ed., *Entry Denied: Exclusion and the Chinese Community in America, 1882–1943*. Philadelphia: Temple University Press.

Chancer, Lynn. 1998. *Reconcilable Differences: Confronting Beauty, Pornography, and the Future of Feminism*. Berkeley: University of California Press.

Chang, Gordon, ed. 2002. *Asian Americans and Politics: Perspectives, Experiences, Prospects*. Palo Alto, Calif.: Stanford University Press.

Chang, Grace. 2000. *Disposable Domestics: Immigrant Women Workers in the Global Economy*. Boston: South End Press.

Chang, Momo. 2005–2006. "Under the Varnish." *ColorLines* 8 (Winter): 49–51.

Chapkis, Wendy. 1986. Beauty Secrets: Women and the Politics of Appearance. Boston: South End Press.

Cheng, Lucie, and Yen Le Espiritu. 1989. "Korean Businesses in Black and Hispanic Neighborhoods: A Study of Inter-Group Relations." *Sociological Perspectives* 32: 521–34.

Chin, Margaret. 2005. *Sewing Women: Immigrants and the New York City Garment Industry*. New York: Columbia University Press.

Chiswick, Barry. 1997. "Soviet Jews in the United States: Language and Labour Market Adjustments Revisited." In Noah Lewin-Epstein, Yaacov Ro'i, and Paul Ritterband, eds. , *Russian Jews on Three Continents: Migration and Resettlement*. New York: Routledge.

Cho, Sumi K. 1993. "Korean Americans vs. African Americans: Conflict and Construction." In Robert Gooding-Williams, ed., *Reading Rodney King/ Reading Urban Uprising*. New York: Routledge.

———. 1997. "Asian Pacific American Women and Racialized Sexual Harassment." In Elaine Kim, ed., *Making More Waves: New Writing by Asian American Women*. Boston: Beacon.

Chou, Rosalind S., and Joe R. Feagin. 2008. *The Myth of the Model Minority: Asian Americans Facing Racism*. Boulder, Colo.: Paradigm.

Chow, Esther, Doris Wilkinson, and Maxine Baca Zinn, eds. 1996. *Race, Class and Gender: Common Bonds, Different Voices*. Newbury Park, Calif.: Sage.

Choy, Catherine Ceniza. 2003. *Empire of Care: Nursing and Migration in Filipino Nursing History*. Durham, N.C.: Duke University Press.

Cogan, Jeanine C. 1999. "Lesbians Walk the Tightrope of Beauty: Thin Is In but Femme Is Out." In Jeanine C. Cogan and Joanie M. Erickson, eds., *Lesbians, Levis and Lipstick: The Meaning of Beauty in Our Lives*. New York: Haworth.

Cohen, Rosalie A. 1996. "Women in the Service Occupation Sector." In Paula J. Dubeck and Kathryn Borman, eds., *Women and Work: A Handbook*. New York: Garland.

Collins, Patricia Hill. 1991. *Black Feminist Thought: Knowledge, Consciousness, and the Politics of Empowerment*. New York: Routledge.

———. 2005. *Black Sexual Politics: African Americans, Gender, and the New Racism*. New York: Routledge.

———. 2006. *From Black Power to Hip Hop: Racism, Nationalism, and Feminism*. Philadelphia: Temple University Press.

Collinson, Margaret, and David L. Collinson. 1996. "'It's Only Dick': The Sexual Harassment of Women Managers in Insurance Sales." *Work, Employment and Society* 10: 29–56.

Congressional Budget Office. 2007. "The Impact of Unauthorized Immigrants on the Budgets of State and Local Governments." A Series on Immigration. December. Washington, D.C., www.cbo.gov/ftpdocs/87xx/doc8711/12–6-Immigration.pdf.

Cortina, L. M., and S. A. Wasti. 2005. "Profiles in Coping: Responses to Sexual Harassment across Persons, Organizations, and Cultures." *Journal of Applied Psychology* 90: 182–92.

Craig, Maxine Leeds. 2002. *Ain't I a Beauty Queen?: Black Women, Beauty, and the Politics of Race*. New York: Oxford University Press.

Crenshaw, Kimberlé. 1991. "Mapping the Margins: Intersectionality, Identity Politics, and Violence against Women of Color." *Stanford Law Review* 43: 1241–99.

Crittenden, Ann. 2001. *The Price of Motherhood: Why the Most Important Job in the World Is Still the Least Valued*. New York: Henry Holt.

Danico, May Yu. 2004. "The Formation of Post-Suburban Communities: Korea-town and Little Saigon, Orange County." *International Journal of Sociology and Social Policy* 24: 15–45.

Daniels, Roger. 1993. *Prisoners without Trial: Japanese Americans in World War II.* New York: Hill and Wang.

Dansky, Bonnie, and Dean Kilpatrick. 1997. "Effects of Sexual Harassment." In William T. O'Donohue, ed., *Sexual Harassment: Theory, Research, and Treatment.* Needham Heights, Mass.: Allyn and Bacon.

Das Gupta, Monisha. 2006. *Unruly Immigrants: Rights, Activism, and Transnational South Asian Politics in the United States.* Durham, N.C.: Duke University Press.

Davis, Kathy. 1995. *Reshaping the Female Body: The Dilemma of Cosmetic Surgery.* New York: Routledge.

De Jong, Gordon F. , and Anna B. Madamba. 2001. "A Double Disadvantage? Minority Group, Immigrant Status, and Underemployment in the United States." *Social Science Quarterly* 82: 117–30.

Dellinger, Kirsten, and Christine L. Williams. 1997. "Makeup at Work: Negotiating Appearances in the Workplace." *Gender and Society* 11: 151–77.

DeVault, Marjorie L. 1999. *Liberating Method: Feminism and Social Research.* Philadelphia: Temple University Press.

Dickson, Akeya. 2005. "There's No Business Like the Nail Business." *Nguoi Viet,* September 28, http://news.newamericamedia.org/news/view_article .html?article_id=4afb34e71cc7be9d530db2492070689c.

Diggs-Brown, Barbara, and Leonard Steinhorn. 2000. *By the Color of Our Skin: The Illusion of Integration and the Reality of Race.* New York: Plume.

Douglas, Susan J., and Meredith W. Michaels. 2004. *The Mommy Myth: The Idealization of Motherhood and How It Has Undermined All Women.* New York: Free Press.

Dower, John. 1986. *War without Mercy: Race and Power in the Pacific War.* New York: Pantheon.

Durand, Jorge, and Douglas Massey. 2004. *Crossing the Border: Research from the Mexican Migration Project.* New York: Russell Sage Foundation.

Edidin, Peter. 2007. "Arts Briefly; More Trouble for Foxy Brown." *New York Times,* August 17, http://query.nytimes.com/gst/fullpage.html?res= 9400EEDF123BF934A2575BC0A9619C8B63&scp=3&sq=foxy+brown+nail+ salon+guilty&st=nyt.

Ehrenreich, Barbara, and Arlie Russell Hochschild, eds., 2004. *Global Woman: Nannies, Maids, and Sex Workers in the New Economy.* New York: Metropolitan.

England, Paula, and Nancy Folbre. 1999. "The Cost of Caring: Emotional Labor in the Service Economy." *Annals of the American Academy of Political and Social Sciences* 561: 39–45.

Environmental Working Group. 2007–2009. "Chemical Families: Phthalates," www.ewg.org/chemindex/term/480.

Espenshade, Thomas, and Gregory A. Huber. 1999. "Fiscal Impacts of Immigrants and the Shrinking Welfare State." In Charles Hirschman, Philip Kasinitz, and Josh DeWind, eds., *The Handbook of International Migration: The American Experience*. New York: Russell Sage Foundation.

Espiritu, Yen Le. 2003. "Gender and Labor in Asian Immigrant Families." In Pierrette Hondagneu-Sotelo, ed., *Gender and U.S. Immigration: Contemporary Trends*. Berkeley: University of California Press.

———. 2008. *Asian American Women and Men*. Lanham, Md.: Rowman and Littlefield.

Farhi, Paul. 2006. "U.S., Media Settle with Wen Ho Lee: News Organizations Pay to Keep Sources Secret." *Washington Post*, June 3, A01, www.washington post.com/wp-dyn/content/article/2006/06/02/AR2006060201060.html.

Farley, Reynolds, and Richard Alba. 2002. "The New Second Generation in the United States." *International Migration Review* 36, no. 3: 669–701.

Feagin, Joe, and Clairece Booher Feagin. 1999. *Racial and Ethnic Relations*. Upper Saddle River, N.J.: Prentice-Hall.

Feagin, Joe, and Karyn D. McKinney. 2002. *The Many Costs of Racism*. Lanham, Md.: Rowman and Littlefield.

Feagin, Joe, and Melvin Sikes. 1994. *Living with Racism: The Black Middle-Class Experience*. Boston: Beacon.

Federman, Maya N., David E. Harrington, and Kathy J. Krynski. 2006. "Vietnamese Manicurists: Are Immigrants Displacing Natives or Finding New Nails to Polish?" *Industrial and Labor Relations Review* 59: 302–18.

Fix, Michael, and Jeffrey Passel. 1994. *Immigration and Immigrants: Setting the Record Straight*. Washington, D.C.: Urban Institute Press.

Foner, Nancy. 1987. Introduction to Nancy Foner, ed., *New Immigrants in New York*. New York: Columbia University Press.

Fong, Timothy P. 2007. *The Contemporary Asian American Experience: Beyond the Model Minority*. Upper Saddle River, N.J.: Prentice Hall.

Fonow, Margaret, and Judith Cook. 1991. *Beyond Methodology*. Bloomington: Indiana University Press.

———. 2005. "Feminist Methodology: New Applications in the Academy and Public Policy." *Signs: Journal of Women in Culture and Society* 30: 2211–36.

Foo, Lora Jo. 2007. *Asian American Women*. New York: iUniverse.

Foucault, Michel. 1979. *Discipline and Punish*. New York: Vintage.

———. 1986. "Disciplinary Power and Subjection." In *Power*, edited by Stephen Lukes. New York: New York University Press.

Frank, Arthur W. 1990. "Bringing Bodies Back In: A Decade Review." *Theory, Culture, and Society* 7: 131–62.

Frankenberg, Ruth. 1993. *White Women, Race Matters: The Social Construction of Whiteness*. Minneapolis: University of Minnesota Press.

Freeman, Carla C. 1999. *High Tech and High Heels in the Global Economy: Women, Work, and Pink-Collar Identities in the Caribbean*. Durham, N.C.: Duke University Press.

Freeman, James. 1991. *Hearts of Sorrow: Vietnamese American Lives*. Palo Alto, Calif.: Stanford University Press.

Friday, Nancy. 1996. *The Power of Beauty*. New York: HarperCollins.

Fujiwara, Lynn. 1998. "The Impact of Welfare Reform on Asian Immigrant Communities." *Social Justice* 25: 62–75.

———. 2005. "Mothers without Citizenship: Asian Immigrant and Refugees Negotiating Poverty and Hunger in Post-Welfare Reform." *Race, Gender, and Class* 12: 121–41.

Furman, Frida Kerner. 1997. *Facing the Mirror: Older Women and the Beauty Shop Culture*. New York: Routledge.

Gagne, Patricia, and Deanna McGaughey. 2002. "Designing Women: Cultural Hegemony and the Exercise of Power among Women Who Have Undergone Elective Mammoplasty." *Gender and Society* 16: 814–38.

Gallagher, Leigh. 2003. "Lather, Rinse, Repeat." *Forbes*, October 13, www.forbes.com/global/2003/1013/022.html.

Gans, Herbert. 1992. "Second Generation Decline: Scenarios for the Economic and Ethnic Futures of the Post-1965 American Immigrants." *Ethnic and Racial Studies* 15, no. 2: 173–92.

Garran, Robert. 1998. *Tigers Tamed: The End of the Asian Miracle*. Honolulu: University of Hawaii Press.

George, Sheba. 2005. *When Women Come First: Gender and Class in Transnational Migration*. Berkeley: University of California Press.

Gilroy, Paul. 1993. *The Black Atlantic: Modernity and Double Consciousness*. Cambridge, Mass.: Harvard University Press.

Gimlin, Debra. 1996. "Pamela's Place: Power and Negotiation in the Hair Salon." *Gender and Society* 10: 505–26.

———. 2002. *Body Work*. Berkeley: University of California Press.

Glass, Jennifer L., and Lisa Riley. 1998. "Family Responsive Policies and Employee Retention Following Childbirth." *Social Forces* 76: 1401–35.

Glenn, Evelyn Nakano. 1986. *Issei, Nisei, War Bride: Three Generations of Japanese American Women in Domestic Service*. Philadelphia: Temple University Press.

———. 1992. "From Servitude to Service Work: Historical Continuities in the Racial Division of Paid Reproductive Labor." *Signs* 18: 1–43.

———. 2002. *Unequal Freedom: How Race and Gender Shaped American Citizenship and Labor*. Cambridge, Mass.: Harvard University Press.

————, ed. 2009. *Shades of Difference: Why Skin Color Matters.* Palo Alto, Calif.: Stanford University Press.

Goffman, Erving. 1959. *The Presentation of Self in Everyday Life.* New York: Doubleday.

————. 1974. *Stigma: Notes on the Management of Spoiled Identity.* New York: Jason Aronson.

Gold, Steven J. 1995. *From the Workers' State to the Golden State: Jews from the Former Soviet Union in California.* Needham Heights, Mass.: Allyn and Bacon.

Goldstein, Morris. 1998. *The Asian Financial Crisis: Causes, Cures, and Systemic Implications.* New York: Institute for International Economics.

Gonnerman, Jennifer. 2007. "The Manicurists' Heroine: Susan Kim Took her Employers to Court, and Catalyzed a Movement for Salon-Workers' Rights." *New York Magazine,* November 25, http://nymag.com/beauty/features/41281/.

Gooding-Williams, Robert, ed. 1993. *Reading Rodney King/Reading Urban Uprising.* New York: Routledge.

Greenhouse, Steven. 2007a. "At Nail Salons, Beauty Treatments Can Have a Distinctly Unglamorous Side." *New York Times,* August 19, p. A22.

————. 2007b. "Studies Highlight Hazards of Manicurists' Chemicals." *New York Times,* August 19, www.nytimes.com/2007/08/19/nyregion/19nailside .html?_r=1&scp=1&sq=Studies%20Highlight%20Hazards%20of%20 Manicurists%E2%80%99%20Chemicals%20&st=cse.

Greer, Germaine. 1999. *The Whole Woman.* London: Paladin.

Grewal, Inderpal, and Caren Kaplan. 2004. *Scattered Hegemonies: Postmodernity and Transnational Feminist Practices.* Minneapolis: University of Minnesota Press.

Hagedorn, Jessica. 1991. *Dogeaters.* New York: Penguin.

Haight, Wendy, Dayna Finet, Sachiko Bamba, and Jesse Helton. 2009. "The Beliefs of Resilient African-American Adolescent Mothers Transitioning from Foster Care to Independent Living: A Case-Based Analysis." *Children and Youth Services Review* 31: 53–62.

Hall, Patricia Wong, and Victor M Hwang. 2001. *Anti-Asian Violence in North America: Asian American and Asian Canadian Reflections on Hate, Healing, and Resistance.* Walnut Creek, Calif.: AltaMira.

Hall, Stuart. 1981. "Notes on Deconstructing the 'Popular.'" In R. Samuel, ed., *People's History and Socialist Theory.* London: Routledge.

————. 1990. *Resistance through Rituals: Youth Subcultures in Post-War Britain.* London: Routledge.

Hamamoto, Darrell Y. 1994. *Monitored Peril: Asian Americans and the Politics of Representation.* Minneapolis: University of Minnesota Press.

Hamilton, Nora and Norma S. Chinchilla. 2001. *Seeking Community in a Global City: Guatemalans and Salvadorans in Los Angeles.* Philadelphia: Temple University Press.

Haney, Lynne. 1996. "The State and the Reproduction of Male Dominance." *American Sociological Review* 61: 759–78.

Hardaway, Cecily R., and Vonnie C. McLoyd. 2009. "Escaping Poverty and Securing Middle-Class Status: How Race and Socioeconomic Status Shape Mobility Prospects for African Americans During the Transition to Adulthood." *Journal of Youth and Adolescence* 38: 242–56.

Harth, Erica. 2003. *Last Witnesses: Reflections on the Wartime Internment of Japanese Americans*. New York: Palgrave Macmillan.

Harvey, Adia M. 2005. "Becoming Entrepreneurs: Intersections of Race, Class, and Gender at the Black Beauty Salon." *Gender and Society* 19: 789–808.

Haughney, Christine. 2003. "Manicure Business Cut to the Quick: Since Terrorist Attacks, Salons Have Suffered Tight-Fisted Times." *Washington Post*, July 6, A3.

Hays, Sharon. 1996. *The Cultural Contradictions of Motherhood*. New Haven, Conn.: Yale University Press.

———. 2003. *Flat Broke with Children: Women in the Age of Welfare Reform*. New York: Oxford University Press.

Herring, Cedric. 2003. "Skin Deep: Race and Complexion in the "Color-Blind" Era." In Cedric Herring, Verna M. Keith, and Hayward Derrick Horton, eds., *Skin Deep: How Race and Complexion Matter in the "Color-Blind" Era*. New York: Institute for Research on Race and Public Policy.

Hill, Suzette. 1997a. "The Asian Influence, Part I." *Nails*, March, 98–107.

———. 1997b. "The Asian Influence, Part II." *Nails*, April, 62–88.

Hing, Bill Ong. 1993. *Making and Remaking Asian America through Immigration Policy, 1850–1990*. Palo Alto, Calif.: Stanford University Press.

Hochschild, Arlie. 1983. *The Managed Heart: The Commercialization of Human Feeling*. Berkeley: University of California Press.

———. 2003. *The Commercialization of Intimate Life: Notes from Home and Work*. Berkeley: University of California Press.

Hochschild, Arlie Russell, and Anne Machung. 1997. *The Second Shift: Working Parents and the Revolution at Home*. New York: Avon.

Hondagneu-Sotelo, Pierrette. 1994. *Gendered Transitions: Mexican Experiences of Immigration*. Berkeley: University of California Press.

———. 2001. *Domestica: Immigrant Workers Cleaning and Caring in the Shadows of Affluence*. Berkeley: University of California Press.

———. 2003. "Gender and Immigration: A Retrospective and Introduction." In Pierrette Hondagneu-Sotelo, ed., *Gender and U.S. Immigration: Contemporary Trends*. Berkeley, CA: University of California Press.

Hondagneu-Sotelo, Pierrette, and Ernestine Avila. 1997. "'I'm Here, but I'm There': The Meanings of Latina Transnational Motherhood." *Gender and Society* 13: 548–71.

hooks, bell. 1981. *Ain't I a Woman: Black Women and Feminism*. Boston: South End.

———. 1990. *Black Looks: Race and Representation.* Boston: South End.

Horkheimer, Max, and T. W. Adorno. 1972. *Dialectic of Enlightenment.* New York: Herder and Herder.

Huerta, Marisela, Lilia M. Cortina, Joyce S. Pang, Cynthia M. Torges, and Vicki J. Magley. 2006. "Sex and Power in the Academy: Modeling Sexual Harassment in the Lives of College Women." *Personality and Social Psychology Bulletin* 32: 616–28.

Huisman, Kim, and Hondagneu-Sotelo, Pierrette. 2005. "Dress Matters: Change and Continuity in the Dress Practices of Bosnian Muslim Refugee Women." *Gender and Society* 19: 44–65.

Hunter, Margaret L. 2005. *Race, Gender, and the Politics of Skin Tone.* New York: Routledge.

Hurtado, Aida. 1989. "Relating to Privilege: Seduction and Rejection in the Subordination of White Women and Women of Color." *Signs* 14: 833–55.

Hyun, Jane. 2006. *Breaking the Bamboo Ceiling: Career Strategies for Asians.* New York: HarperCollins.

Inkelas, Karen K. 2006. *Racial Attitudes and Asian Pacific Americans: Demystifying the Model Minority.* New York: Routledge.

Jervis, Lori L. 2001. "The Pollution of Incontinence and the Dirty Work of Caregiving in a U.S. Nursing Home." *Medical Anthropology Quarterly* 15: 84–99.

Jo, M. H. 1992. "Korean Merchants in the Black Community: Prejudice among the Victims of Prejudice." *Ethnic and Racial Studies* 15: 395–411.

Johnson, Kevin. 2007. *Opening the Floodgates: Why America Needs to Rethink Its Borders and Immigration Laws.* New York: New York University Press.

Jonas, Susanne. 2006. "Reflections on the Great Immigration Battle of 2006 and the Future of the Americas." *Social Justice* 33: 6–15.

Kang, Miliann. 1997. "Manicuring Race, Gender, and Class: Service Interactions in New York City Korean Nail Salons." *Race, Gender, and Class* 4: 143–64.

———. 2000. "Researching One's Own: Negotiating Co-Ethnicity in the Field." In Martin Manalansan, ed., *Cultural Compass: Ethnographic Explorations of Asian America.* Philadelphia: Temple University Press.

———. 2003. "The Managed Hand: The Commercialization of Bodies and Emotions in Korean Immigrant-owned Nail Salons." *Gender and Society* 17: 820–39.

Kaplan, Caren, Norma Alarcon, and Minoo Moallem. 1999. *Between Woman and Nation: Nationalism, Transnational Feminism, and the State.* Durham, N.C.: Duke University Press.

Kaplan, Elaine Bell. 1997. *Not Our Kind of Girl: Unraveling the Myths of Black Teenage Motherhood.* Berkeley: University of California Press.

Kasinitz, Philip. 2008. "Becoming American, Becoming Minority, Getting Ahead: The Role of Racial and Ethnic Status in the Upward Mobility of the

Children of Immigrants." *Annals of the American Academy of Political and Social Science* 620 (November 1): 253–69.

Kawai, Yuko. 2005. "Stereotyping Asian Americans: The Dialectic of the Model Minority and the Yellow Peril." *Howard Journal of Communications* 16: 109–30.

Kempadoo, Kamala, and Jo Doezema. 1998. *Global Sex Workers: Rights, Resistance, and Redefinition.* London: Routledge.

Kibria, Nazli. 1993. *Family Tightrope: The Changing Lives of Vietnamese Americans.* Princeton, N.J.: Princeton University Press.

———. 1994. "Household Structure and Family Ideologies: The Dynamics of Immigrant Economic Adaptation among Vietnamese Refugees." *Social Problems* 41: 81–96.

Kim, Bok-Lim C. 1977. "Asian Wives of U.S. Servicemen: Women in Shadows." *Amerasia Journal* 4: 91–114.

Kim, Claire Jean. 2000. *Bitter Fruit: The Politics of Black-Korean Conflict in New York City.* New Haven, Conn.: Yale University Press.

Kim, Elaine, and Eui-Young Yu. 1996. *East to America: Korean American Life Stories.* New York: New Press.

Kim, Eun Mee. 1999. *The Four Asian Tigers: Economic Development and the Global Political Economy.* New York: Academic Press.

Kim, Kwang Chung, and Won Moo Hurh. 1988. "The Burden of Double Roles: Korean Wives in the USA." *Ethnic and Racial Studies* 11: 151–67.

Kim, Kwang Chung, ed. 1999. *Koreans in the Hood: Conflict with African Americans.* Baltimore: Johns Hopkins University Press.

Kim, Minjeong, and Angie Chung. 2005. "Consuming Orientalism: Images of Asian/American Women in Multicultural Advertising." *Qualitative Sociology* 28: 67–73.

Kim, Nadia Y. 2006a. "'Patriarchy Is So Third World': Korean Immigrant Women and 'Migrating' White Western Masculinity." *Social Problems* 53: 519–36.

———. 2006b. "'Seoul-America' on America's 'Soul': South Koreans and Korean Immigrants Navigate Global White Racial Ideology." *Critical Sociology* 28: 67–73.

———. 2008. *Imperial Citizens: Koreans and Race from Seoul to LA.* Palo Alto, Calif.: Stanford University Press.

Kim, Pan Suk, and Gregory Lewis. 1994. "Asian Americans in the Public Service: Success, Diversity, and Discrimination." *Public Administration Review* 54: 285–300.

King, Deborah K. 1988. "Multiple Jeopardy, Multiple Consciousness: The Context of a Black Feminist Ideology." *Signs* 14: 42–72.

King-O'Riain, Rebecca Chiyoko. 2006. *Pure Beauty: Judging Race in Japanese American Beauty Pageants.* Minneapolis: University of Minnesota Press.

Kishinevsky, Vera. 2004. *Russian Immigrants in the United States: Adapting to American Culture.* New York: LFB Scholarly.

Kraut, Alan. 1994. *Silent Travelers: Germs, Genes, and the "Immigrant Menace."* New York: Basic Books.

———. 2006. "Bodies from Abroad: Immigration, Health, and Disease." In Reed Ueda, ed., *A Companion to American Immigration.* Malden, Mass.: Blackwell.

Kwapniewski, Rachel, Sarah Kozaczka, Russ Hauser, Manori Silva, Antonia Calafat, and Susan Duty. 2008. "Occupational Exposure to Dibutyl Phthalate among Manicurists." *Journal of Occupational and Environmental Medicine* 50, no. 6 (June): 705–11.

Kwong, Peter, and Dusanka Miscevic. 2007. *Chinese America: The Untold Story of America's Oldest New Community.* New York: New Press.

Lamphere, Louise, Patricia Zavella, Felipe Gonzalez, and Peter B. Evans. 1993. *Sunbelt Working Mothers: Reconciling Family and Factory.* Ithaca, N.Y.: Cornell University Press.

Lan, Pei-Chia. 2000. "The Body as a Contested Terrain for Labor Control: Cosmetics Retailers in Department Stores and Direct Selling." In Rick Baldoz, Chuck Koeber, and Phil Kraft, eds., *The Critical Study of Work: Labor, Technology, and Global Production.* Philadelphia: Temple University Press.

———. 2003. "Working in a Neon Cage: 'Bodily Labor' of Cosmetics Saleswomen in Taiwan." *Feminist Studies* 29: 1–25.

———. 2006. *Global Cinderellas: Migrant Domestics and Newly Rich Employers in Taiwan.* Durham, N.C.: Duke University Press.

Lareau, Annette. 2002. "Invisible Inequalities: Class, Race, and Child Rearing in Black Families and White Families." *American Sociological Review* 67: 747–76.

Le, C. N. 2007a. *Asian American Assimilation: Ethnicity, Immigration, and Socioeconomic Attainment.* New York: LFB Scholarly.

———. 2007b. "China as a Political Issue." Asian Nation: APA News Blog, August 15, www.asian-nation.org/headlines/2007/08/china-as-a-political-issue.

Lee, Chisun. 2000. "Not a Chinaman's Chance: Advocates Doubt Wen Ho Lee Release Will Change Anti-Asian Politics." *Village Voice,* September 19, www.villagevoice.com/2000-09-19/news/not-a-chinaman-s-chance/3.

Lee, Don. 1999. "The State of Small Business in L.A. County: Divergent Trends for Entrepreneurs: Times Poll Finds That Chinese Americans Are More Likely to Tap Technology While Korean Americans Favor Involvement in Retail and Service Businesses." *Los Angeles Times,* September 25, p. 1.

Lee, Eunju. 2005. *Gendered Processes: Korean Immigrant Small Business Ownership.* New York: LFB Scholarly.

Lee, Heon Cheol. 1993. "Black-Korean Conflict in New York City: A Sociological Analysis." Ph.D. diss., Department of Sociology, Columbia University.

Lee, Janet. 1994. "Menarche and the (Hetero)sexualization of the Female Body." *Gender and Society* 8: 343–62.

Lee, Jennifer. 1999. "Striving for the American Dream: Struggle, Success, and Intergroup Conflict among Korean Immigrant Entrepreneurs." In Min Zhou and James V. Gatewood, eds., *Contemporary Asian America*. New York: New York University Press.

———. 2000. "The Salience of Race in Everyday Life: Black Customers' Shopping Experiences in Black and White Neighborhoods." *Work and Occupations* 27: 353–76.

———. 2002a. *Civility in the City: Blacks, Jews, and Koreans in Urban America.* Cambridge, Mass.: Harvard University Press.

———. 2002b. "From Civil Rights Relations to Racial Conflict: Merchant-Customer Interactions in Urban America." *American Sociological Review* 67: 77–98.

Lee, Jennifer 8. 2007. "Vindication and Then Some for a Nail Salon Worker." *New York Times,* October 31, http://cityroom.blogs.nytimes.com/2007/10/31/vindication-and-then-some-for-a-nail-salon-worker/.

———. 2009. "Former Nail Salon Owner Files for Bankruptcy." *New York Times,* June 17, http://cityroom.blogs.nytimes.com/2009/06/17/former-nail-salon-owner-files-for-bankruptcy/#more-48705.

Lee, Namhee. 2007. *The Making of Minjung: Democracy and the Politics of Representation in South Korea.* Ithaca, N.Y.: Cornell University Press.

Lee, Robert. 1999. *Orientals: Asian Americans in Popular Culture.* Philadelphia: Temple University Press.

Leidner, Robin. 1993. *Fast Food, Fast Talk: Service Work and the Routinization of Everyday Life.* Berkeley: University of California Press.

Levitt, Peggy, and Mary Waters, eds. 2002. *The Changing Face of Home: The Transnational Lives of the Second Generation.* New York: Russell Sage Foundation.

Light, Ivan, and Edna Bonacich. 1988. *Immigrant Entrepreneurs: Koreans in Los Angeles: 1965–1982.* Berkeley: University of California Press.

Light, Ivan, Hadas Har-Chvi, and Kenneth Kan. 1994. "Black/Korean Conflict in Los Angeles." In Seamus Dunn, ed., *Managing Social Conflicts.* Newbury Park, Calif.: Sage.

Lin, Lynda. 2008. "What Happens to Asian American Identity When the 'Home Country' Is Criticized?" *Pacific Citizen,* May 14, http://news.newamericamedia.org/news/view_article.html?article_id=120436d0e5f33cb9a92edcdd45badb27.

Logan, John, and Richard Alba. 1999. "Minority Niches and Immigrant Enclaves in New York and Los Angeles: Trends and Impacts." In Frank D. Bean and Stephanie Bell-Rose, eds., *Immigration and Opportunity: Race, Ethnicity, and Employment in the United States.* New York: Russell Sage Foundation.

Lorber, Judith, and Lisa Jean Moore. 2007. *Gendered Bodies: Feminist Perspectives.* Los Angeles: Roxbury.

Lorde, Audre. 1984. *Sister Outsider.* Freedom, Calif.: Crossing Press.

Lowe, Lisa. 1996. *Immigrant Acts: On Asian American Cultural Politics.* Durham, N.C.: Duke University Press.

Luibhéid, Eithne. 2002. *Entry Denied: Controlling Sexuality at the Border.* Minneapolis: University of Minnesota Press.

Ma, Sheng-mei. 2000. *The Deathly Embrace: Orientalism and Asian American Identity.* Minneapolis: University of Minnesota Press.

Macedo, Donaldo, Panayota Gounari, and Bessie Dendrinos. 2003. *The Hegemony of English.* New York: Paradigm.

Macdonald, Cameron Lynne, and Cathy Sirianni. 1996. "The Service Society and the Changing Experience of Work." In Cameron Lynne Macdonald and Cathy Sirianni, eds., *Working in the Service Society.* Philadelphia: Temple University Press.

Mahler, Sarah J. 1996. *American Dreaming: Immigrant Life on the Margins.* Princeton, N.J.: Princeton University Press.

Marchetti, Gina. 1993. *Romance and the "Yellow Peril": Race, Sex, and Discursive Strategies in Hollywood Fiction.* Berkeley: University of California Press.

Martin, Emily. 1987. *The Woman in the Body: A Cultural Analysis of Reproduction.* Boston: Beacon.

———. 1996. "The Body at Work: Boundaries and Collectivities in the Late Twentieth Century." In Wolfgang Natter and Theodore R. Schatzki, eds. , *The Social and Political Body.* New York: Guilford.

Martin, Susan Ehrlich. 1999. "Police Force or Police Service? Gender and Emotional Labor." *Annals of the American Academy of Political and Social Science* 561: 111–26.

Massey, Douglas, and J. Edward Taylor. 2004. *International Migration: Prospects and Policies in a Global Market.* New York: Oxford University Press.

Massey, Douglas, Joaquin Arango, Graeme Hugo, Ali Kouaouci, Adela Pellegrino, and J. Edward Taylor. 2005. *Worlds in Motion: Understanding International Migration at the End of the Millennium.* New York: Oxford University Press.

Massey, Douglas, Jorge Durand, and Nolan J. Malone. 2002. *Beyond Smoke and Mirrors: Mexican Immigration in an Era of Economic Integration.* New York: Russell Sage Foundation.

McCall, Leslie. 2005. "The Complexity of Intersectionality." *Signs* 30: 1771–1880.

McCormack, Karen. 2005. "Stratified Reproduction and Poor Women's Resistance." *Gender and Society* 19: 660–79.

McDonnell, Patrick J. 1997. "San Salvador Mayor Visits Expatriots in L.A." *Los Angeles Times Nuestro Tiempo,* November 19.

Mellor, William H. 1996. "Is New York City Killing Entrepreneurship?" Institute for Justice, www.ij.org/index.php?option=com_content&task=view&id=2568&Itemid=245.

Menjivar, Cecilia. 2000. *Fragmented Ties: Salvadoran Immigrant Networks in America*. Berkeley: University of California Press.

———. 2003. "The Intersection of Work and Gender: Central American Immigrant Women and Employment in California." In Pierrette Hondagneu-Sotelo, ed., *Gender and U.S. Immigration: Contemporary Trends*. Berkeley: University of California Press.

Min, Pyong Gap. 1990. "Problems of Korean Immigrant Entrepreneurs." *International Migration Review* 24: 436–55.

———. 1996. *Caught in the Middle: Korean Communities in New York and Los Angeles*. Berkeley: University of California Press.

———. 1997. *Changes and Conflicts: Korean Immigrant Families in New York*. Boston: Allyn and Bacon.

Minh-ha, Trinh T. 1989. *Woman, Native, Other: Writing Postcoloniality and Feminism*. Bloomington: Indiana University Press.

Model, Suzanne. 1988. "The Economic Progress of European and East Asian Americans." In Norman Yetman, ed., *Majority and Minority: The Dynamics of Race and Ethnicity in American Life*. Boston: Allyn and Bacon.

Mohanty, Chandra Talpade. 1991. "Under Western Eyes: Feminist Scholarship and Colonial Discourse." In Chandra Talpade Mohanty, Ann Russo, and Lourdes Torres, eds., *Third World Women and the Politics of Feminism*. Bloomington: Indiana University Press.

———. 2003. *Feminism without Borders: Decolonizing Theory, Practicing Solidarity*. Durham, N.C.: Duke University Press.

Mollenkopf, John. 2009. "The Neighbourhood Context for Second-Generation Education and Labour Market Outcomes in New York." *Journal of Ethnic and Migration Studies* 35:1181–99.

Mollenkopf, John, and Manuel Castells, eds. 1991. *Dual City: Restructuring New York*. New York: Russell Sage Foundation.

Moon, Katherine. 1997. *Sex among Allies: Military Prostitution and U.S.-Korea Relations*. New York: Columbia University Press.

Moon, Seungseuk. 2005. *Militarized Modernity and Gendered Citizenship in South Korea*. Durham, N.C.: Duke University Press.

Moraga, Cherríe, and Gloria Anzaldúa, eds. 1981. *This Bridge Called My Back. Writings by Radical Women of Color*. New York: Kitchen Table/Women of Color Press.

Morgan, Kathryn Pauly. 1991. "Women and the Knife: Cosmetic Surgery and the Colonization of Women's Bodies." *Hypatia* 6: 25–53.

Morris, Narelle. 2005. *Anti-Japanism since the 1980s: The Politics and Culture of Japan-Bashing.* New York: Routledge.

Moya, Jose C. 2007. "Domestic Service in a Global Perspective: Gender, Migration, and Ethnic Niches." *Journal of Ethnic and Migration Studies* 33: 559–79.

Nadadur, Ramanujan. 2009. "Illegal Immigration: A Positive Economic Contribution to the United States." *Journal of Ethnic and Migration Studies* 33, no. 6: 1037–52.

Nakanishi, Don. 1993. "Surviving Democracy's 'Mistake': Japanese Americans and the Enduring Legacy of Executive Order 9066." *Amerasia Journal* 19: 7–35.

Nails. 2002. "Industry Statistics." In *Nails Big Book 2001–2002.* Torrance, Calif.: Nails [magazine].

———. 2005. "Industry Outlook and Trends." In *Nails Big Book 2004–2005.* Torrance, Calif.: Nails [magazine].

———. 2008. "Regional Analysis, Nail Techs and Nail Salons, 2006 and 2007." In *Nails Big Book 2007–2008.* Torrance, Calif.: Nails [magazine], www.nailsmag.com/pdfView.aspx?pdfName=NAILS20072008stats.pdf.

Naples, Nancy. 2003. *Feminism and Method: Ethnography, Discourse Analysis and Activist Research.* New York: Routledge.

Narayan, Uma. 1997. *Dislocating Cultures: Identities, Traditions, and Third World Feminism.* New York: Routledge.

Nash, June, and Maria Patricia Fernandez-Kelly. 1983. *Women, Men, and the International Division of Labor.* Albany: State University of New York Press.

Neckerman, Catherine, Prudence Carter, and Jennifer Lee. 1999. "Segmented Assimilation and Minority Cultures of Mobility." *Ethnic and Racial Studies* 22: 945–65.

Ngai, Mae. 2004: *Impossible Subjects: Illegal Aliens and the Making of Modern America.* Princeton, N.J.: Princeton University Press.

Oerton, Sarah. 2004. "Bodywork Boundaries: Power,. Politics and Professionalism in Therapeutic Massage." *Gender, Work and Organization* 11: 544–65.

Oerton, Sarah, and Joanna Phoenix. 2001. *Sex/Bodywork: Discourses and Practices. Sexualities* 4: 387–412.

Ogbar, Jeffrey O. G. 1999. "Slouching toward Bork: The Culture Wars and Self-Criticism in Hip-Hop Music." *Journal of Black Studies* 30: 164–83.

Oh, Joong-Hwan. 2007. "Economic Incentive, Embeddedness, and Social Support: A Study of Korean-owned Nail Salon Workers' Rotating Credit Associations." *International Migration Review* 41: 623–55.

Okihiro, Gary Y. 1994. *Margins and Mainstreams: Asian in American History and Culture.* Seattle: University of Washington Press.

———. 1995. "Reading Asian Bodies, Reading Anxieties." Paper presented at the University of California, San Diego Ethnic Studies Colloquium, La Jolla.

Ong, Aihwa. 2003. *Buddha Is Hiding: Refugees, Citizenship, the New America.* Berkeley: University of California Press.

Ong, Paul, Kyeyoung Park, and Yasmin Tong. 1994. "The Korean-Black Conflict and the State." In Paul Ong, Edna Bonacich, and Lucie Cheng, eds., *The New Asian Immigration in Los Angeles and Global Restructuring.* Philadelphia: Temple University Press.

Osajima, K. 1988. "Asian Americans as the Model Minority: An Analysis of the Popular Press Image in the 1960s and 1980s." In G. Y. Okihiro, S. Hune, A. A. Hansen, and J. M. Liu, eds., *Reflections on Shattered Windows: Promises and Prospects for Asian American Studies.* Pullman: Washington State University Press.

Padavic, Irene, and Barbara Reskin. 2002. *Women and Men at Work.* Thousand Oaks, Calif.: Pine Forge Press.

Palumbo-Liu, David. 1999. *Asian/American: Historical Crossings of a Racial Frontier.* Palo Alto, Calif.: Stanford University Press.

Park, Ishle. 2004. *The Temperature of This Water.* New York: Kaya/Muae.

Park, Kyeyoung. 1991. "Conceptions of Ethnicities by Koreans: Workplace Encounters." In Shirley Hune et al., *Asian Americans: Comparative and Global Perspectives.* Pullman: Washington State University Press.

———. 1996. "Use and Abuse of Race and Culture: Black-Korean Tension in America." *American Anthropologist* 98: 492–99.

———. 1997. *The Korean American Dream: Immigrants and Small Business in New York City.* Ithaca, N.Y.: Cornell University Press.

Park, Lisa. 2005. *Consuming Citizenship: Children of Asian Immigrant Entrepreneurs.* Palo Alto, Calif.: Stanford University Press.

Parreñas, Rhacel S. 2000. "Migrant Filipina Domestic Workers and the International Division of Reproductive Labor." *Gender and Society* 14: 560–80.

———. 2001. *Servants of Globalization: Women, Migration and Domestic Work.* Palo Alto, Calif.: Stanford University Press.

———. 2005. *Children of Global Migration: Transnational Families and Gendered Woes.* Palo Alto, Calif.: Stanford University Press.

Pascale, Celine-Marie. 2006. *Making Sense of Race, Class, and Gender: Commonsense, Power, and Privilege in the United States.* New York: Routledge.

Passel, Jeffrey S. 1999. "Undocumented Immigration to the United States: Numbers, Trends, and Characteristics." In David W. Haines and Karen E. Rosenblum, eds., *Illegal Immigration in America: A Reference Handbook.* New York: Greenwood.

Passel, Jeffrey, and D'Vera Cohn. 2008. "Trends in Unauthorized Immigration: Undocumented Inflow Now Trails Legal Inflow." Report for Pew Hispanic Center, October 2, http://pewhispanic.org/reports/report.php?ReportID=94.

Peffer, George. 1999. *If They Don't Bring Their Women Here: Chinese Female Immigration before Exclusion.* Champagne-Urbana: University of Illinois Press.

Peiss, Kathy. 1998. *Hope in a Jar: The Making of America's Beauty Culture.* New York: Metropolitan Books.

Pennycook, Alast. 1998. *English and the Discourses of Colonialism.* New York: Routledge.

Perea, Juan, ed. 1997. *Immigrants Out: The New Nativism and the Anti-Immigrant Impulse in the United States.* New York: New York University Press.

Perlmann, Joel, and Roger Waldinger. 1997. "Second Generation Decline? Children of Immigrants, Past and Present—A Reconsideration." *International Migration Review* 31: 893–922.

Peskowitz, Miriam. 2005. *The Truth behind the Mommy Wars: Who Decides What Makes a Good Mother?* Emeryville, Calif.: Seal Press.

Pessar, Patricia. 2003. "Engendering Migration Studies." In Pierrette Hondagneu-Sotelo, ed., *Gender and U.S. Migration: Contemporary Trends.* Berkeley: University of California Press.

Pierce, Jennifer L. 1995. *Gender Trials: Emotional Lives in Contemporary Law Firms.* Berkeley: University of California Press.

Portes, Alejandro, and Min Zhou. 1993. "The New Second Generation: Segmented Assimilation and its Variants." *Annals* 503: 74–96.

Portes, Alejandro, and Rubén Rumbaut. 2001. *Legacies: The Story of the Immigrant Second Generation.* Berkeley: University of California Press.

Portes, Alejandro, Patricia Fernandez-Kelly, and William Haller. 2009. "The Adaptation of the Immigrant Second Generation in America: A Theoretical Overview and Recent Evidence." *Journal of Ethnic and Migration Studies* 35: 1077–1104.

Postrel, Virginia. 1997. "The Nail File: The Economic Meaning of Manicures." *Reason,* October, www.reason.com/news/show/30400.html.

———. 2004. "A Prettier Jobs Picture?" *New York Times,* February 22, , p. 16.

Putnam, Robert D. 2000. *Bowling Alone: The Collapse and Revival of American Community.* New York: Simon and Schuster.

Pyke, Karen D., and Denise L. Johnson. 2003. "Asian American Women and Racialized Femininities: 'Doing' Gender across Cultural Worlds." *Gender and Society* 17: 33–53.

Reinharz, Shulamit. 1992. *Feminist Methods in Social Research.* New York: Oxford University Press.

Retkwa, Rosalyn. 1993. "Korean Salons' Polish Chipped; Manicurists Menaced by State Rules." *Crain's New York Business,* November 1, p. 46.

Reutter, Linda, Miriam J. Stewart, Gerry Veenstra, Rhonda Love, Dennis Raphael, and Edward Makwarimba. 2009. "'Who Do They Think We Are,

Anyway?' Perceptions of and Responses to Poverty Stigma." *Qualitative Health Research* 19: 297–311.

Rhee, Jong-Chan. 1994. *The State and Industry in South Korea: The Limits of the Authoritarian State.* New York: Routledge.

Richardson, Laurel. 1997. *Fields of Play: Constructing an Academic Life.* New Brunswick, N.J.: Rutgers University Press.

Roberts, Dorothy E. 1997. *Killing the Black Body: Race, Reproduction, and the Meaning of Liberty.* New York: Pantheon.

Roelofs, Cora, Lenore S. Azaroff, Christina Holcroft, Huong Nguyen, and Tam Doan. 2008. "Results from a Community-based Occupational Health Survey of Vietnamese-American Nail Salon Workers." *Journal of Immigrant and Minority Health* 10, no. 4 (August): 353–61.

Romero, Mary. 2002. *Maid in the U.S.A.* New York: Routledge.

Rost, Allison. 2008. "Ripped from the Headlines." *Nailpro,* May, 72–89.

Rupert, G.G. 1911. *The Yellow Peril; or, the Orient vs. the Occident as Viewed by Modern Statesmen and Ancient Prophets.* Britton, Okla.: Union Publishing.

Sachs, Susan. 2001. "Success, at a Price, at Nail Salons; Anxiety Tempers Good Times for Koreans in Business." *New York Times,* February 21, p. B1.

Said, Edward. 1979. *Orientalism.* New York: Vintage.

Sakamoto, Arthur, and Yu Xie. 2006. "The Socioeconomic Attainments of Asian Americans." In Pyong Gap Min, ed., *Asian Americans: Contemporary Trends and Issues.* Thousand Oaks, Calif.: Pine Forge Press.

Sanders, Jimy M., and Victor Nee. 1987. "The Limits of Ethnic Solidarity in the Enclave Economy." *American Sociological Review* 52: 745–73.

Sassen, Saskia. 1989. "New York City's Informal Economy." In Alejando Portes, Manuel Castells, and Lauren A. Benton, eds., *The Informal Economy: Studies in Advanced and Less Developed Countries.* Baltimore: Johns Hopkins University Press.

———. 1998. *Globalization and Its Discontents: Essays on the Mobility of People and Money.* New York: New Press.

———. 2001. *The Global City: New York, London, Tokyo.* Princeton, N.J.: Princeton University Press.

Scanlon, Jennifer. 2007. "'If My Husband Calls I'm Not Here': The Beauty Parlor as Real and Representational Female Space." *Feminist Studies* 33: 308–34.

Sennett, Richard, and Jonathan Cobb. 1993. *The Hidden Injuries of Class.* New York: W.W. Norton.

Sethi, Rita Chaudry. 1994. "Smells Like Racism: A Plan for Mobilizing against Anti-Asian Bias." In Karin Aguilar San-Juan, ed., *The State of Asian America: Activism and Resistance in the 1990s.* Boston: South End.

Shah, Nayan. 2001. *Contagious Divides: Epidemics and Race in San Francisco's Chinatown.* Berkeley: University of California Press.

Shim, Doobo. 1998. "From Yellow Peril through Model Minority to Renewed Yellow Peril." *Journal of Communication Inquiry* 22: 385–409.

Shim, T. Youn-ja, Min-Sun Kim, and Judith N. Martin. 2008. *Changing Korea: Understanding Culture and Communication*. New York: Peter Lang.

Shin, Doh C. 1999. *Mass Politics and Culture in Democratizing Korea*. London: Cambridge University Press.

Shohat, Ella. 1999. *Talking Visions: Multicultural Feminism in a Transnational Age*. Cambridge, Mass.: MIT Press.

Sidel, Ruth. 1998. *Keeping Women and Children Last: America's War on the Poor*. New York: Penguin.

Smith, Dorothy. 1998. *Writing the Social: Critique, Theory and Investigations*. Toronto: University of Toronto Press.

Smith, James, and Barry Edmonson. 1998. *The Immigration Debate: Studies on the Economic, Demographic, and Fiscal Effects of Immigration*. Washington, D.C.: National Academy Press.

Sole-Smith, Virginia. 2007. "The High Price of Beauty." *Nation*, October 8, www.thenation.com/doc/20071008/sole-smith.

Solomon, Andrew. 2002. *The Noonday Demon: An Atlas of Depression*. New York: Scribner's.

Spivak, Gayatri. 1988. "Can the Subaltern Speak?" In Cary Nelson and Lawrence Grossberg, eds., *Marxism and the Interpretation of Culture*. London: Macmillan.

Standley, Leigh. 2007. "Life Is Tough." Curly Girl Design (SKU# SQLT13), www.curlygirldesign.com.

Steiner, Leslie Morgan, ed. 2006. *Mommy Wars: Stay-at-Home and Career Moms Face Off on Their Choices, Their Lives, Their Families*. New York: Random House.

Stevenson, Brenda. 2004. "Latasha Harlins, Soon Ja Du, and Joyce Karlin: A Case Study of Multicultural Female Violence and Justice on the Urban Frontier." *Journal of African American History* 89: 152–76.

Stone, Pamela. 2007. *Opting Out? Why Women Really Quit Careers and Head Home*. Berkeley: University of California Press.

Sturdevant, Saundra Pollack, and Brenda Stoltzfus. 1993. *Let the Good Times Roll: Prostitution and the U.S. Military in Asia*. New York: New Press.

Sullivan, Shannon. 2006. *Revealing Whiteness: The Unconscious Habits of Racial Privilege*. Bloomington: Indiana University Press.

Sun, Wei, and William J. Starosta. 2006. "Perceptions of Minority Invisibility among Asian American Professionals." *Howard Journal of Communications* 17: 119–42.

Swarns, Rachel L., and Christopher Drew. 2003. "Aftereffects: Immigrants; Fearful, Angry or Confused, Muslim Immigrants Register." *New York Times*, April

25, http://query.nytimes.com/gst/fullpage.html?res=9C0CE5D9173DF936A 15757C0A9659C8B63.

Takagi, Dana. 1992. *The Retreat from Race: Asian American Admissions and Racial Politics.* New Brunswick, N.J.: Rutgers University Press.

Takaki, Ronald. 1989. *Strangers from a Different Shore: A History of Asian Americans.* New York: Penguin.

———. 1995. *Strangers at the Gates Again: Asian American Immigration after 1965.* New York: Chelsea House.

Tang, Joyce. 1993. "Caucasians and Asians in Engineering: A Study in Occupational Mobility and Departure." *Research in the Sociology of Organizations* 11: 217–56.

Tavernise, Sabrina. 2005. "Rapper's Visit to Nail Salon Leads to Fight and Day in Court." *New York Times,* April 12, http://query.nytimes.com/gst/fullpage .html?res=9406E2DD123EF931A25757C0A9639C8B63.

Taylor, Charles R., Stacy Landreth, and Hae-Kyong Bang. 2005. "Asian Americans in Magazine Advertising: Portrayals of the 'Model Minority.'" *Journal of Macromarketing* 25: 163–74.

Tchen, John Kuo Wei. 2001. *New York before Chinatown: Orientalism and the Shaping of American Culture, 1776–1882.* Baltimore: Johns Hopkins University Press.

Torres, McNelly. 2007. "Is Your Nail Salon Safe?" *South Florida Sun-Sentinel,* January 21, www.sun-sentinel.com/business/custom/consumer/sfl-0121nail salons,0,1515810.story.

Townsend, Alair A. 1989. "The Old American Dream with a Special Korean Polish," *Crain's New York Business,* April 17), p. 11.

Tuan, Mia. 1998. *Forever Foreigners or Honorary Whites? The Asian Ethnic Experience Today.* New Brunswick, N.J.: Rutgers University Press.

Twigg, Julia. 2000. "Carework as a Form of Bodywork." *Ageing and Society* 20: 389–411.

Tyner, James J. 2006. *Oriental Bodies: Discourse and Discipline in U.S. Immigration Policy, 1875–1942.* Lanham, Md.: Lexington Books.

Uchida, Aki. 1998. "The Orientalization of Asian Women in America." *Women's Studies International Forum* 21: 161–74.

United Nations Economic and Social Commission for Asia and the Pacific. 1999. "Empowerment of Women in Asia and the Pacific." April, www.unescap .org/55/e1133e.htm#_1_8.

U.S. Bureau of Labor Statistics. 2000. "Changes in Women's Labor Force Participation in the Twentieth Century." *Monthly Labor Review,* February, www.bls .gov/opub/ted/2000/feb/wk3/art03.htm.

U.S. Bureau of Labor Statistics. U.S. Department of Labor. 2007. "Barbers, Cosmetologists, and Other Personal Appearance Workers." In *Occupational*

Outlook Handbook, 2008–2009 Edition, December, www.bls.gov/oco/ocos169
.htm#earnings.

U.S. Census Bureau. 2004. "Geographic Distribution—Nail Salons: 1997." In
*Industry Statistics Sampler: North American Industry Classification System
(NAICS) 812113 Nail Salons, 2002 Economic Census Data,* December 2, www
.census.gov/epcd/ec97/industry/E812113.HTM.

U.S. Department of Labor. 2006. "New York City Spas and Nail Salons Agree
to Pay More Than $222,000 in Back Wages and Interest to Settle U.S. Labor
Department Lawsuit." Press release no. 06–1581-NEW/BOS 2006–288,
October 12, www.dol.gov/esa/whd/media/press/whdpressVB2.asp?
pressdoc=Northeast/20061588.xml.

U.S. Office of Immigration Statistics. 2007. "2007 Yearbook of Immigration
Statistics." Department of Homeland Security, September, www.dhs.gov/
xlibrary/assets/statistics/yearbook/2007/ois_2007_yearbook.pdf.

Vineyard, Jennifer, with Audrey Kim. 2008. "Mariah Carey, Fergie Promise to
'Love You Long Time'—But Is the Phrase Empowering or Insensitive?" MTV
.com, July 30, www.mtv.com/news/articles/1591868/20080730/story.jhtml.

Visweswaran, Kamala. 1994. *Fictions of Feminist Ethnography.* Minneapolis:
University of Minnesota Press.

Vo, Linda Trinh, and Marian Sciachitano. 2000. "Moving beyond 'Exotic Whores
and Nimble Fingers': Asian Americans Women in a New Era of Globalization and Resistance." *Frontiers* 21: 1–19.

Waldinger, Roger. 1987. "Changing Ladders and Musical Chairs: Ethnicity
and Opportunity in Post-Industrial New York." *Politics and Society* 15:
369–401.

———. 1989. "Structural Opportunity or Ethnic Advantage? Immigrant Business Development in New York." *International Migration Review* 23: 48–72.

Wang, L. Ling-chi. 1998. "Race, Class, Citizenship, and Extraterritoriality: Asian
Americans and the 1996 Campaign Finance Scandal." *Amerasia* 24: 1–21.

Waters, Mary C. 1990. *Ethnic Options: Choosing Identities in America.* Berkeley:
University of California Press.

———. 2001. *Black Identities: West Indian Immigrant Dreams and American Realities.* Cambridge, Mass.: Harvard University Press.

Weber, Lynn. 2004. "A Conceptual Framework for Understanding Race, Class,
Gender, and Sexuality." In Sharlene Nagy Hesse-Biber and Michelle L.
Yaiser, eds., *Feminist Perspectives on Social Research.* New York: Oxford Uni-
versity Press.

Weglyn, Michi Nishiura. 1996. *Years of Infamy: The Untold Story of America's Concentration Camps.* Seattle: University of Washington Press.

Weitz, Rose, ed. 1998. *The Politics of Women's Bodies: Sexuality, Appearance and
Behavior.* New York: Oxford University Press.

———. 2001. "Women and their Hair: Seeking Power through Resistance and Accommodation." *Gender and Society* 15: 667–86.

West, Candace, and Sarah Fenstermaker. 1995. "Doing Difference." *Gender and Society* 9: 8–37.

Willett, Julie. 2000. *Permanent Waves: The Making of the American Beauty Shop.* New York: New York University Press.

———. 2005. "'Hands across the Table': A Short History of the Manicurist in the Twentieth Century." *Journal of Women's History* 17: 59–80.

Williams, Christine. 2006. *Inside Toyland: Working, Shopping and Social Inequality.* Berkeley: University of California Press.

Wolf, Naomi. 1991. *The Beauty Myth: How Images of Beauty Are Used against Women.* New York: William Morrow.

Wolkowitz, Carol. 2006. *Bodies at Work.* London: Sage.

Women's Voices for the Earth. 2007. "Leading Nail Polish Manufacturer Removes Toxic Ingredients: Report Finds Regulations Still Needed for Health and Safety of Salon Workers." Press release, March 29, www.coalition forcleanair.org/pdf/pressreleases/press-release-leading-nail-polish-manu facturer-removes-toxic-ingredients.pdf.

Wong, Jan. 1986. "Asia Bashing: Bias against Orientals Increases with Rivalry of Nations' Economies." *Wall Street Journal,* November 28, p. 1.

Woo, Deborah. 2000. "The Inventing and Reinventing of 'Model Minorities': The Cultural Veil Obscuring Structural Sources of Inequality." In Timothy Fong and Larry H. Shinagawa, eds., *Asian Americans: Experiences and Perspectives.* Upper Saddle River, N.J.: Prentice-Hall.

———. 2002. *Glass Ceilings and Asian Americans: The New Face of Workplace Barriers.* Walnut Creek, Calif.: AltaMira.

Wu, Diana Ting Liu. 1997. *Asian Pacific Americans in the Workplace.* Walnut Creek, Calif.: AltaMira.

Wurdinger, Victoria. 1992. "The Korean Influence," *Nails,* December, 36–42.

Xie, Yu, and Kimberly Goyette. 2004. *A Demographic Portrait of Asian Americans.* New York: Russell Sage Foundation.

Yamanaka, Keiko, and Kent McClelland. 1994. "Earning the Model-Minority Image: Diverse Strategies of Economic Adaptation by Asian American Women." *Ethnic and Racial Studies* 17: 79–114.

Yanagisako, Sylvia. 1995. "Transforming Orientalism: Gender, Nationality, and Class in Asian American Studies." In Sylvia Yanagisako and Carol Delaney, eds., *Naturalizing Power: Essays in Feminist Cultural Analysis.* New York: Routledge.

Yoon, In-Jin. 1997. *On My Own: Korean Businesses and Race Relations in America.* Chicago: University of Chicago Press.

Young, I. Phillip, and Julie A. Fox. 2002. "Asian, Hispanic, and Native American Job Candidates: Prescreened or Screened within the Selection Process." *Educational Administration Quarterly* 38: 530–54.

Yu, Henry. 2000. *Thinking Orientals: Migration, Contact, and Exoticism in Modern America.* London: Oxford University Press.

Yu, Tianlong. 2006. "Challenging the Politics of the 'Model Minority' Stereotype: A Case for Educational Equality." *Equity and Excellence in Education* 39: 325–33.

Yuh, Ji-Yeon. 2002. *Beyond the Shadow of Camptown: Korean Military Brides in America.* New York: New York University Press.

Yung, Judy. 1995. *Unbound Feet: A Social History of Chinese Women in San Francisco.* Berkeley: University of California Press.

Zelizer, Viviana A. 2005. *The Purchase of Intimacy.* Princeton, N.J.: Princeton University Press.

Zhou, Min, and Carl L. Bankston. 1995. "Asian-American Entrepreneurship: The Causes and Consequences." *National Journal of Sociology* 9: 1–35.

Zhou, Min, and John Logan. 1989. "Returns on Human Capital in Ethnic Enclaves." *American Sociological Review* 54: 809–20.

Zinn, Maxine Baca, and Bonnie Thornton Dill. 1996. "Theorizing Difference from Multiracial Feminism." *Feminist Studies* 22: 321–31.

Zolberg, Aristide R. 2006. *A Nation by Design: Immigration Policy in the Fashioning of America.* Cambridge, Mass.: Harvard University Press.

Index

Page numbers in italics indicate a photograph.

Abelmann, Nancy, 165, 169
Adorno, T. W., 264n5
African American women. *See* black women
Ahn, Cynthia, 232–33
"Anatomy of a Fish Store" (Park), 133
anti-immigrant sentiments: Asian Americans and, 203, 205–10, 236, 243, 270n10, 270n22; economic fears and, 31, 34, 85, 203, 206, 231–36; legislation, and support for, 242–43; media representations and, 205, 208–10, 243, 270n22; nativism, 20, 87, 242–43; racial tensions and, 192; working conditions and, 34. *See also* immigrants
Aoki, Guy, 209
Asian Americans: bamboo ceiling and, 81–83; history in the United States of, 203, 205–8, 212, 270n10; racialization of, 25, 142, 171–72, 189. *See also* model minority stereotype; yellow peril; *specific Asian nationalities*
Asian Communities for Reproductive Justice, 233
"The Asian Influence" (Hill), 201
Asian Law Caucus, 227
Asian women: explanations for clustering in manicuring work, 84, 139–41, 171–73, 244; gendered experiences of, 138, 141, 143, 160, 163, 203–8, 244–45; globalization of service economy and, 4–5, 33, 42, 246–48; labor migration flows for, 5, 48–50, 55; in nail salon industry, 5, 29, 33, 46–47, 52, 171, 255n4; pathologization of, 206–7; racialization of, 4–5, 42; sexual harassment of, 88–90, *89*, 95; sexualization of, 207–8, 210. *See also* women; *specific Asian nationalities*
Atwood, Margaret, 96–98

Baldwin, James N., 232–33
bamboo ceiling, 81–83
Banet-Weiser, Sarah, 130
Bartky, Sandra, 135
Baumgardner, Jennifer, 12–13
beauty: age and, 104–5; "beauty myth," 14–16; black women's constructions of, 96, 105–9, 115, 122, 124, 128–29, 130, *131*; class difference and, 105, 110–18; commodification of, 33, 35, 247; exploitative nature of, 99–100; feminine norms and, 38, 96, 100–101, 103, 105–9, 115, 119, 122, 124, 128–30, *131*, 245–46, 264n5; hairstyles and, 126, 245–46, 265n21; identity and, 42, *97*; marginalization and, 100–101, 104, 128–29; masculinity and, 106; motherhood and, 105, 110–18, 127–28; pedicures and, *97*; power and limitations in, 128–31, *131*, 245–46; racialization of, 100–109, 110–18; social and historical contexts for, 129–30, 265n23; socioeconomic mobility and, 107–8; third shift and, 15–16; white women's constructions of, 96, 101–3, 106–7, 109, 119, 129, 130; women in paid labor force and, 111–13
beauty salons, 4, 41, 140, 256n5
Belkin, Lisa, 264n13
Bettie, Julie, 100–101

black, as racial category, 256n10

"Black Korea" (song), 166, 267n3

black-Korean relations: gender and, 169–70, 187–89, 190–93, 198–99; media represen-tations of, 166; in nail art salons, 165–67, 169, 170–77, 187, 267n3, 267–68n4

Black Sexual Politics (Collins), 100

black women, middle-class, 118, 120–22, 129

black women, working-class: acrylic nails and, 7–8, 17, 42, 104, 195; airbrushed acrylic nails and, 28, *39*, 42, 100, 103–5, 179; beauty and, 96, 100, 105–9, 115, 122, 124, 128–29, 130, *131*; beauty salons owned by, 4, 256n5; Caribbean and African American relations and, 15, 22, 179, 192–93, 256n12; class difference and, 173–74; communal experience in salons for, 114–15, 117–18; as customers, 179–80, 268n8; hair salons and, 41; motherhood and, 113–18; nail art designs for, 81, 83, *131*, 179, 181, 195; nails as race marker for, 42; racialization of, 142, 171–72, 174–77, 189; self-definition by, 105–7, 115; service interactions with, 178–81. *See also* nail art salons

Blue Dreams (Abelmann and Lie), 165

Board of Barbering and Cosmetology, 234

Bodies at Work (Wolkowitz), 163–64

the body: agency versus social control of, 125; beauty and, 2, 11, 15, 125; commer-cialization of, 32, 33, 35–38; in feminist theory, 2–3, 19, 258n25; food, and politics of, 150–52; manicuring of, 2, 11; presenta-tions of, 118–20, 129, 149–50; yellow peril and, 205–8

body labor: agency and, 157–58; commercial-ized exchanges of, 1–2, 18, *19*, 21, 28–29; defined, 20–21, 258–59n27; disciplinary technologies of, 9, 147–50, *149*; expres-sive, 167, 174–76, 182–84, 188–90, 193–99; hygiene regimens of, 32, 133; labor rights and, 240–41, 273n1; manicurists and, 59, 60, 63–64, 88–90, 208; in nail salon indus-try, 36–37, 247–48; in nail spas, 134, 135, 144–47, 153–58; owners' and managers' control of, 145, 150, 152; as pampering service, 97, 134, 144–46; physical labor and, 20, 182–84, 188–90, 214, 216, 221, 226–28; resistance to performance of, 153–58; routinized, 201, 205, 208, 211–16, 214, 237; valuation of, 146–47

body work, 20, 247, 258–59n27. *See also* body labor

Body Work (Gimlin), 129

Borstein, Alex, 208–9, 243

Bourdieu, Pierre, 98–99, 131

Boushey, Heather, 264n13

Brown, Foxy (Inga Marchand), 165–66, 267n1

Burawoy, Michael, 256n12

California: nail salon industry in, 3, 43, 255n4; Proposition 187, 242; Vietnamese women in nail salon industry in, 3, 44, 46, 51–52, 222–23, 231–32, 233–34, 255n4, 272n45

California Department of Public Health, 271n31

California Healthy Nail Salon Collaborative, 222–23, 225, 271n30

California Safe Cosmetics Act, 271n31

Candelario, Ginetta, 41

Caplan, Jeremy, 201

care work, 249–54

Caribbean women, 15, 22, 179, 192, 256n12

Chan, Sucheng, 207

Chancer, Lynn, 109

Chang, Young Ku, 47–48

chemical exposures, in nail salons, 202, *221*, 222–26, 269n1

child care, 71–75, 79–80

Children of Global Migration (Parreñas), 70

Chin, Vincent, 270n10

Chinese Americans, 25, 44, 51, 52, 91, 203, 205–8

Chinese Exclusion Act, 203, 205

Cho, Margaret, 5–6, 8

Cho, Sumi K., 88–89

chop shop, use of term, 202, 269nn3. *See also* discount nail salons

class: beauty and, 100–109, 110–18; black middle-class women and, 173–74; black working-class motherhood and, 105, 110–18; bodily presentations and, 118–20, 129; customers and, 112, 264n12; discount nail salons and, 216–21; immigrant-owned small businesses and, 170, 268n6; inequal-ities and, 11; model minority stereotype and, 138–39; in nail art salons, 173–74; in nail salon industry, 12, 83, 256n11; own-ers and, 256n11; professional women's appearance expectations and, 118–22, 119, 129; white middle class and, 118–20, 129

Cobb, Jonathan, 80–81

Collins, Patricia Hill, 5, 100, 106, 256n8

The Commercialization of Intimate Life (Hoch-schild), 1

commercialization of women's bodies, 32, 33, 35–38

commercialized intimacy, 35, 37, 247, 250–51
Committee Against Anti-Asian Violence (CAAAV), 22, 259n29
Community Occupational Health Project, 227
community relations: in discount nail salons, 219–20; managers' efforts in, 165–66, 197–98, 200; nail art salons and, 117–18, 181, 184–90, 195–98, 265n18
Contagious Divides (Shah), 205–6
controlling images, 4–9, 27, 216, 256n8
Cook, Judith, 2
Craig, Maxine Leeds, 245–46
customer relations: in discount nail salons, 219, 251; in Korean grocery stores, 169, 186, 187, 189–90, 199, 212; managers' efforts in, 165–66, 197–98, 200; in nail art salons, 195–98; pedicurists and, 196; personal ties between customers and manicurists, 8, 63–64, 158–60, 250–51, 254
customers: Alexandra case study, 96, 101–3, 106–7, 109, 119, 129, 130; appreciation and respect, for services, 146–47, 240, 242, 250; black working-class women as, 179–80, 268n8; Brianna case study, 113–18, 124–25; Cheryl case study, 118–20, 129; communal experience in salons for, 114–15, 117, 117–18, 265n18; Ella case study, 118, 120–22, 129; emotional and physical needs of, 8, 27–28, 37, 38, 105, 111, 130; expectations of, 26–27; Jamilla case study, 96, 105–9, 115, 122, 124, 128–29, 130; labor rights and, 239–40; male attention, and role of manicures for, 122–28; men as, 88–90; model minority stereotype, views of, 139; motherhood and, 105, 110–18, 124–25, 127–28, 264n13; personal ties between manicurists and, 8, 63, 64, 158–60, 250–51, 254; reforms, and role of, 251–52, 254; summary, 96–100, 131–32, 241, 244; Theresa case study, 110–13, 115–16; women in paid labor force as, 37–38, 111–13, 118–22, 129, 260n8. *See also* beauty; black women; class; racialization; white women

Davis, Kathy, 19, 258n24
Dellinger, Kirsten, 118
discount nail salons: body labor routinized in, 201, 205, 208, 211–16, 214, 237; chemical exposures in, 202, 221, 222–26, 269n1; chop shop, use of term, 202, 269nn3; class difference and, 216–21; community relations and, 219–20; Convenient Nails

case study, 201, 214, 235; Crosstown Nails case study, 211–21; customer health issues, 201–6, 221, 226–27, 234–35, 269n3; customer relations in, 219, 251; economic threat posed by, 231–36; emotional labor and, 205, 210, 211, 213–14, 216, 219–21, 226–28; gendered experiences in, 205–8; hygiene regimens in, 201–2, 213, 219, 228, 234–35, 236–37; labor rights in, 202, 204–5, 221, 221–25, 228–31, 237, 272n40; Lee, Susan owner case study and, 211–12; model minority stereotype in, 206–7; multiracial relations, 216–21, 236; occupational health in, 224, 225–28; personal ties with customers in, 212; physical labor in, 214, 216, 221, 226–28; racialization of, 202–3, 206–11, 216–21, 228, 231; regulation and licensing in, 232–33, 236; in socioeconomically mixed neighborhood, 40, 244; summary, 9, 40–41, 201–5, 235–37, 244, 249; wages and, 229; yellow peril and, 202–3, 205–8, 228, 231, 235, 236, 269n4
Distinction (Bourdieu), 98–99
Doerlamm, Debbie, 231
Dogeaters (Hagedorn), 155, 267n20

earnings and wages. *See* wages and earnings
Edidin, Peter, 367n1
Ehrenreich, Barbara, 15
embodied labor. *See* body labor
emotional labor: defined, 20, 21, 258–59n27; in discount nail salons, 205, 210, 211, 213–14, 216, 219–21, 226–28; Hochschild on, 3, 9, 18, 20, 21, 247, 258–59n27, 259n28; lunchtime meals, 68–69, 69, 79; for manicurists, 3, 18, 19, 63–64, 80–81, 84, 92, 94; for owners, 3, 18, 19, 60, 66–69, 69, 79, 96
emotional management, 258–59n27
emotions and feelings. *See* emotional labor
emotion work, 258–59n27
employees. *See* managers; manicurists
employment patterns: gendered, 52, 55–56, 81–82, 241, 258n23; immigrants and, 10, 83–85; manicurists and, 10, 63, 83–85
"Engendering Migration Studies" (Pessar), 57
England, Paula, 251
entrepreneurship, immigrant, 62, 65–66, 91–92, 170, 263n36, 268n6
Entry Denied (Luibhéid), 207
Environmental Working Group, 271n31
Espiritu, Yen Le, 52, 77, 138

family relations, 58, 59, 61–62, 69–72, 74–77, 180, 187–88, *188*
Farhi, Paul, 269n4
Fast Food, Fast Talk (Leidner), 152, 267n19
Federman, Maya, 231–32, 272n45
feelings and emotions. *See* emotional labor
feminism: debates and scholarship on, 2–3, 12–13, 16–19, 24, 257n20, 258nn21–22; intersectional, 16–18, 257n20, 258nn21–22; postcolonial, 17, 257n20; transnational, 17, 257n20
Filipina Americans, 70, 203, 263n25
Fitzpatrick, Laura, 201
Folbre, Nancy, 251
Fong, Eric, 136
Fonow, Margaret, 2
Foucault, Michel, 135, 266n3
French manicures, 42, 100, 101, 120, 145
"From Servitude to Service Work" (Glenn), 1
Fujiwara, Lynn, 242
Full Metal Jacket, 210

gender: Asian women and constructions of, 138, 141, 143, 160, 163, 203–8, 244–45; black-Korean relations and, 169–70, 187–89, 190–93, 198–99; division of labor and, 76, 77, 180, 187–88, *188*; employment patterns and, 52, 55–56, 81–82, 241, 258n23; inequalities and, 29, 57, 70, 75–80, 143, 158, 160, 245; manicuring work and, 2–3, 11–12, 16–18, 256–57n12, 258n23; migration and, 5, 48–50, 58–59; model minority stereotype and, 30, 47, 138–39; in nail spas, 144–46; Orientalism and, 140, 266n11; racialization and, 17, 170, 258n22; yellow peril and, 205–8
Gendered Bodies (Lorber and Moore), 1
Gilroy, Paul, 11–12
Gimlin, Debra, 129
Glenn, Evelyn Nakano, 1, 14, 251
globalization of service economy, 4–5, 33, 35, 42, 55, 246–48
Global Woman (Hochschild and Ehrenreich), 15
"Glossed Over" (Gorman and O'Connor), 222–23, 271n29
Goffman, Erving, 149
Gorman Scranton, Alexandra, 222–23, 230–31, 271n29
grocery stores, Korean: black boycotts of, 142, 166, 186–87; child-care strategies and, 73; customer and community relations and, 169, 186, 187, 189–90, 199, 212; economic security and, 51, 52, 53;

patriarchal power in, 79, 187; shooting of Latasha Harlins in, 199, 268n9

Hagedorn, Jessica, 155, 267n20
hair salons, 41–42
Hall, Stuart, 264n5
The Handmaid's Tale (Atwood), 96
Harlins, Latasha, 199, 268n9
Harrington, David, 231–32, 272n45
Haughney, Christine, 32
Hays, Sharon, 115–16
health: body labor and, 32, 133; chemical exposures and, 202, 221, 222–26, 269n1; discount nail salons and, 201–2, 213, 219, 228, 234–35, 236–37; immigrants and, 20, 206–7; occupational health risks, 146–47, 224, 225–28; pedicurists and, 219; public health issues, 201–6, 221, 226–27, 234–35, 269n3; racialization of, 20, 104, 105, 206–7, 219; regulations and, 232; stress of manicurists and, 80–81, 91, 95
The Hidden Injuries of Class (Sennett and Cobb), 80–81
Hill, Suzette, 201
Hochschild, Arlie Russell: *The Commercialization of Intimate Life*, 1; on commercialization of intimacy, 35, 247, 260n3; on emotional labor, 3, 9, 18, 20, 21, 247, 258–59n27, 259n28; on emotion work, 20, 258–59n27; flight attendants, study of, 258n23, 259n28; on gendered employment experiences, 258n23; *Global Woman*, 15; *The Managed Heart*, 3; *The Second Shift*, 15, 69–70
Hondagneu-Sotelo, Pierrette, 58–59, 130
Horkheimer, Max, 264n5
Huisman, Kim, 130
Hurh, Won Moo, 76

Ice Cube, 166, 267n3
Illegal Immigrant Reform and Immigrant Responsibility Act, 242
immigrants: aspirations of, 58, 60, 62–63, 82–84; economic fears about, 31, 34, 85, 203, 206, 231–36; employment patterns and, 10, 83–85; entrepreneurship and, 62, 65–66, 91–92, 170, 263n36, 268n6; gains and losses for, 62–63, 93; labor migration flows for, 5, 44, 48–50, 55; legal status for, 85–87, 180, 263n28; manicuring work, and role of, 9, 15–16, 20; negative stereotypes of, 5–6, 20, 202–3, 206–7, 228, 231, 236; regulations and credentialing requirements for, 47, 49; scholarship on

gender and, 58–59; secondary migration for, 86–87; third shift, and role of, 15–16; yellow peril and, 202–3, 205–8, 228, 231, 235, 236, 269n4. *See also* anti-immigrant sentiments

Immigration Reform Act, 205

inequalities: gendered experiences and, 29, 57, 70, 75–80, 143, 158, 160, 245; in nail salon industry, 240, 246, 247–48, 250; racialization and, 5, 11, 172, 203–4; between women, 12–14, 31, 163, 164, 246, 250–52

intimacy, commercialized, 35, 37, 247, 250–51

"Is New York City Killing Entrepreneurship?" (report), 233

Italian American women, 104–5, 118–22, 126–27

"Jamaican" women, 15, 22, 179, 192, 256n12

Japanese Americans, 140, 203, 205, 207, 212, 270n10

Jewish Americans, 77–78, 142

Kaplan, Elaine Bell, 117–18, 265n18

Kim, Claire Jean, 166

Kim, Do Yea (Susan), 239–40, 248–49, 273n7

Kim, Kwang Chung, 76

Kim, Nadia Y., 62

Korean Americans: churches and, 53–54; ethnic community resources, 10, 29, 35, 46, 51–55, 229–30; marginalization experiences of, 90–93; in New York, 50–55; rotating credit associations (*kye*) and, 53; U.S.-Korean relations and, 48–50. *See also* Asian Americans; black-Korean relations; model minority stereotype; yellow peril

The Korean American Dream (Park), 48

Kraut, Alan, 19–20

Krynski, Kathy, 231–32, 272n45

Kubrick, Stanley, 210

kye (rotating credit association), 53

labor migration flows, 5, 44, 48–50, 55

labor rights: customer loyalty versus, 239–40; in discount nail salons, 202, 204–5, 221, 221–25, 228–31, 237, 272n40; organizing in nail salon industry, 225–31, 239–40, 248–252; relations between women and, 246–47; violations in nail salon industry, 239–40, 248–49, 273n7

language skills, 8, 22, 26, 47, 49, 53, 141

Latina immigrants, in nail salon industry, 25, 41, 42, 52, 87, 180, 212

Lee, Eunju, 65–66

Lee, Jennifer, 267–68n4

Lee, Kye Song, 51

Lee, Robert, 151

legislation, anti-immigrant, 242–43. See also *specific legislation and acts*

Leidner, Robin, 152, 267n19

licensing, and regulations, 45, 47, 49, 52–53, 232–33, 236, 261n25

Lie, John, 165, 169

Liou, Julia, 222–23, 225, 226

Lorber, Judith, 1

Lowe, Lisa, 4–5

Luibhéid, Eithne, 207

MAD TV, 208–9

Maid in the U.S.A. (Romero), 249

the managed hand, 3, 18–20

The Managed Heart (Hochschild), 3

managers: body labor, and control efforts by, 145, 150, 152; customer relations, and efforts by, 165–66, 197–98, 200; racial constructions by, 176–77; social status difference in nail salons and, 83, 256n11. *See also* manicuring work

manicures: about, 2, 241; as class markers, 218; French, 42, 100, 101, 120, 145; prices for, 39–40, 43, 91, 119, 204, 213, 216–17, 269n3; racialization of, 17, 42, 104. *See also* nails

manicuring work: agency in, 9–12, 256n11; exploitative nature of, 94, 128, 171; racialization of, 84, 139–41, 171–72, 244; reflexivity in research on, 24–28, 259n30, 266n15; research described, 11, 21–23, 256–57n12; research directions for, 31, 259n32; sisterhood concept in, 4, 12; as therapeutic practice, 252–54. *See also* manicurists

manicurists: agency in manicuring work and, 9–12, 256n11; body labor and, 59, 60, 63–64, 88–90, 149–50, 208; child-care strategies for, 71–75, 79–80; class difference and, 173–74; communal relations between, 68–69, 69, 79, 150–52; commuting experiences for, 66–67, 69; customer relations and, 63–64, 178–79, 183–84, 186–88, 189, 192–93, 251; described, 14, 256n11; emigrant dreams and, 58, 60, 62–63, 82–84; emotional labor for, 3, 18, 19, 63–64, 80–81, 84, 92, 94; employment patterns and, 10, 63, 83–85; family life and, 58, 59, 76, 77; gains and losses from immigration and, 62–63, 93; gendered division of labor and, 76, 77,

manicurists (*continued*)
180, 187–88, *188*; Kim, Jinny, case study,
59, 60, 80–93, 95; language skills for, 8,
22, 26, 47, 49, 53, 141; legal status for,
85–87, 180, 263n28; marginalization of,
90–93; men as co-owners, and relations
with, 66–67; ownership possibilities for,
91–92; patriarchal power and, 57, 70,
75–80; personal ties between customers
and, 8, 63–64, 158–60, 250–51, 254; racial
relations and, 174–76; racialized sexual
harassment of, 88–90, *89*, 95; service work
by, 146–47, 240, 242, 250; skills and training for, 64–65, 86, 263n28; social status
difference and, 92, 157, 256n11, 263n36;
socioeconomic mobility patterns for,
71–72, 81–84, 120, 130, 262n11, 263n25;
statistics, 38, 260nn12–13; stress related
to, 80–81, 91, 95; summary, 57–60, 94–95,
241–42; wages for, 31, 40, 47, 51, 58, 75,
83, 229, 249–50, 261n38. *See also* manicuring work; pedicurists
massages, 139–40
McCormack, Karen, 110, 116
media representations, 4, 166, 205, 207–10,
243, 270n22
medicalized nativism, 20
men: commuting experiences for manicurists, and role of, 66–67; as customers,
88–90; as hypermasculinized and feminized, 138; manicures, and role in getting
attention, 125–26; manicurists, and relations with co-owner, 66–67; middleman
minority, use of term, 170; as owners and
co-owners, 52, 66–67, 180, 187–88, *188*;
patriarchal power and, 52, 57, 70, 75–80,
187
Menjivar, Cecilia, 75
middleman minority theory, 170, 268n6
Min, Pyong Gap, 51, 79, 232, 268n6
model minority stereotype: class difference
and, 138–39; controlling images and, 4–9,
27, 216, 256n8; customers, and role in,
139; described, 136–38; in discount nail
salons, 206–7; gender and, 30, 47, 138–39;
in nail salon industry, 32, 47, 52; in nail
spas, 30, 134, 136–46, 266n11; owners
and, 71, 94, 139; racialization and, 138–40,
266n11; yellow peril and, 206–7
"mommy wars," 112, 264n13
Moon, Seungsook, 48–49
Moore, Lisa Jean, 1
motherhood, construction of, 105, 110–18,
124–25, 127–28, 264n13

nail art salons: artistic nails and, 7–8, 17,
28, 38, *39*, 42, 81, 100, 103–5, 179, 182,
195, 260n13, 260n14; Artistic Nails case
study, 194–98; class difference in, 173–74;
community relations and, 181, 184–90,
195–98; customer relations in, 178–79,
183–84, 186–88, 189, 192–93, 195–98, 251;
customers in, 179–80, 268n8; Downtown
Nails case study, 178–93; expressive body
labor in, 167, 174–76, 182–84, 188–90,
193–99; gendered experience in, 190–93;
managers in, 83, 165–66, 176–77, 197–98,
200; nail art in, 81, 83, *131*, 179, 181, 195;
owners and co-owners of, 180–81, 187–88,
188, 193–96; photograph of, *168*; physical labor dimensions in, 182–84, 188–90;
racialization of, 142, 171, 189; racial relations in, 171–72, 174–76, 189, 190–93, 197;
statistics, 260n13; structural conditions
for, 196–97; summary, 7, 9, 40–41, 165–68,
199–200, 244; as women-dominated
spaces, 180, 187, *188*. *See also* black–
Korean relations; black women
Nail Plaza protest, 239–40, 248–49, 273n1
Nailpro (magazine), 202
nails: acrylic, 7–8, 17, 38, *39*, 42, 81, 104, 195,
260n13, 260n14; airbrushed acrylic, 28,
39, 42, 100, 103–5, 179; artists' distinctive
designs for, 81, 83, 179, 181, 195; French
manicures for, 42, 100, 101, 120, 145;
nailed metaphor, 2; racialization of, 17,
42, 104
Nails (magazine), 38, *39*, 201, 255n4
nail salon industry: advocacy and organizing in, 225–31, 239–40, 248–52; Asian
women in, 3, 5, 29, 33, 46–47, 51–52,
91, 171, 222–23, 231–32, 233–34, 255n4,
272n45; body labor in, 36–37, 247–48; in
California, 3, 43, 255n4; churches, and
role in, 53–54; class difference in, 12, 83,
256n11; commercialization of women's
bodies and, 32, 33, 35–38, 247, 250–51;
community resource mobilization and,
10, 29, 35, 46, 51–55, 229–30; earnings in,
51, 65, 261n38; ethnic domination and
competition in, 33–35, 40–42, 44, 45–47,
51–56, 172; gendered employment patterns in, 52, 55–56, 241; globalization of
service economy and, 33, 35, 55, 247–48;
as growth industry, 38–41, 260n12; hair
versus nail salons and, 41–42; inequalities in, 240, 246, 247–48, 250; innovations
in, 38, *39*, 40, 46; labor migration flows,
48–50, 55; Latina immigrants in, 25, 41,

42, 52, 87, 180, 212; model minority stereotype in, 32, 47, 52; in New York City, 3, 35, 42–50, 255n4; polishes display, 34; racialization of, 34, 42, 46, 50, 52, 55–56, 82, 88–90, 89, 94–95, 141, 263n34; reforms in, 249–54, 251–52, 253–54; regulation and licensing in, 45, 47, 49, 52–53, 232–33, 261n25; routinization of, 39–40; Russian women in, 52, 141; service interactions in, 2–6, 9, 11, 14, 241; skills and training in, 44–45, 53; social contexts and relations in, 243–45; statistics on, 38, 39, 260nn12–13; summary, 32–35, 55–56, 241; types of services in, 40–42; women-dominated spaces in, 180, 187, 188; women in paid labor force, and effects on, 37–38, 260n8; working conditions in, 239–40, 248–49, 273n7. *See also* discount nail salons; nail art salons; nail spas

nail schools. *See* skills and training

nail spas: bodily self-presentations in, 149–50; body labor in, 134, 135, 144–50, 153–58; chairs, and equipment in, 149, 196; class difference in, 138–39; customers in, 6–7, 147, 157, 266–67n16; emotional attentiveness in, 134–35, 143–44; Exclusive Nails case study, 61–62, 158–60, 163; food management in, 150–52; gendered experience in, 144–46; language of service in, 134–35, 152–56, 267n19; massages and, 139–40; model minority stereotype and, 30, 134, 136–46, 139–40, 144–46, 266n11; occupational health risks in, 146–47; owner case study, 59, 61–80, 93, 95, 158–62; pampering services in, 97, 134, 144–46; personal ties in, 8, 158–60, 251, 254; photographs, 136, 149; racialized interactions in, 138–43, 161–62, 266n11; summary, 9, 40–41, 133–36, 162–64, 163, 244; tips and tipping in, 146–47; Uptown Nails case study, 6–7, 144–158, 162–63

nail technicians. *See* manicurists

National Healthy Nail Salon Alliance, 226

nativism, 20, 87, 242–43

New York: as global city, 44; Korean immigrants in, 50–55; nail salon industry in, 3, 35, 42–50, 255n4; service economy in, 42–44

Ngai, Mae, 85

Nguyen, Trang, 233–34

The Noonday Demon (Solomon), 252–53

Nordstrom, Stuart, 260n14

Nuon, Phaly, 252–53, 273n12

occupational health. *See* health

Ogbar, Jeffrey O. G., 267n3

Okihiro, Gary, 206

Onasch, Joy, 228

"opting out" for motherhood, 112, 264n13

Orientalism, 140, 266n11

Orientals, as racial category, 140, 142, 171–72, 189, 266n11

Orientals (Lee), 151

OSHA (U.S. Occupational Safety and Health Administration), 226

owners: assimilation and, 160–62; black women as, 173; control of workers by, 145, 150, 152; characteristics of, 61–66, 180–81, 193–96, 211–12; child care by, 71–75, 79–80; Choi, Charlie, case study, 59, 61–80, 93, 95, 158–62; as co-ethnic employers, 256n11; commuting experiences of, 66–67, 69; earnings for, 65; emigrant dreams and, 62–63; emotional labor by, 60, 66–69, 69, 79, 94; family relations and, 61–62, 69–72; gendered division of labor for, 76, 77; labor rights, and role of, 239–40, 248–49, 273n7; lunchtime communal meals and, 68–69, 69, 79; men as co-owners and, 52, 66–67, 180, 187–88, 188; model minority stereotype and, 71, 94, 139; patriarchal power and, 52, 57, 70, 75–80; small business possibilities and, 65–66, 91–92; status differences and, 92, 256n11, 263n36; summary, 57–60, 94–95, 241. *See also* entrepreneurship, immigrant; manicuring work

Page Law, 207

Palumbo-Liu, David, 137

Park, Ishle, 133, 134

Park, Kyeyoung, 48, 87, 263n36

Park, Lisa Sun-Hee, 71, 157

Parreñas, Rhacel, 70, 83, 263n25

Pascale, Celine-Marie, 258n21

patriarchal power, 52, 57, 70, 75–80, 187

pedicurists: customer relations and, 196; emotions and feelings of, 64, 92; equipment for, 149, 196; hygiene regimens and, 219; pampering services and, 97, 144–45; wages for, 261n38. *See also* manicurists

Perea, Juan, 87

Personal Responsibility and Work Opportunity Act, 242

Pessar, Patricia, 57

Postrel, Virginia, 260n12

power: beauty and, 128–31, 131, 245–46; patriarchal, 57, 70, 75–80, 187

professional women. *See* women in paid
labor force
Proposition 187, 242
public health. *See* health
The Purchase of Intimacy (Zelizer), 37

Rabin, Richard, 226
racialization: of Asian women, 3–5, 142–43,
174–77; beauty and, 100–109, 110–18;
body and, 20, 104, 105, 206–7, 219;
customer relations and, 219; discount
nail salons and, 208–11, 216–21, 219–20;
discrimination and, 34, 42, 46, 50, 55–56,
82, 88–90, *89*, 94–95, 263n34; economic
mobility and, 81–82; food and body
politics and, 150–52; gender and, 17, 170,
192–93, 258n22; hairstyles and, 41–42,
126, 245–46; immigrants and, 5–6, 192,
202–3, 206–7, 228, 231, 236; Internet sites
and, 12, 202, 209; manicures and, 17, 42,
104; manicuring work and, 12, 41–42,
139–42, 171–72, 189, 244; model minority stereotype and, 138–40; motherhood
and, 105, 110–18; multiracial relations,
216–21; in nail art salons, 171–72, 174–76,
189, 190–93, 197; nail styles and, 7–8, 17,
28, 38, 39, 42, 81, 100–101, 103–5, 120–22,
129, 145, 179, 182, 195, 260n13, 260n14;
racial categories, 256n10; representations
and, 4–6, 8–9, 27, 166, 205, 207–10, 216,
243, 256n8, 270n22; sexual harassment
and, 88–90, *89*, 95; white defined,
256n10. *See also* Asian Americans; black-
Korean relations; black women; model
minority stereotype; white women;
yellow peril
racialized sexual harassment, 88–90, *89*, 95
Reconcilable Differences (Chancer), 109
reforms, in nail salon industry, 249–54
regulations and licensing, 45, 47, 49, 52–53,
232–33, 236, 261n25
Republic of Korea, 48–50
"Revolution" (comedy tour), 5
Roberts, Dorothy, 110
Roh Park, Allison, 210, 270n22
Romero, Mary, 249
Rost, Allison, 269n3
rotating credit association *(kye)*, 53
Russian women, in nail salon industry, 52,
141

Said, Edward, 266n11
salon owners. *See* owners
Sassen, Saskia, 44, 45

schools. *See* skills and training
second shift, 15, 69–70
Seinfeld (television show), 134, 153, 266n2
Sennett, Richard, 80–81
service work: ethos of, 178–81; inequalities
in, 94, 99–100, 128, 171, 250; interactions
in, 2–6, 9, 11, 14, 178–81, 241; language
and, 134–35, 152–56, 267n19; tips and
tipping, 146–47
sexual harassment, 88–90, *89*, 95
sexualization, of Asian women, 88–90, *89*, 95,
207–8, 210
Shah, Nayan, 205–6, 207
Silent Travelers (Kraut), 19–20
skills and training: language skills, 8, 22, 26,
47, 49, 53, 141; for manicurists, 53, 64–65,
86, 263n28
small business ownership. *See* entrepreneurship, immigrant
socioeconomic status: beauty and, 107–8;
discount nail salons, and mixed, 40, 244;
of immigrants, 162, 167, 179; manicurists and, 71–72, 81–84, 120, 130, 262n11,
263n25; service work, and effects on, 192,
244. *See also* class
Solomon, Andrew, 252–53
Stone, Pamela, 264n13
Swan, Bunny (television character), 208–9,
243

Takagi, Dana, 137
third shift, 15–16
Time, 202, 269n1
tips and tipping, 146–47
Townsend, Alair A., 32, 34
toxic products. *See* chemical exposures;
health
training and skills. *See* skills and training
Tuan, Mia, 265n1

United Nations Economic and Social Com-
mission for Asia and the Pacific, 50
USA PATRIOT Act, 243
U.S. Bureau of Labor Statistics, 38, 260n8,
260n12, 261n25, 261n38
U.S. Census Bureau, 43, 51, 262n5
U.S. Department of Labor, 229
U.S. Occupational Safety and Health Admin-
istration (OSHA), 226

Vietnamese women, in nail salon industry,
3, 44, 46, 51–52, 222–23, 231–32, 233–34,
255n4, 272n45
Vineyard, Jennifer, 270n22

wages and earnings: immigrants, and effects on, 31, 34; for manicurists, 31, 40, 47, 51, 58, 75, 83, 229, 249–50, 261n38; owners and, 65; for pedicurists, 261n38; upgrades in nail salon industry, and effects on, 225, 226, 234, 250

Weitz, Rose, 265n21

West Indians, 185, 192

white women, middle-class: Alexandra case study, 96, 101–3, 106–7, 109, 119, 129, 130, 161–62; appearance expectations for professional, 118–20, 129; Asian ethnicities construct and, 142–43; beauty and, 42, 96, 100, 101–3, 106–7, 109, 119, 129, 130; bodily presentations of, 118–20, 129; class difference and, 118–20, 129; customer experience for, 6–7; male attention, and role of manicures for, 125–26; manicurists, and relations, 175–76; model minority stereotype and, 139–40; motherhood and, 110–13, 115–16; racial constructions of, 42, 100, 139–40, 142, 175–76, 266n11; white, as racial category, 256n10

white women, upper-class: beauty and, 42, 100; customer experience of, 6–7; Gwen case study, 144–46; model minority stereotype and, 139–40; racialization and, 42, 100, 139–40, 142, 266n11; white, as race category, 256n10

Willett, Julie, 41, 261n25, 264n12

Williams, Christine L., 118, 140

Wolf, Naomi, 15

Wolkowitz, Carol, 163–64

women: inequalities between, 12–14, 31, 163, 164, 246, 250–52; marginalization of, 90–93, 104, 128–29; second shift and, 15, 69–70; sisterhood concept and, 4, 12; spaces dominated by, 180, 187, 188; third shift and, 15–16. See also Asian women; beauty; black women; the body; feminism; white women

women in paid labor force: appearance expectations for, 118–22, 129; customers as, 37–38, 111–13, 118–22, 129, 260n8; nail salon industry, and effects of, 37–38, 260n8; "opting out" for motherhood by, 112, 264n13

Women's Voices for the Earth (organization), 224–25, 271nn29–30

Wong, Michelle, 88, 230

workers. See managers; manicurists; owners

work-family scholarship, 74–75

"The Worst Jobs in America" (Caplan and Fitzpatrick), 201

yellow peril, 202–3, 205–8, 228, 231, 235, 236, 269n4

Zelizer, Viviana, 37

Text:	10/14 Palatino
Display:	Univers Condensed Light, Bauer Bodoni
Compositor:	BookComp, Inc.
Indexer:	Naomi Linzer
Printer/Binder:	Maple-Vail Book Manufacturing Group